Firstfruits

365 Days of Blessing from
the Book of Genesis

BroadStreet
PUBLISHING

BroadStreet Publishing® Group, LLC
Savage, Minnesota, USA
BroadStreetPublishing.com

Firstfruits: 365 Days of Blessing from the Book of Genesis

Copyright © 2020 Brian Simmons and Gretchen Rodriguez

978-1-4245-6045-5 (faux leather)
978-1-4245-4245-6046-2 (e-book)

Unless indicated otherwise, all Scripture quotations are from The Passion Translation®. Copyright © 2017, 2018 by Passion & Fire Ministries, Inc. Used by permission. All rights reserved. ThePassionTranslation.com. Scripture quotations marked NIV are taken from The Holy Bible, New International Version® NIV® Copyright © 1973 1978 1984 2011 by Biblica, Inc.™ Used by permission. All rights reserved worldwide.

Stock or custom editions of BroadStreet Publishing titles may be purchased in bulk for educational, business, ministry, fundraising, or sales promotional use. For information, please email orders@broadstreetpublishing.com.

Cover and interior by Garborg Design at GarborgDesign.com

Printed in China

20 21 22 23 24 5 4 3 2 1

I will establish

my eternal covenant of love

between me and you.

GENESIS 17:7

January

His Story

When God created the heavens and the earth...

GENESIS 1:1

*G*enesis is God's autobiography. It is his story. His account of turning extraordinary desire into something tangible. He created us because he longed to share his unlimited love. He formed the heavens, the earth, and all that they contain to demonstrate his extravagance, wisdom, creativity, and generosity. God wanted us to know to what lengths he went to bring all that we see and all that we are into being. From his eternal dwelling, he created everything from nothing.

The story of creation pulls us into mystery. With no answers to our curiosity, we can only worship. Man wasn't made to analyze God. First and foremost, he was created to be a worshiper (John 4:24). We will never be able to take the mystery out of creation, for a God who is incomprehensible in his greatness accomplished it.

Father, from the beginning, you have wanted me to be blessed by your extravagance. All that I see, from the skies above me to the waters beneath, is a testimony of not only your desire to bless me but also of your absolute power and wisdom. As I start this journey through Genesis, I open myself to experience your love in ways I've never known before.

He Fills Empty Spaces

The earth was *completely* formless and empty,
with nothing but darkness draped over the deep.

GENESIS 1:2

*O*ur brilliant, all-powerful God doesn't need a starter kit. He isn't at a loss for how to turn dark situations into something glorious. Perfect beauty and harmony fill empty spaces, void of life, when he enters the scene—just look at what his glory has done in us! Obscurity is merely a blank canvas awaiting the touch of the Master's hand.

Let this encourage you. This magnificent One doesn't listen to our difficult prayers or look at our desolation and stand by feeling stumped. No! He confidently steps into the darkness and wraps it around himself like a robe. With perfect wisdom and uncontainable glory, he infuses every inch with light until not even a shadow exists. Not one single atom remains the same when it comes in contact with him.

Father, I'm so glad my trials don't repel you. Thank you for reminding me that the areas of my life that seem dark and empty are only opportunities awaiting your splendor. So come. Breathe upon every hollow and lifeless situation. As you do, I know life itself will radiate with your glory once again.

His Fluttering Spirit

God's Spirit hovered over the face of the waters.

GENESIS 1:2

The word *hovered* can also be translated "to brood, to vibrate, to flutter." It signifies a gentle, intentional movement. Imagine a mother eagle tending to her young, wings flapping with both gentleness and power as she hovers above. On the morning of creation, God's Spirit fluttered over the waters. Air, land, and sea were set perfectly into place.

Now the Holy Spirit has set his intention upon you—gently brooding with fierce love and approval because of what Jesus has done. He looks at your life and, with unmatched wisdom, knows exactly how to bring every area into heavenly order. You can be confident, fully trusting him, knowing he has set his attention upon you. Imagine his Spirit gently sweeping over you as you rest in his presence. Notice the way his love greets you in the morning and tucks you in at night. With loving affection, he is there—with you now and always. Gently brooding over you.

Father, my heart rises to meet you. Overshadow me like you did the Virgin Mary—creating something out of nothing. Take my life, every part of me, and make me eternally yours. Refresh me with your Spirit wind and fan the flames of holy devotion.

God Is Light

God announced, "Let there be light," and light burst forth!

GENESIS 1:3

God shaped all things by his word and spoke them into being with intricate detail and skill. Light was his first expression released on the earth—bursting forth though the sun had not graced the sky! Before the natural sun existed, the light of God filled the earth with glory. The very essence of God illuminated the world.

God spoke, and an explosion of light appeared that still races through the darkness! Darkness heard his command and bowed. And that word still proceeds out of the mouth of God today. In fact, everything he speaks accomplishes his purpose. Darkness continues to submit to light. Remember that when it opposes you. Your life is bursting with creation glory, and you stand victorious! When God announces his desires, his words carry the power to make them a reality. Light always overcomes darkness.

Father, you have filled my life with the brilliance of your love. The desire to know you consumes me. To see the One whose light illuminates every dark crevice. May the glory of your presence be prevalent in my life. And may I shine the beauty and power of your love into the world around me.

Made Beautiful

God saw the light as pleasing and beautiful.

GENESIS 1:4

God wants us to see ourselves the way he sees us. As we position ourselves in Jesus, in the glory that comes from him, we discover our true identity. Spiritual light floods our vision so we can see a surprising reality: he has made us beautiful. Not bearable or tolerable. Not loved because God's a good Father and *has* to love us. But so pleasant, treasured, and desirable that we were worth the price of the cross.

When God looks at us, he sees the light of his presence within us. He loved us long before the cross ever happened. He sees us— every inch of us, every flaw and bad attitude—yet still delights in us. He who created the light and then stepped back to admire it has created *you*. God sees with perfect vision, and nothing hides from his gaze. It's time for you to see yourself the way he does—wholly beautiful in his sight.

Father, open my eyes and spiritual understanding. Help me to see myself the way you do. You created me in your image—to be full of light and to stand separate from darkness. As I look into your eyes, I discover my true identity. I am your child—beautiful and valued in your sight.

Morning Always Comes

He used the light to dispel the darkness.
God called the light "Day," and the darkness "Night."
And so, evening gave way to morning—the first day.

GENESIS 1:4–5

The Light of the World has come onto the scene and ruined the intensity of darkness forever. Every day, when morning casts its golden glow, darkness bows. It resigns itself to the power of God's command that there would be light. This is an astounding message of hope given at the start of every day to remind us of God's faithfulness. Light always comes. Evening always gives way to morning.

Darkness helps us recognize the importance, beauty, and power of light. Whether on the earth and in the skies or through the trials of life, even shadows seek out the light. Shadows point to the fact that light must exist. Difficulties cause us to lift our eyes and await the dawn with hope, faith, and expectation. Even in our most difficult seasons, the Glorious One still shines. His magnificence glistens through the deepest night, turning darkness into day and chaos into order.

Jesus, you are the Light of the World. Illuminate my life. Let the valley of shadows bow to your majesty and come into alignment with your Word. Shine brightly so that even in the fog, I will see clearly. I set my eyes on you so my vision will adjust. Eclipse this obscurity with your glory.

The Sky Above

God said, "Let there be a dome between the waters
to separate the water above from the water below."
He made the dome and called it "Sky."

GENESIS 1:6–8

It doesn't matter where you live—a bustling city or a tropical island—
the sky above us declares the brilliance and wisdom of God. The
stars glisten as a reminder of his grace, and the sun burns with
samples of his fiery love. The clouds swell with refreshing rain. The
wind teaches us that we can feel invisible things. It demonstrates
that we don't need to see, bottle, or understand something to know
it's there.

The height of the heavens reminds us of God's supremacy and
the infinite span of his power. The brightness of the sky reminds us
of his purity and glory. Its vastness teaches us the immensity and
grandeur of his majesty. He is the God of the heavens who has
stretched out this dome over us!

*Father, thank you for giving me glimpses of your greatness and
then reminding me that it has been set in place for my enjoyment.
When I feel the sun on my face or enjoy the night sky, I stand
in awe. Your brilliance stirs my soul to worship. Your generosity
ignites my passionate praise.*

New Life

God said, "Let the land burst forth with growth."

GENESIS 1:11

God's words still carry power! His declaration that the ground would burst forth is still applicable to our lives today. Every dry, cracked, dusty area of your soul thirsts for the quenching rains of his love. He can turn a desert into a blossoming oasis.

It's time to believe again. To ask this loving, gracious Father to pour out his glory into every lifeless chasm. To turn our desolation into something beautiful and fruitful. To stop agreeing with a victim mentality and remember that he created us for beauty. Destined to fit into this crown he has placed upon our heads. We are not defined by our trials but by the glory that makes us whole and causes us to shine.

Father, this year I'm going to see things from your point of view. Instead of allowing circumstances, busyness, or disappointments to dictate how I feel, I'm going to agree with the words you've spoken. Saturate my dry ground with your love so I will burst forth with new life!

Seeds of Glory

God said, "Let the land burst forth with growth:
plants that bear seeds of their own kind,
and every variety of fruit tree,
each with power to multiply from its own seed."

GENESIS 1:11

God raised the land up from the waters and clothed it with life. In the place of desolation and barrenness, God, the author of life, blanketed the earth with vegetation. He gave the trees and flowers the ability to seed themselves in the land so they could blossom, bloom, and feed the soon coming creatures and humans. He didn't hand us something ugly, useless, and tolerable. He gave us something beautiful and useful.

God raised us up and clothed us with himself. He took our barrenness and wrapped it in his glory. Now, the seeds we sow—these actions in the form of prayer, compassion, and kind deeds—bear fruit in his name. He has given us the privilege of spreading his glory seeds across the earth.

Father, I love reading the comparisons of what you did on the earth and how they apply to my life. You astound me. Nothing you do is accidental, and I know when I get to heaven, I will learn even more about the intricacies of creation I don't yet understand. Thank you for inviting me on this journey to discover you in all that I see around me.

You Move His Heart

God loved what he saw,
for it was beautiful.

GENESIS 1:12

There was a void that once reverberated in silent need of its Creator yet now stands in confident awe at what it's become. Creation wasn't always the glorious masterpiece we see today, yet from the moment God held its design in his heart, he knew it was beautiful.

When God looks at you, your beauty moves him. He is overcome by the love he has for you. You, who were once in desperate need of his cleansing, now glisten with the splendor of God himself. He made you in his image, and he loves what he sees. Your life of devotion has become a beautiful poem. The very heartbeat of love he knew you would be.

Father, your love has made me confident. I am becoming the person you've always known I could be. I am your perfect design. Your glorious bride and honored friend. In you, I am beautiful. Because of your mercy, I shine with holy purity. I move the heart of God.

Created to Shine

God said, "Let there be bright lights to shine in space
to bathe the earth with their light.
Let them serve as signs to separate the day from night."

GENESIS 1:14

God did not mean for the distinction between light and darkness
to intimidate us. It was always God's idea for these two opposing
expressions to teach us great truth and to reveal our position in
Christ. Darkness, seen as worldly views, sin, and man-made ideas,
won't bully us when we know our identity in the Lord. Instead, we
see these as invitations to shine.

As the sun, moon, and stars bathe the earth in light, we who radiate
the glory of God pour out the purifying love of God into the world.
He created us to shine. To be radiant, full of compassion and
courage, just as our Father is. We are glorious when we keep our
minds fixed on the Lord. The One whose face is like the brightness
of the sun reminds us that we are his bride. As we step from the
chambers of his love onto the platform for which he created us, we
radiate with his glory so all the world can see.

*Father, keep me close to you. Near enough to see the brilliance
of your smile and feel the warmth of your embrace. Consume
my fears so I may boldly shine into the darkness. Absorb my
weaknesses with the glory of your love. I embrace the truth of who
I am—glorious and filled with light!*

Present in Every Moment

"...and signify the days,
seasons, and years."

GENESIS 1:15

God did not create time to rule over us. It was meant to be a gift, a way to watch our lives progress in knowledge of the One we love, serve, and run alongside. Time can serve as a reminder of its importance, so we don't squander it, but it is not our master. God is.

Our heavenly Father is the Creator of our days, seasons, and years. It's time for us to change our perspective of time. Instead of looking back at what we haven't accomplished or focusing on what has gone wrong, let's set our hearts on the Lord. Let's live by faith, believing that our time is in his hands. The Lord knows our seasons, and when we fully surrender each day, moment, and decision to him, he will set them in order. He will take us by the hand and give us the grace and wisdom necessary to do all that is in our hearts. It's not too late. There is always enough time when we follow the Lord's leading and see each moment as a blessing instead of a curse.

Father, I repent for behaving as though time is my master. I don't serve time; I serve you! You are my Master, and you hold my seasons with care. Release to me the grace to find purpose, peace, and joy in each day. Help me to be present in every moment, discovering the blessing you've hidden in each one.

Illuminate

He also spread the tapestry of shining stars
and set them all in the sky to illuminate the earth.

GENESIS 1:16–17

Look at how extravagantly the Lord has dressed the sky! Before he
ever created you, he taught the stars to dance on the edge of his
fingertips. To release pinpricks—samples of his glory to illuminate
the night sky. But the stars in their brilliant wonder don't compare to
the mystery of his light in you.

You are a vessel of the highest honor. The one who houses the
very glory of God himself. The same Holy Spirit who raised Christ
from the dead dwells in you. God created you to brighten every
room you walk into. To sparkle and shine with joyous praise that the
enemy cannot silence. To speak words of life that awaken sleeping
hearts. You are radiant.

*Father, thank you for filling me with the light of your Spirit. Help
me to remember how much glory and power I carry. I am your
child—a beautiful masterpiece with an eternal purpose. You delight
in me. You love me, and I am an extension of your love on this
earth. I will shine with the glory you've entrusted to me.*

Empowered by Love

To rule over the day and to rule over the night...

GENESIS 1:18

Do not hide in a corner bewildered at this darkness all around you. It wasn't created to take you out. It is there to demonstrate how powerful you really are. To allow you an opportunity to release the majesty of God and see his will manifest on the earth.

When you stand in the midst of the unknown, let faith be the posture of your heart. Remember who lives inside of you, and let him lead, even if your legs are shaking with those first steps. Soon, you'll realize how trustworthy he is. How much fun it is to rule and reign with him. How strong you really are when you choose to believe despite the screaming lies of hell. Don't give up! You carry the power of breakthrough inside.

Father, thank you for reminding me that I am not a victim but a victor. I can do all things because you are on my side. You are in me, with me, and leading me. Fear is the enemy of love, and from now on, I will not agree with it. Trusting your love is what empowers me!

Let There Be Life

God said, "Let there be life!"

GENESIS 1:20

God will breathe life into every dead and lifeless situation. No matter how dark and gloomy things are, he can turn them around in an instant. His light shines brightest in darkness. Trials are merely opportunities to see God do amazing things. Don't run from trials, face them head-on and laugh in their faces. Allow them to build patience as you trust God and wait for his hand of breakthrough.

Let this trial become a testimony of victory. Lift your voice in joyful anticipation of what God is about to do. He has declared life, so agree with his Word! He is encouraging you to believe despite what you see, so shake off discouragement and trample it with your faith. God is good, he loves you, and in his presence is fullness of life.

Father, I see the light of hope shining on the horizon. It's the testimony of breakthrough that you released over me from the beginning of time. Even when an answer to my prayer is different than I expect, your love is worth trusting. You always breathe new life into my soul.

The Gift of Creativity

God created huge sea creatures and every living creature that moves of every kind—swarming in the water and flying in the sky, according to their species. God loved what he saw, for it was beautiful.

GENESIS 1:21

Our all-wise God is also fun and unique. His creativity has no limits. The extravagance of creating sky, planets, oceans, trees, and flowers wasn't enough. God wanted to gift us with more. To live in awestruck wonder of his originality and wisdom. It seems he wants us to know creativity can be fun, intriguing, and extraordinary—expressions of our own ideas, emotions, and beauty.

He filled the world with multitudes of living creatures. Animals that are wild, weird, and brilliant! And we are to be like him when we create. Let's not hold back for fear of what others may think. We are an expression of him on this earth, so let's not fear to be unique in our gifts of creativity.

Father, all you've created is astounding! I stand in awe of your artistic brilliance and perfect wisdom. You created all that I see and don't see, yet you knew exactly how it would tie together to make up this wonderful world. Grace me with the ability to express my creativity with freedom, joy, and uniqueness, just as you did.

His Word Is Alive

God said...
And so it happened. ...
And God loved what he saw,
for it was beautiful.

GENESIS 1:24–25

We often say God created out of nothing. But God didn't create things out of nothing; he created everything from his word. He took the invisible substance of his words and made them visible. Elohim took what had never been seen and made it known. All things came to life through the word of God.

Like our Father, our words carry the power of life or death. God's unchanging Word, spoken through our lips, releases life and beauty even now. It is still alive and powerful—continuing to create. Let's soak in the truth of the Scriptures until they saturate us with faith and assurance. Soon the power of his Word will overflow into all we say, faith will frame our perspective, and the truth will fill our lives with beauty.

Father, inhabit the areas of my life that are barren and dull and make them beautiful. I trust the power of your Word that flows with eternal, creative power. Saturate my thinking with the life-giving truths that will transform my way of speaking, doing, and believing. Thank you for your Word that continues to bring all things into divine order and causes my life to blossom with heavenly beauty.

In His Image

God said, "Let us make a man and a woman in our image."

GENESIS 1:26

Image can be translated "representation, resemblance." We not only represent God, but we also look like him! More than anything else he created, we are the ones who bring his beauty into the earth. Reflecting the nature, authority, power, and compassion of who he is into creation. We are walking examples of God upon the earth.

Think about the painted sunset, majestic mountains, and the brilliance of a starry sky. As stunning as creation is, you are more beautiful still. The glory of his Spirit is in you and releases from you. The master artist, this perfect Creator who breathed the world's most exquisite sights into existence, says that you are his most beautiful creation. Nothing compares to the delight he feels when he gazes upon you.

Father, I love that you put so much care into the way you created everything around me. Yet you bestowed me with the honor of carrying your glory. I'm undone by the grace you've shown. I stand in awe of your beauty within me. Delighted to represent you and to live in this holy union.

Like Him

"...in our image to be like us.
Let them reign."

GENESIS 1:26

It was God's original intent that we would be like the Father, Son, and Holy Spirit. Sin attempted to usurp our rightful place of rulership, but God, through Jesus, redeemed our calling. Through a humble display of extravagant love, Jesus took our sinful nature upon himself and gave us his righteousness. We are the bride who has been chosen to rule and reign with Christ.

We are not only created in his image, but we also have become the perfect partner for Jesus—loved by the Father the same way he loves his Son. We have an equal role with Jesus upon the earth. We present his glory, his merciful and joyous personality, his hope, his wisdom, and his redemption to the world. What an honor it is to be like him!

Father, let every motive of my heart be fine-tuned, flowing in unison with you. I want to look like you, see like you, and walk like you. I want to know you more than any person ever has. Strengthen me with your presence and transform every part of me into your image

One with Him

God created man and woman and shaped them with his image inside them. In his own beautiful image, he created his masterpiece. Yes, male and female he created them.

GENESIS 1:27

God is vast and mysterious. Being neither male nor female, he had to create two genders to reveal the dimensions of his nature and character. Everything that exists contains demonstrations of his creativity and brilliance, but we are the ones who radiate the very beauty of God. We are his masterpiece, formed to have communion and relationship with our Creator.

The Lord took his own nature and likeness and fashioned a creature to be like him—one he could love with unlimited passion. Humans who were created from dust yet filled with the divinity and nature of a holy, omnipotent God. We are meant to enjoy him in the warmth of mutual love. Freely and openly, we stand in his presence and commune. Being one has been his divine idea since the beginning.

Father, I'm overwhelmed by the desire of your heart to be one with me. You literally filled me with yourself. You love me so much that you want to continually commune with me. To enjoy the beauty of our relationship at all times and to experience our oneness as your presence greets me each day.

Blessed in His Love

God blessed them in his love.

GENESIS 1:28

The blessing of God implies love. Love that empowers us to live with joy. Love that expects and cannot fear. Love that is fruitful and established in him. This blessing gives us all we need to succeed. Walking hand in hand with the Lord equips us for all we face. This relationship infuses us with the power and favor necessary to succeed. His love is the stabilizing force that anchors us in the ways of peace.

God created us to live *in his love*. This is the place of continued blessing where safety and stability are the norms. In the cocoon of his wraparound glory, we are equipped and soon emerge transformed. Able to face anything that comes our way. When we remain near his heart, the blessing of his presence melts away anything that contradicts this holy blessing.

Father, there is nothing sweeter than remaining in the bliss of your presence. You have become my strength and song. When everything else feels out of sorts, I can rest in the confidence that you love me. Nothing else matters when I'm aware of you. Thank you for the blessing of your passionate desire for me.

God's Delight

God surveyed all he had made and said, "I love it!"
For it pleased him greatly.
Evening gave way to morning—day six.

GENESIS 1:31

Take a moment and imagine our Father leaning back in his throne and surveying the vast beauty of all he created. The waters abundant with life lapping at the shores. The creatures spreading out upon the earth, running and playing for the first time. Wind partnering with the trees, making the leaves dance under glimmering stars. Perfectly green grass and fragrant flowers untainted by pollution. Imagine the sounds filling the atmosphere. Sounds of life never heard before. And then there we were—the ones who would contain the uncontainable One. What did the angels do to celebrate the birth of creation? What must it have been like to see it all unfold?

The story of creation doesn't end with God feeling disappointed or dissatisfied. From the beginning, we (the entirety of creation) pleased him *greatly*. Before we could possibly do anything to please him, he loved us. We are his delight.

Father, thinking about the wonder of creation leaves me awestruck. How glorious and brilliant you are! Thank you for blessing me with such beautiful things. No one could ever gift me with planets, oceans, and life itself. You are the epitome of perfection, yet you look at me and call me beautiful.

Flow in Harmony

The creation of the heavens and the earth
were completed in all their vast array.

GENESIS 2:1

Our Father designed all of creation in heaven and earth as a visual representation of his perfect power and unlimited generosity. Nothing was an accident. Everything he created is beautiful and filled with purpose. It all flows together in harmony.

When we look at the diversity around us, it should excite us because each of us is a portrayal of the One we worship. Our differences and uniqueness aren't meant to push us apart but serve to reveal God's vastness. If he had made us all alike, it wouldn't have conveyed who he is. He desires that we flow in harmony, becoming stronger and more beautiful as we embrace who God created us to be without shaming or criticizing each other. We are whole when we function as a whole and embrace each other in the light of God's love.

Father, thank you for reminding me of the importance and beauty of our diversity. Help me to see others, even those I don't agree with, as valued, important, and as a reflection of you. Teach me to look beyond what makes us different and to remember the power of uniting despite those differences.

Time with God

God had completed creating his masterpiece,
so on the seventh day, he rested from all his work.

GENESIS 2:2

Like an artist who has finished his masterpiece, God took the time to admire his work. The Omnipotent One didn't rest because he was weary. There is no mention of evening and morning completing the seventh day, which implies that God's Sabbath rest endures forever. On the sixth day, the Lord created man, and on the seventh, he rested. God took the day off to be with him.

Man started his life by enjoying his Father in the place of rest. He wasn't taken into the fields and taught the importance of each animal, plant, or seed. He wasn't versed in the science of the cosmos. God didn't put him to work. Man learned the importance of rest by watching his Creator demonstrate it firsthand. Adam's first day was to be the foundation for the rest of his life! It centered on nearness to his Father and the value of resting with him.

Father, I want to follow your example. I long to find this place of rest and enjoyment with you. When I want to rush and get the day started, remind me to start in the stillness of your presence. Bless me with the grace to quiet my mind and find this rest again.

Seasons and Times

God blessed the seventh day.

GENESIS 2:3

The Hebrew word for "day" is *yom* and can be translated into over fifty different words, such as "today, time, forever, continually, age, life, season, perpetually, or a period of time." The Hebraic mindset doesn't view *yom* as a twenty-four-hour period. Scriptures frequently speak of the day of the Lord, which points to a time period of God's divine activity, not a day with a sunrise and sunset. Both Moses and Peter spoke of a thousand years being like one day (Psalm 90:4; 2 Peter 3:8).

God's ways are higher than ours. His wisdom is far greater than the wisdom of man. When we feel confined by the limits of time, God sees unlimited possibilities. He isn't restricted to our timetables. When we commit our days, seasons, and lives to the Lord's care, there is always enough time. He knows how to lead us in his perfect timing, even if it doesn't make sense to our natural understanding.

Father, forgive me for my unbelief. For putting limits on what I think can or cannot happen based on my age or the restrictions of time. I know my seasons are safe in your hands. I don't need to sacrifice my dreams just because they haven't happened yet. You are a faithful God—the keeper of my days.

Sacred Days

God blessed the seventh day and made it sacred,
because on it, he paused to rest.

GENESIS 2:3

Since Scripture never references the end of the seventh day, we should pause and acknowledge the eternal truth of sacred rest. This isn't necessarily a ceasing of action but an internal, ongoing enjoyment of this spiritual relationship with the Lord that never ends.

God has provided everything we need to live a full and satisfying life. We are now complete in Christ. Created to enjoy his provision. Our busy or mundane days, each breath, and every moment are sacred. Each nanosecond, a gift from our heavenly Father. Let's not take life for granted but instead learn to embrace it fully. To live for eternity with an awareness of the Holy Spirit's continual abiding presence. These are sacred days.

Father, give me eyes to see from eternity's perspective. To enjoy these sacred days with you that will continue forever. To never take for granted the blessing of our holy union. To not only acknowledge your presence but also to stay tuned into it throughout the day. You are the way, the truth, and the life that transforms every moment.

Awestruck

This is the account of the heavens and the earth.

GENESIS 2:4

God loves to share things with us. To let us in on family secrets and ideas that move his heart. He wasn't obligated to divulge the mysteries of creation. He wanted to. And yet even in this account, as he breaks it down into bite-sized pieces, we can only stand and wonder at his brilliance.

The wisdom of our Father is vast and glorious, yet he tells us to ask for it. To search out the unsearchable. To dip our toes in an ocean of understanding that has existed before time began. He wants us to reach while being comfortable with the mystery of the unreachable. He is not only our Creator and King, but he is also our friend and Savior. Our brother and Father. He is the beginning and the end. The One who abides within the very beings he created.

Father, I'm astounded by the brilliance of your creation. Left awestruck by the beauty you have entrusted within this vessel of flesh and blood. Each day you give me glimpses of glory and snapshots of revelation. And when I think of all there is to know, I'm grateful that we have eternity to spend together.

A Holy Spirit Deluge

Yahweh-God had not yet sent rain. In those days, a mist arose from the soil and watered the whole face of the ground.

GENESIS 2:5–6

Rain often stands as a symbol of the Holy Spirit. Before God sent the Holy Spirit to live inside us, he was already there—enveloping us like a mist. Drawing us to himself. Before our souls were ever watered, he wet our lips and awakened our thirst.

God, in his mercy, poured out the refreshing rain of his love upon our dry, dusty ground. What once was a trickle has become a downpour! Every day of our lives, we're invited to splash about as we dance in the rain with our beloved. To laugh and sing as he satisfies our parched souls. His love is the remedy. His grace is our refreshing. We never need to complain of feeling spiritually dry when the fountain of living water lives inside of us!

Father, I'm diving in! Worshiping you without restraint. You are the One who quenches my thirsty soul. You are the river that cascades through my being with refreshing, healing love. Pour out your presence into every dry and cracked crevice so I will never thirst again.

Awaken

Yahweh-God scooped up a lump of soil, sculpted a man,
and blew into his nostrils the breath of life.

GENESIS 2:7

God created everything else through an act of speech. He
sculpted only man with his hands. Take a moment and imagine the
tenderness and care that went into forming us. God knelt in the soil
and delicately sculpted his most desired offspring. With each brush
of his hand, he meticulously created Adam, who would become his
firstborn on the earth.

We are a reflection of our Father, mysteriously complex and
beautifully woven together. We were chosen to be his vessels—
containers of his presence and glory. Face-to-face, as close as one
gets to another, God breathed the breath of life into Adam. In
essence, Adam was awakened by a kiss from his Father. Imagine
being kissed into existence! Today, our Father's presence is the kiss
of love that awakens us to life.

*Father, kiss me with holy awakening. Meet me face-to-face as I
set time aside to enjoy you and breathe deeply of your love. Your
nearness reminds me how much you care for me. You have been
with me since the beginning. In these moments of encounter, you
continue to pour over me with loving attention, telling me how
desired and beautiful I am.*

To Be One

> In the Land of Delight...he placed the man he had formed.
> In the middle of the garden, he planted the Tree of Life.
>
> GENESIS 2:8–9

At the start, God gave us a peek at his perfect will. Man was placed *in* the Land of Delight (*Jesus*—our home and true delight). Then life itself was planted in the middle of the garden (*we* are his garden). From the very beginning, we see God's heart. We catch a glimpse of our prophetic destiny—man and God were meant to live in perfect union.

Today, this is our reality. *In him,* we live, move, and have our being (Acts 7:28). And inside of us dwells the Holy Spirit (1 Corinthians 3:16). Our Father held this heavenly design close to his heart before Adam ever sinned. God, in his perfect wisdom and sin-shattering love, set a plan in motion that nothing could stop. Before anyone would ever challenge love, it had already won.

Father, it's mind-boggling to think that from the very start, you knew we would be one. You loved me and had a plan to rescue me before I needed rescuing. Each day, as I live in the reality of your presence, I know I've found my perfect home.

Garden of Delight

Yahweh-God planted a lush garden paradise in the East, in the Land
of Delight; and there he placed the man he had formed.

GENESIS 2:8

Mankind's first home wasn't a palace of gold but a garden planted
by the Lord on the third day. It was furnished with freedom and
creativity. Set in an environment of peace and love. Our birthplace
was one of delight and desire. The whole earth was a paradise.
A pleasurable garden. A wonderland. This is life in its highest
perfection. All that God provides for us is pleasurable.

Set in the East, man would eventually see the day when the *Son*
would rise after Adam's fall. The man who was placed in a garden
was meant to *be* a garden. *We* become a sanctuary of God's delight
when we live in the place of holy intimacy. As we yield our spirits,
souls, and bodies to the Lord, he prepares us to be a garden where
beautiful fruit springs forth. We are the desired, fragrant place
where God's Spirit dwells.

*Father, I long to dwell in the paradise of your love. To know you.
To see you. To have nothing hindering our relationship. Stir up
the fragrance of your presence in my life so all will partake of the
beauty springing up from within me. Teach me how to remain in
the paradise of your presence, free to be who you created me to
be. Let me become your garden of delight.*

February

The Tree of Life

In the middle of the garden he planted the Tree of Life
and the Tree of the Knowledge of Good and Evil.

GENESIS 2:9

In the lush, beautiful garden, God gave Adam a choice to eat from
the Tree of Life, a symbol of Christ, or eat what would provide him
with knowledge apart from God. Today the invitation to eat from
the Tree of Life is still available. We are free to fill our heads with
philosophies, theories, and worldly intelligence, outside of the
presence of God, or we can seek the One who is wisdom.

As we fix our gaze on the One who was crucified on a tree, we are
changed into his image. We are invited to enjoy a relationship that
isn't separate from the wisdom he imparts. The Lord *is* our source
of virtue and understanding. He satisfies our souls with something
much more profound than mental ascension. The greatest need of
the human heart is life (relationship), not knowledge. Relationship
with Jesus gives us the glories of a fulfilling life *and* the ability to
discern between good and evil.

*Father, you are the wisdom I need. Worldly wisdom could never
satisfy this longing in my soul. Help me to keep my heart set upon
you today. To turn to you in every decision and to humbly bow
before you with every question. I find in you all I need to run this
race with wisdom and discernment.*

The River Is Alive

Flowing from the Land of Delight
was a river to water the garden.

GENESIS 2:10

Right now, a river flows from the Land of Delight straight into the gardens of our souls. It is the river that proceeds from the throne of God and of the Lamb. A river that's alive—the very outflow of God's presence cascading into every dry and thirsty heart. Its waters are deep enough to swim in, and life comes by drowning in its expanse.

As we dive into Jesus, the source of our refreshing, we come alive. He is a well that never runs dry. The One who satisfies our deepest longings. We become a reservoir of divine water so that the life pouring into us spills out everywhere we go. It is this overflow that waters the path we are on, leaving behind a beautiful legacy for others to follow.

Father, I thirst for the rivers of living water. Saturate every part of me. Drown every motive, thought, and desire that doesn't reflect you. In the rivers of your glorious love, I am changed. Sustained. Reminded that grace is ready to meet me every day. Your presence satisfies my greatest desires. Here I will wait.

Healing Waters

Flowing from the Land of Delight was a river to water the garden, and from there, it divided into four branches.

GENESIS 2:10

The number four speaks of the four corners of the earth. Before mankind filled the planet, God already loved us. Regardless of how we would rebel, despite our cultures, colors, and beliefs, he would pour out. He would provide a pure river of cleansing for every heart.

Our merciful God never restricts himself. He isn't biased. He isn't stressed about our differences. He isn't wringing his hands, wondering how to reach lost souls or how to correct wrong theology. Jesus is perfect wisdom. He is our river of provision. He sees everything that is happening around the globe and has a solution. He is cascading into his garden (us), and we are waking up! We are learning to love despite the differences. We are finally watering the earth with the glory he has entrusted to us.

Father, thank you for reminding me that your love is limitless. It is honest, wise, and carries itself with integrity. But it is also compassionate, caring, and sincere. I am filled with the healing waters of this love, and I will release it every place you lead me.

Encircled with Grace

The first river, Overflowing Increase,
encircles the gold-laden land of Havilah.

GENESIS 2:11

Havilah has a number of possible meanings: "to cause to grow, to give birth out of pain, a stretch of sandy land, mud, to writhe or fall grievously in pain or fear, to grieve, be sorrowful, to tremble." All of the possible meanings seem to point to our human nature. But facing our humanity mercifully reminds us of our humble need for God.

In the most difficult seasons of our lives when we fall before the Lord in absolute dependence, he comes. The Lord rushes to our side and encircles us with grace. When we're on the verge of giving up, sorrowful, and exhausted, Jesus becomes our everything. He strengthens, heals, and reveals his faithfulness. He lifts us up and uncovers the gold within us that was hidden beneath the muck of fear and pain.

Lord, encircle me with your overflowing increase. Wipe away the dirt and grime that has hidden the true beauty within me—the glory I didn't realize was there. Though trials have sought to steal my resolve, your strength is becoming my own.

You Are His Treasure

The gold of that land is pure,
with many pearls and onyx found there.

GENESIS 2:12

You are God's most valued treasure, worth more than the purest gold or most precious stones. The river of his cleansing has cascaded over your soul and has revealed your true beauty. Nothing holds more significance in the heart of God than his children.

Like gold, pearls, and precious stones, you have been transformed. The work of his Spirit in your life has made you beautiful. Despite what you believe or what anyone else tells you, God loves you, wants you, and created you with a purpose. You captivate his heart and have his full attention. God sought you more than the finest gems or costly gold. He paid a great price so nothing could ever separate you from him. You are his treasure.

Father, tuck me away like a valuable treasure so I will remain protected and humble. Keep me close to your heart so I will radiate with purity and glory. You have transformed me by your mercy. You have made me beautiful by your love.

Swift-Flowing Truth

The third river, Swift Flowing,
flows east of Assyria.

GENESIS 2:14

The third river mentioned here is Tigris. It signifies a swift flowing of truth meant to stream from us, the children of God's delight. We are the answer for stuffy religious systems that seem successful on the outside but inside are void of life. We are the ones who release the River of God into every stagnant and dead belief.

What a blessing it is to know we carry the life-giving Spirit of God inside us. We have the honor of releasing the captives and setting people free by the power of his might and love. Nothing can stop the swiftly flying arrows of truth from hitting their mark. Religious walls crumble when hearts are loosened from their restrictive chains.

Father, I want rivers of freedom to stream from me everywhere I go. I long to release swift-flying arrows of truth that pierce deep into the heart of man. Your glory in me is unstoppable. Your freedom is meant for us all. Drown me in the rivers of your love and never let me emerge.

Fruitful

The fourth is the river Fruitfulness.

GENESIS 2:14

A fruitful life doesn't always equal a successful one by the world's standards. We cannot measure it by the number of followers we have on social media. We cannot define it by titles, accolades, or the praises of men. It is much more significant than these temporary things.

A fruitful life is one that blossoms from our relationship with the Lord, not our desire for fame or fortune. In the Lord's eyes, we're successful when we follow the leading of his Spirit. When we love him with every fiber of our being and allow our actions to reflect this love. When we pour out of our fullness instead of our need for attention. When we inspire others, maintain a thankful heart, and do everything from a posture of love. Let's live with these aspirations in mind.

Father, as long as I'm fruitful in your eyes, it doesn't matter what the world thinks. Bless the work of my hands as I seek you for wisdom and guidance. I live to honor you in all my ways. To love you and love those you place in my life. That makes me a true success.

Rooted in Love

Yahweh-God took the man
and placed him in the garden of Eden
to work and watch over it.

GENESIS 2:15

The same word used for working the ground (*avoda*) is used for
the service or worship of God. God's intention is that man would
be a gardener who tills the very ground from which he came. It is a
picture of how man must guard his heart and his life. God charging
man to till the land can also be taken symbolically—breaking up and
preparing the soil of his heart for the Tree of Life to grow in him.

Let's become those whose hard, dry ground has been loosened—
opened to the rain of God. Always willing to receive his correction
and continuously surrendering to his will—especially when fleshly
desires get in the way. As we allow the Holy Spirit to have his
way in us, the roots of commitment grow deep, stabilizing us
and grounding us in love. In the garden of God's presence, life
crowds out the weeds until all that remains is the beauty of a fully
surrendered heart.

*Father, show me any areas where my heart has become hardened
by doubt, fear, or impurities. Till the soil of my soul so I will remain
tender and pliable in your hands. Remove the weeds so nothing
will hinder the work of your Spirit in my life. May my garden be a
fragrant offering of absolute devotion.*

All You Need

> Yahweh-God commanded him,
> "You may freely eat of every fruit of the garden."
>
> GENESIS 2:16

God's original intent was for us to freely enjoy his blessings. Throughout this garden of delight, he laid out a smorgasbord and invited us into abundant life. He didn't focus on what we couldn't have but on the vastness of his provision. He created us for this lifestyle.

The person of Jesus has given us all we need—peace, joy, wisdom, relationships, provision, healing, etc. When we establish ourselves *in him*, seeking his mind on every subject, he leads. The fruit of knowledge doesn't come when we grasp for it apart from God. But it's freely given when *he* is our delight. As we feast on him, all other blessings are generously supplied.

Father, everything I need is provided in the bounty of your presence. Instead of being sidetracked by the things I don't have and racking my brain to think of how to obtain them, I will enjoy you. I will present my needs and trust you to lead me. Feasting on your love has no restrictions! And it is here in your presence that all blessings flow.

Surrender Is a Joy

"You must not eat of the Tree
that gives the knowledge of good and evil,
for when you eat from it you will most certainly die."

GENESIS 2:17

God is neither unkind nor harsh. He knows what's best for us.
We can choose to step outside of his boundaries and reach for
what appeases our selfish desires, or we can find true freedom
in surrender. Deciding for ourselves what is right and what is not
means we have a limited understanding of our Father's good
intentions. Anytime we live according to our own desires, we
experience life outside of God's best, which is a type of death
because life is found in him.

Trusting God means knowing his heart. When we are convinced of his
love, we don't question his instructions. That doesn't mean we always
understand the details. But surrender is a joy when it flows from
intimacy. We aren't afraid to obey because we believe in his love.

*Father, I let go of my need to understand the reasons behind the
things you ask. All I need to know is that you love me and care for
me. You desire to bless me with a full and victorious life. So I will
obey. I will trust. I will free-fall into love and taste the fruit of your
glorious garden.*

Find Your Tribe

Yahweh-God said, "It is not good for the man to be alone.
Therefore, I will fashion a suitable partner
to be his help and strength."

GENESIS 2:18

Our relationship with the Lord is the center around which all other relationships should flow. Though we walk with God in the cool of the day and find fulfillment by being with him, he knew we would need others. When God created Adam, he wanted him to have a partner, friend, and companion. From this marriage would come children, and from this family would come community. Friendship is God's idea. Man was made to be in relationship with others to fulfill the purposes of God. He created us for each other.

An important way of tending the gardens of our souls is by finding like-minded believers and surrounding ourselves with them. Let's call this *finding our tribe*, or finding people who we're comfortable around, people we can open up to and be vulnerable with. People who mutually encourage and support each other. It takes time to find people who you're willing to invite into the protected garden of your life. But if you ask the Lord, he'll faithfully help you find your tribe.

Father, lead me to those who make me feel known and those I can be a blessing to. Show me where to find those who will reflect your acceptance and strength. Enable me to be this for others as well. I desire friendships that are anchored in you. Show me where to find my tribe.

Spend the Day with Him

Whatever the man called the living creature,
that was its name.

GENESIS 2:19

Imagine how much fun it was to spend the day with God. To walk the land with the Father as he introduced Adam to every species he had created. Think of what it was like to hear God's heart regarding each creature. What type of information did the Father disclose as Adam considered what each animal should be called?

While it is rare for people to physically walk with God or audibly hear his voice, we have the privilege of enjoying his fellowship, every day. This Father who showed Adam around and entrusted him with secrets of creation is nearer now than before. He is closer than the wisps of breath encircling us on a winter day. He is in us. Longing for us to shift our attention to him so we can spend the day together. Here in the quiet of our lovesick hearts, he still speaks.

Father, let's spend the day together. I sense you inviting me to start each day with you. To set aside the distractions that deafen me to your voice. To notice the subtle ways you interact with me and try to catch my attention. Lord, hold my heart near yours in holy union. Speak. I'm listening.

Made Whole

Yahweh-God used the portion of Adam's side
and skillfully crafted a woman and presented her to him.
Then Adam said, "At last! One like me!"

GENESIS 2:22–23

Adam's response to Eve was bursting with excitement and
acceptance. God had given him someone to complete him.
Someone to cherish and love. Eve wasn't formed from Adam's
head, signifying his rule over her, nor out of his feet to trample her,
but out of his side, as an equal. His side—under his arm as a symbol
of protection. Next to his heart to be loved. What a beautiful
depiction of God's desire to protect and love those he forms.

Adam and Eve were two halves who came together to form a
complete picture of God. It wasn't until woman was formed that
God looked at creation and declared his great delight. Woman
completes man as the bride completes the Lord. You are that bridal
partner. You are the one who fulfills the Lord's deepest desire. Hear
the Lord's cry of excitement over you today! You are the one he's
longed for.

*Father, your love is mysterious and divine. To think that I move
your heart and that you desire me leaves me undone and eternally
grateful. I want to be with you forever. To be the bride you've
always had in mind. Here in the safety of your love, I am complete.*

Be Yourself

The man and his wife felt no shame,
unaware that they were both naked.

GENESIS 2:25

In the garden of paradise, Adam and Eve walked in majestic splendor covered by nothing but the glory of God. Imagine walking with each other and with God, with no thoughts of pride, shame, or fear. No pretense. Nothing hiding who they truly were. Free to be exactly who God created them to be without worrying if they would be accepted.

This nakedness—this vulnerability—and assurance that we can be ourselves and still be loved is God's idea. He created us for authenticity and honest connection. It's time we shed the charade that has wrapped our identity. Time to stop succumbing to the pressure of being what we *think* others want us to be and rest confidently in the person God has created each of us to be. As we walk with the Lord, he untangles us from the facades we've embraced, and we discover the joy of being ourselves.

Father, I invite you to unravel any pretense or insincerity in my life. I don't want to wear a mask. I want to be myself. To grow in wisdom, compassion, and joy as I walk with you and flourish into the best version of me that I can be. In you, I am fully alive and thoroughly known.

Continual Surrender

The snake was the most cunning
of all living beings that Yahweh-God had made.
He deviously asked the woman,
"Did God really tell you…"

GENESIS 3:1

In the center of this beautiful paradise, doubt crept in. Many of us have been there—in seasons of unspeakable glory yet feeling sidetracked by murmurs of uncertainty. One moment we're soaring upon the breath of faith, and the next, we're crashing into walls of fear and mistrust.

It's hard to believe that the enemy could have tricked Adam and Eve into listening when they were enjoying unhindered fellowship with God. It's equally unsettling that although the Spirit of God is both in and around us, we do the same. We doubt. We're duped into reasoning away God's promises. The cure? A continual quest for truth. For his presence. To instantly recognize what draws us away. Though the enemy and our own murky thoughts fight for authority, we rise victorious when we lay every doubt at the Lord's feet as an offering of love.

Father, I choose a lifestyle of continual surrender. When doubts blur my vision, remind me to turn my eyes to you. You will help me see clearly. Your presence will clear the air. May my devotion and desire to live in truth surround me like an impenetrable shield. May faith frame my perspective, and may your love conquer my fear and doubt.

Power over Temptation

The snake said to her, "You certainly won't die. ..."
When the woman saw that the tree produced delicious fruit...
she took its fruit and ate it.

GENESIS 3:4, 6

The moment Eve entered into a discussion with the enemy, trying to reason away deception, she fell victim to its entrapment. It is never a good idea to wrap our fingers around lures of enticement. It is never wise to inspect the hooks that seek to snare our souls. It's better to walk away. What is most beneficial is to run into the arms of he who strengthens our resolve.

Reasoning is a trap of the enemy. He crawls into our desert seasons when he thinks we're too tired to resist and tempts us, as he did with Jesus. Like Jesus, we overcome by speaking truth. Eve could have done this. Instead, she *considered* what the enemy said. The moment we entertain temptation, playing with the consequences as if they're optional, we fall victim. But when we submit every confusing idea to the Lord, he comes with grace and leads us to safety.

Father, in the safety of truth I find my footing. Enable me to resist temptation by softening my heart to the beauty of effortless submission. With my thoughts drenched in desire for you, I remain free from the enemy's subtle lies. As I keep my heart in tune with you, your melody of love drowns out the enemy's enticing lullaby.

Unashamed

Immediately, their eyes were opened,
and they realized they were naked, vulnerable, and ashamed;
so they sewed fig leaves together for coverings.

GENESIS 3:7

Eating the fruit opened Adam and Eve's eyes to their true condition: "miserable, poor, blind, barren, and naked!" (Revelation 3:17). Having chosen disobedience, they plunged into spiritual darkness, which only Jesus' redeeming light could illuminate. Instead of running to God, they hid. Tried to camouflage sin by covering it with fig leaves. But the works of man will never cover sinfulness.

When we sin, shame tries to drag us further away from the Lord. It tempts us to hide or scramble to find ways to heal our own misery. But the only thing that will cover our spiritual nakedness is the provision made for us at the cross. Through the blood of Jesus, we are washed. We emerge cleansed, whole, and fully restored. On our own, we cannot remedy our sinful condition. Only Jesus can. If we're honest and humble, he will clothe us in the robe of righteousness only he can provide.

Father, you are the light that shines into every darkened crevice of my soul. Every beautiful thing about me comes from you. All that I am, every shining portrayal of righteousness, comes from the glory of your Spirit within me. Thank you for opening your arms wide enough to fit me inside. For reminding me that I never need to hide.

The Garden of Your Soul

Adam and his wife heard the sound of Yahweh-God passing
through the garden in the breeze of the day.

GENESIS 3:8

Still yourself and imagine hearing God walk in the garden. Imagine
the fragrance of the flowers wafting through the air. The sounds of
the animals roaming freely. The breeze stirring the trees. Picture
yourself in this garden paradise where nothing hinders you from the
Lord's presence. There is no doubt when he approaches.

Though mankind no longer lives in a physical paradise, our
communion with God can be more powerful and perceptible.
Although sin took us out of the garden, the Lord, in his redeeming
love, made us *to be* his garden. Now, he meets with us in the most
delightful, pleasant, appealing enclosure of all: the gardens of
our souls. We tap into his love, perspective, wisdom, voice, and
friendship by tuning out the external and communing with him in a
place that we alone are responsible for tending. Within us is a place
of promise. A garden he calls home.

*Father, I want my life to be an offering of fragrant devotion.
Come with your gentle hand and remove the weeds that seek to
suffocate our love. I want to be a place where love dwells. To be a
delight and joy. To live in a way that continually makes you feel as
cherished as you make me feel.*

The Beauty Inside

They hid among the trees concealing themselves
from the face of Yahweh-God.

GENESIS 3:8

Jesus has paid the price to bring you close—right up to the face of God. There is no need to hide. No reason to keep secrets from our Father who knows and sees it all. Every sin, shame, doubt, and fear stand at attention, ready to be purged by his glory light.

Come out of hiding. He's reaching for you. Smiling at you with love that carries no demands. No criticisms. No restrictions. Right now, exactly as you are, the Father longs to spend time with you. To pour the healing waters of his love into every nook and cranny of your once dry soul. You don't have to feign religious piety. You simply come and accept the gift of perfect love. Everything else will fall into place. Come.

Father, I'm done pretending to be something I'm not. Only you can make me whole. It's only by receiving your love that I can love myself and love others. Instead of staring at my many imperfections, I will behold your glory. And as I do, I will be transformed into your image. You are the beauty inside me.

Confess Your Need

Yahweh-God called Adam's name and asked,
"Where are you?"

GENESIS 3:9

Instead of rushing to meet with the Father when Adam sinned, he hid. But God, in his perfect love, didn't angrily demand an explanation. The first words out of the Father's mouth were words of yearning love. *Where are you?* In other words, "What is the condition of your heart that causes you to hide from me?" This is the question the Lord holds before us today.

God longs for each of us to examine our lives, be honest about the areas we'd rather hide from him, and confess our need. God's words to fallen man speak of grace, not judgment. His question is meant to remind us where he longs for us to be: by his side. He wants to draw us out of hiding. In the place of perfect love, there is no shame. When we sin, we can run to the Father who pulls us in close and restores our fellowship.

Father, here I am! In seasons of weariness and confusion, I am yours. In times of doubt and temptation, I ask that you never leave my side. And if the enemy ever casts shadows upon my soul and I lose my way, rush in to rescue me. I depend on you entirely. I desire to remain close to you forever.

Hear Him

"I heard your powerful presence
moving in the garden."

GENESIS 3:10

Quiet yourself in the presence of God. You were created for this. Beautifully woven in the heart of God long before time began. You aren't an accident. You don't need to be afraid of his glory when it is a part of you.

Listen and you will hear him moving in the garden of your soul. He's awakening you to your destiny. To the joyous freedom found in sweet fellowship. Unending communion that will last for eternity. The glory of his presence compels you to pay attention. To lift your head, bow your knees, open your arms, and welcome him home. He is the song rising from your heart. He is the love that drives away fear. He is the light in the darkness. Do you hear him?

Father, I hear you! I sense you in the atmosphere. I feel you in my bones. Your glory is unmistakable, and I'm running straight for you. You are the One I long for. The One I give my life to. Nothing matters more than being with you and experiencing the sweetness and life-altering power of your love.

Honesty

Adam pointed to the woman and said, "The woman you placed
alongside me—she gave me fruit from the tree."
So Yahweh-God said to the woman, "What have you done?"
The woman pointed to the snake and said, "The shining snake
tricked me."

GENESIS 3:12–13

Blame-shifting began in the garden. Adam laid the blame for his
actions upon someone else and indirectly upon God. The enemy
tricks us into thinking that if we sugarcoat sin or get away with it,
no one will hold us responsible. We want to point the finger and
cast responsibility for sin on anyone but ourselves. But God already
knows the truth.

Honesty is the road to integrity. Without it, we will never know
where we need to mature. And we most likely won't have anything
more than a superficial relationship with the Lord. True repentance
flows from a humble heart. Jesus is faithful to cleanse us from
unrighteousness but only when we confess our sins, great and small.
Let's be honest about the things we'd rather sweep under the rug. It
not only invites God's presence but also sets us up for a powerful life.

*Father, sometimes it's difficult accepting responsibility for the
areas of my life that fall into disarray. Give me the courage to be
honest about my sins, bad judgments, and selfish decisions. I want
to live without blockages in our relationship. Though pride tries to
hold me captive, your truth sets me free.*

Never Forget

Yahweh-God then said to the snake, "Because you have done this...
You will slither on your belly and eat dust all the days of your life!"

GENESIS 3:14

You were fearfully and wonderfully made. The very essence of
God's love and power. A beautiful combination of grace and glory.
You were created to live from a heavenly perspective. Designed to
walk confidently through the landmines of life—those circumstances
and temptations that once opened like hungry craters ready to
devour you. It's time to see the path God has cleared before you.

In the place of spiritual awareness, where our eyes are fixed upon
the Lord, we see the snares the enemy sets. He wants us to walk
in our *dust-nature* so he has something to feast on. When we hold
on to our old mindsets and ways of living, we become the enemy's
food. But when our hearts are set higher, on the revelation of who
we are in Christ, temptation cannot hold us. Vessels created for
God's glory only get covered in the dirt and grime of this world
when we forget who we are.

*Father, I stand confident in who you made me to be. Not because
I think I can live one moment without you but because I know
you never leave. Every day I spend with you changes me. I become
more and more like you with each encounter. And here in the
safety of my identity in Christ, the enemy holds no ground.*

Under His Feet

"I will place great hostility between you and the woman,
and between her seed and yours.
He will crush your head as you crush his heel."

GENESIS 3:15

From the very beginning, God had a plan of redemption. Sin never stumped him. His joy wasn't quelled by the fear of how everything he made might be ruined. We read no record of his surprise or confusion over what to do next. He showed his irrefutable wisdom, incomparable power, and unlimited compassion the very first time man rejected his instructions. God didn't cross his arms over his chest and, with a look of disgust, tell us to clean up our mess. He already had a plan, and he wasn't worried about a thing. Mercy would provide the way.

Jesus would become the incorruptible seed born of woman. He would be the One capable of crushing the sin barrier that could have blocked us from a relationship with our heavenly Father. Love found a way. Love continues to find ways to stomp out the enemy's attempts at hindering this divine connection.

Father, no one loves me the way you do. From the beginning of time, you have proven your faithfulness to those you love. My redeeming Savior, I'm bowed low, overcome by the ways you draw me close. May the posture of my heart forever demonstrate my absolute gratefulness and unrestrained devotion.

Life-giving Creativity

God said to the woman,
"I will cause your labor pains in childbirth to be intensified;
with pain, you will give birth to children."

GENESIS 3:16

Most children are birthed through pain. The Hebrew word for *pain* is *'etsev*, a homophone that can also mean *creativity*. Isn't it incredible that some of the most brilliant, life-giving creativity is birthed through the labor pains of life? God enjoys using our most difficult trials as a canvas to display his redemptive genius.

Pain can be an incubator for creativity. In the moments we are left with nothing, we find that Jesus is enough. In our most raw and vulnerable anguish, we tap into the strength of the One who breathes hope into hopelessness. It is in the discovery of God's grace that we find beauty powerful enough to make our music, writing, painting, and dancing come alive. We create works of art that are not only pure and meaningful but also anointed with his healing virtue.

Father, for too long I viewed my trials from a perspective of disappointment. I wanted to hide from them and get as far away from the memories of hardship as I could. But now, I understand that beauty can blossom from the ashes of suffering and heartache. The ways you greeted me in my pain is a testimony that can set others free. Turn every heartache into a masterpiece of creativity that demonstrates your faithfulness.

Garments of Grace

Yahweh-God made garments from animal skins
to clothe Adam and Eve.

GENESIS 3:21

God didn't ignore Adam and Eve's feelings of shame over their nakedness. He didn't wag his finger of judgment and tell them to endure their embarrassment as punishment. He didn't even force them to continue wearing fig leaves—their pitiful attempts at covering themselves. Instead he provided the soft, beautiful clothing made from animal skins—the first animal sacrifice mentioned in the Bible.

What a beautiful example of God's compassion. Our endeavors to cover our sin will always fall short. Only the robe of righteousness that God provides will do. This merciful God never leaves us to fend for ourselves. He never holds us at a distance when we reek of failure. He always provides an answer. He carefully and lovingly finds the best way to keep us close when our hearts long for truth and atonement. Wrapped in the Lord's garments of grace, we look just like our Father.

Father, thank you for your mercy. For always making a way for me to remain close. For stripping away my sin-stained garments and wrapping me in love. May I always stay aware of your redemption. Always feel the warmth of your nearness as I linger in your presence. I want to look and sound like you. To bring you glory by accepting every provision of grace you extend.

The Fiery Sword

> He drove them out of the garden, and placed fearsome angelic sentries east of the garden of Eden, with a turning fiery sword to guard the way to the Tree of Life.

GENESIS 3:24

When we read this passage, it's easy to think God was barring man from the Tree of Life forever. But that's not true. The way of returning leads us through a spiritual path—through the One who is *the way*. Again, we see both the wisdom and mercy of God as he provides a way for us to live forever, not in our frail human condition, but once we've shed our bodies and step into heaven.

This fiery sword that guarded the way gives us a glimpse of the sword we refer to as the Word of God. Now, in order to get to the Tree of Life, we first go through this flaming sword, which judges the secret motives of our hearts. We invite the fires of purification to separate our fleshly, sinful nature from our redeemed, awakened spirits. The Word of God is more than a map that shows the way to the Tree of Life. It is a holy, living, powerful force examining our deepest desires, so we may be set free.

Father, I invite your fiery truth to cut away anything in me that would separate me from you. I long to eat from the Tree of Life. To have unbroken fellowship. I yearn to be with you forever with no limits restricting our interaction.

In the Garden

He drove them out of the garden.

GENESIS 3:24

Sin separated us from God. It forced us from the garden until Jesus carried us back in on the shoulders of redemption. We are blessed once again with the sweetness of holy fellowship. In the holy place, this secret garden of his presence, we can experience the closeness of our Father in ways Adam and Eve didn't.

Our very lives have become the Lord's most precious vineyard. Now the garden of encounter is found in the quiet of our hearts. We've been invited to meet with him here. To enjoy the honor of garden walks with our Father, Savior, and friend. To savor these moments of devotion, worship, prayer, or simply resting in his presence. To breathe in the fragrance of divine love. To simply be with him every day.

Father, I love meeting with you in our private garden—the secret place of your holy presence. When the world feels like it's spinning out of control, it's here that I find solitude and grace. You pull me close and wrap me in the warmth of your love. Holy Spirit, walk with me today.

March

Mercy's Gift

Yahweh was very pleased with Abel and accepted his offering,
but with Cain and his offering, Yahweh was not pleased,
making Cain very furious and resentful.

GENESIS 4:4–5

Many have tried to understand why God would accept Abel's
offering but not Cain's. We know Abel sacrificed an animal while
Cain brought an offering of fruit. And because the Bible is full of
hidden treasure, when we dig, we see glints of prophetic insight.
Redeeming sacrifice must proceed fruit. In other words, we must
accept the sacrifice of the Lamb of God in our hearts before any of
our works are worth offering to the Lord.

We also notice that Cain's reaction was one of anger. Of course,
we didn't see the true musings of his heart until after things didn't
go his way. But God saw his heart from the beginning. We shouldn't
judge him. No one has perfect motives all the time. Remember, our
Father sees into the deepest caverns of our souls, even the areas
we've yet to face. This is why we bow low and confess our great
need for mercy's kiss.

*Father, I long for your cleansing flow to wash my life. I cry out for
mercy's gift. Create a clean heart within me. Let every thought,
desire, and deed be founded on the truth of who you are. May my
focus not be on the trinkets I offer you but on the beauty of what
you have given me.*

Vulnerable Moments

"If you refuse to offer what is right, sin, the predator, is crouching in wait outside the door of your heart. It desires to have you, yet you must be its master."

GENESIS 4:7

Our reactions to disappointment and frustration pique the enemy's attention. Sin crouches outside the doors of our hearts, waiting for an opportunity to root itself and skew our objectivity. It's easier to justify bad attitudes than to prostrate ourselves before the Lord. It takes zero effort to yield to fleshly reactions. Confessing bad attitudes takes honesty and vulnerability. But an honest and contrite heart draws the strengthening grace of God.

When we choose to yield our will and our right to defend ourselves, we're empowered to overcome. This ongoing decision to embrace a Christlike mindset becomes easier each time. Falling at the feet of Jesus with messy tears of surrender invites the glory of his grace. And when we're smeared with the oil of God's presence, burdens slide right off.

Father, pour out your empowering grace. When storms rage against my soul and injustices push me to react, help me to remember that there is something greater at risk—my sensitivity to your Spirit. I don't want to become accustomed to reacting but to be acquainted with the higher ways of your Spirit. Give me the courage to inspect my attitudes and to get to the root of them with you.

Sin's Debt

Cain said to Yahweh,
"My punishment is more than I can bear!"

GENESIS 4:13

It's easy to look at the actions of others and declare that they deserve to be disciplined. While it is true that evil deserves punishment, restoration is at the heart of each of God's corrections. Even though we read no record of Cain crying out for forgiveness, we still see the Lord's compassion. God promises Cain that if anyone kills him, there will be a sevenfold vengeance upon his or her life. Mercy reached out to Cain even though he didn't deserve it.

Mercy and grace drip from the cross in a flow of costly blood. Blood that Jesus shed for all who have sinned. None of us deserves it. No matter how insignificant we think our sins are, they are powerful enough to separate us from the presence of God. Sin is a burden too heavy for us to bear on our own, so Jesus bore it for us. When we are tempted to judge others' sin as worse than our own, let's remember that if not for the cross, God would banish us from his presence too.

Father, I'm undone by the power of your compassion. You continue to reach out your hand of mercy even when I mistakenly think I don't need it. But I will always need your mercy. And by your grace, my heart will remain humble. Forever I will worship you for this love that paid my ransom.

A Listening Heart

Yahweh responded.

GENESIS 4:15

We could quickly pass over these two powerful words. Perhaps it's because we're so used to doing all the talking in our times of prayer. Maybe it's because we don't actually expect God to respond. Sadly, many people spend enormous amounts of time venting to God and the rest of the time wondering why they don't hear him. But this can change in an instant!

We were created to hear the voice of our Father. He longs to commune with us, and there is only one requirement—a listening heart. We desire his wisdom, but to hear it, we must be still. Let's make quiet time a priority each day. Instead of doing all of the talking, let's tap into his presence and wait there until truth and wisdom rise from the depths of our spirit. He's there. He's speaking. He's responding to your lovesick heart.

Father, I honor the beauty of your presence with me right now. Forgive me for doubting. For talking more than I listen. I quiet myself in your presence and ask for the grace to do this often. I'm listening, Lord.

Wandering

Cain left the presence of Yahweh
and journeyed to the Land of Wandering.

GENESIS 4:16

Stand inside the expanse of God's glorious presence and you will experience life to the fullest. This is what the Lord created you for—to dwell in the safety of his wraparound love and to know that he is good.

His presence is home. All that you need or could ever desire flows from the heart of God. Many have searched for shortcuts to riches, fame, and pleasures of this world only to lose themselves in the process. Guard your heart and don't let it wander. Though his path may lead you on a journey that takes longer than you anticipate, stay the course. God, in his perfect wisdom, will never steer you wrong. He knows exactly how to get you where you need to go. Stay focused. Stay fixated on the beauty of his ever-present love and you won't be led astray.

Father, don't let my own wandering thoughts pull me away from the awareness of you. I want to remain here in the sanctuary of your presence, regardless of what the day brings. Faith overrides fear when I abide with you. Your presence is the meeting place for indescribable peace. Your love is a perfect home.

Yahweh

People began to worship Yahweh and pray to him.

GENESIS 4:26

The name *Yahweh* was once considered the unspeakable name. Too holy to put on our lips. Constructed of consonants in Hebrew that aren't actually articulated by the tongue or mouth, God's name is more accurately pronounced by breathing. With lips parted, we inhale *Yah* and exhale *weh*.

Even our unconscious breathing, which sustains our lives, reminds us of the sovereignty of God. With every breath, we declare his eternal splendor and wisdom. We unwittingly declare his existence just by being alive. With each inhale, we take in his glory. With every exhale, we confess our absolute dependence. His name is like a whisper. It is heard on the wind. It is gentle, powerful, and alive. Just saying *Yahweh* stirs our souls with longing. He is the only One who is with us in every breath we take.

Yahweh—simply saying your name draws me into the mystery of your love. From before I was conceived in my mother's womb, you have known me. Been with me. Breathed life into my being and never left. Every inhale and exhale reminds me of your great care. Oh, how I love to say your name!

He Sees You

Here is the family history of Adam and Eve.

GENESIS 5:2

Throughout the Bible are scattered lists of family history. Long lists of names, lifespans, and reflections of how people lived either for the Lord or for themselves. For some readers, it may be a tad boring to scroll through the names that, for us, don't appear to have a reason for being there. But let's think about the fact that our Father knew each person. By including snapshots of different lives, he seems to be letting us know that no one escapes his eye. He knows us all.

Your life matters. You have been born into an eternal family. Every sigh of your heart, each joyous laugh, and every person you touch is important to the Lord. You are not insignificant. God has not bypassed you. In truth, he is wooing you to come closer. He's willing to let you peek at the chapters he is writing about you. Regardless of how your life has gone so far, each day has the potential for something new and exciting when you walk with him.

Father, I want to live each day to its fullest potential. That may mean changing my plans and seeking your will before forging ahead. It may mean resting when I want to run. But in all things, I seek to please you in all I do and think.

He Knows You

After he had created them, he lovingly blessed them
and named them "humanity."
So here is the family history of Adam and Eve.

GENESIS 5:2–3

Nothing in the Bible is there by mistake. The long lists of names
and ages aren't simply a record of historical lineage. They give us
another glimpse into the heart of God. Only a Father who loves his
children takes the time to mention each one by name.

God sees you and knows not only your name but also every
movement of your heart and each dream you long to fulfill. He
knows the number of hairs on your head and what you're thinking
at this very moment. You are desired and cherished. You are the
beloved bride he has chosen for his Son. You are the one Jesus died
for. You're the temple he's elected to house his Holy Spirit. Nothing
about you is mundane or uninteresting to him. He enjoys being
with you so much that he's created eternity so this holy relationship
will never end.

*Father, you always know just how to encourage me. When I think
about the way you tenderly care for me, I can't help but smile.
Every time I call to you, you take the time to listen. I'm so honored
to be a part of your family. I feel known, celebrated, and desired.
Thank you for being a Father who loves without any strings
attached. For accepting me just as I am.*

Imparting to Future Generations

The life span of Adam was nine hundred and thirty years,
and then he died.

GENESIS 5:5

Adam and Enoch were alive at the same time. This means that Enoch very likely grew up hearing stories from his elder family member. Imagine what that was like, hearing Adam share stories of God walking in the garden and speaking with them in the cool of the day. Perhaps Enoch's desire for intimacy came from hearing these incredible accounts.

It's so vital that we don't overlook our own stories of encounter, breakthrough, and discovery of the faithfulness of God. Every fiery trial we have walked through with him is a testimony we should share with those we love. These are the golden treasures of our inheritance. They are more valuable than any financial blessing we can leave behind. Our encounters and intimate experiences of God's holy presence can create longing in the hearts of others and set the course of their lives.

Father, help me to be a good steward of my relationship with you. Remind me to keep track of the wisdom, revelations, and the many ways you've led me so it can be passed down for generations to come. The reality of your tangible love is a gift I long to impart.

Walk with God

Enoch walked with God for three hundred years
after Methuselah was born.

GENESIS 5:22

Every day we are invited to walk with God as Enoch did. Sometimes we read stories of those who were blessed with close relationships with the Lord, and instead of allowing our sense of wonder to draw us in, we stand awestruck and immovable. We aren't mean to linger outside of God's chambers, feeling satisfied with casual conversations as he walks by. We are called to enter in. To savor each day and count it as an immense blessing. To tune in to the whispers of his voice. To recognize his laugh. To perceive his fragrance as he wraps us in his arms.

Walking closely with the Lord implies setting aside our agendas to follow his. We notice when his steps slow or speed up, turn when he turns, and pause when he pauses. We commune with him in the intimate sharing of hearts.

Father, I want to know you. To remain so near to you that I never wonder where you've gone or why you're so quiet. I don't want to waste one moment on a path that you're not on. Take my hand. Lead me as we walk together.

Be His Friend

Enoch and God walked together as intimate friends.

GENESIS 5:24

God made sure that Scripture recorded his friendship with Enoch. Can you imagine having your name etched forever in history as one of God's close friends? To be known as his intimate friend sounds like one of the highest honors we could ask for!

Let's make it our life's quest to live as one of God's favorites. To start our day with heart and mind fixed on his nearness. To anticipate our quiet times of communion before we rush about. To not only pour out prayers but to also lean in close to listen. Friends laugh, joke, share secrets, and are there for each other during trying times. We were created for a relationship like this with the Lord. To live so aware of him that we expect his voice and anticipate his guidance and encouragement throughout the day. To enjoy the sweetness of fellowship with God as our intimate friend.

Father, I want to be known as someone who has captured your attention with my surrendered life. For the angels of heaven and the demons of hell to notice that we are inseparable. To hear your whispers as I fall asleep and feel the radiance of your smile when I awake. I want my yearning heart to please you and my actions to reflect my absolute gratitude and unrivaled devotion.

Sweet Fellowship

God took him to himself,
and he was seen no more.

GENESIS 5:24

Imagine walking so closely with the Lord that when you suddenly disappear, people automatically know the Lord has taken you. Many respected Enoch's relationship with the Lord. Then one day, God took him because he delighted in Enoch. He left behind a legacy of holy intimacy, integrity, and miraculous encounter. Wow! That's the kind of legacy we should all strive for.

This man whose life pleased God during days of wickedness and corruption is an example for us. We don't have to live in isolation to have an intimate walk with our Father. Enoch was a husband and father with a long list of relatives. Yet he was known as God's friend. How we live and speak reflect the desires of our hearts. We don't have to impress people with Bible knowledge or strive to appear holy. When sweet fellowship with God is our norm, we effortlessly reflect the beauty of the One we love.

Father, I delight in you. Your presence warms my soul, wraps me like a blanket of peace on a cold day. Your laughter exhilarates me like a refreshing breeze. You are my best friend. You're the reason I sing and the One who occupies my mind. I pray this love that consumes me will overflow into the lives of everyone I meet.

Moved to Love Him

Yahweh was saddened that he had made humanity,
and his heart was filled with pain.

GENESIS 6:6

What does this verse do to your heart? It's hard to imagine the perfect, Almighty God anguished over us. Our creative minds may imagine darkness, stars falling from the sky, planets colliding, the very earth itself dropping because of the heaviness of his sorrow. Of course, this was not the case. But when we think of God's heart being filled with pain, it should affect us profoundly and cause us to take notice.

God does not stand far off, unaffected by us. He loves us. The ideal, flawless, ever-loving Father allows himself to be moved by our actions and heart intent. This should cause us to love him even more. To know that, individually, we matter to him. Oh, that our love and absolute devotion would rise as fragrant offerings to bless him. That we would be known as people who have ravished his heart and caused him joy.

Lord, may it never be said of me that I caused you pain. I want my life to be saturated with a holy desire to honor and love you. May every cell, every fiber of my being swell with holy longing to bless you. I want to fill you with joy. I want you to be as overwhelmed by my love as I am by yours.

By Grace Alone

One man found grace in the sight of Yahweh: Noah.

GENESIS 6:8

Our choices, our everyday decisions to walk before the Lord with pure hearts capture his attention. Everything we do matters. Idle words, judgments, the way we joke, our patience levels, everything. He overlooks nothing. Noah's heart and lifestyle must have stood in harsh contrast to the people of his day. He was the one who found grace in the sight of God.

Noah would be God's hands to build the ark and save mankind. This favor extended to his family. By grace alone, they would escape divine judgment. When God finds people whose hearts are toward him, he draws them close and pours out even more grace to do his will. Works alone cannot fulfill his mandate on the earth. It was the grace of God, not the virtue of Noah, that preserved him and his family from the devastation of judgment. Grace is the foundation of every life that pleases him.

Father, no matter how hard I try, I will never deserve the grace you give. Even with your Spirit within me, my humanity rears its ugly head. My heart is toward you, and my greatest desire is to live in a way that honors and pleases you. Extend your grace to me and draw me closer. Thank you for inviting me to partner with you on the earth. I know it is by your grace alone I stand.

Our Story

This is the story of Noah.

GENESIS 6:9

Since Genesis is like God's autobiography, it should excite us to read the way he references people. We hear of those who were evil and those who stood out as favorites. God sees it all—every thought and intent of our hearts. Every decision, conversation, and desire is known and important enough for him to remember. And when he wants people to know who we are and what our story is, he finds a way.

Have you ever considered the story God may share about you? Knowing he is loving and merciful and sees the deepest intentions of the heart should cause hope to rise in you. Imagine hearing that you brought him tears of joy when you thought you failed. Or hearing him call you faithful even though it took years to overcome fear and doubt. Noah wasn't perfect. Only Jesus was without sin. Yet God says Noah was without fault. God doesn't see as man does. He sees our hearts. Let's be encouraged and inspired to live our story from God's viewpoint.

Father, when I feel like I'm disappointing you, I can run to you and find grace and mercy in time of need. You don't highlight my failures; you shout my victories from heaven. You are kind and merciful, and I want to be the type of person you love to write about.

Honor Him

Noah was a godly man of integrity,
without fault in his generation,
and he lived close to God.

GENESIS 6:9

Noah was described as a godly man in a perverse generation. Since we know only Jesus was without sin, we know Noah wasn't perfect. Still, he was honored as someone whose integrity and lifestyle caught the Lord's attention.

Living close to the Lord gives us a different perspective on what is essential. While others are enticed by lust, greed, and selfish pride, our relationship with him keeps our hearts soft and pliable. No matter how evil the world may be, God's grace purifies us and enables us to live in righteousness. It provides us with the grace to stand out, not for the sole purpose of being different, but because our entire focus is living to honor him.

Father, I long to please you with a life of holy devotion. To stand apart from the crowd as one whose deepest desires reflect your heart. To exist within the masses in order to shine your love, holiness, and compassion. To live in godliness, wholly dependent upon your empowering grace.

The Way of Faith

God said to Noah...
"Build a boat for yourself—an ark of sturdy timber.
And this is how you are to design it."

GENESIS 6:13–14

It's interesting to imagine the details of God speaking to Noah.
Did he appear to him? Did Noah hear an audible voice? Perhaps
the Lord spoke in a dream or through an angel. We aren't told,
but regardless of how he warned Noah, it took faith to act on the
revelation he received. Most of the things God leads us to require
risk. The only way to know if we're really hearing God is to take that
risk and wait for the result.

Faith can be scary, but following him becomes a journey of
testimony for others to follow. Noah's family certainly had their faith
tested! Not only did God protect them, but later, he also honored
Noah by mentioning him as a man of faith (Hebrews 11:7). Trusting
the Lord opens our hearts to receive revelation. Obedience to
those revelations, no matter how shaky those steps feel, causes us
to grow. We were created to know the voice of our Father. This is
the way of faith.

*Father, sometimes the things you ask me to do seem outrageous.
You move me in directions I don't feel qualified to handle, tell me
to wait when I want to run, or ask me to believe when everything I
see contradicts your truth. Though my mind rarely grasps spiritual
matters, you have my "yes!" You have my heart.*

Sealed

"And seal it inside and out with thick tar."

GENESIS 6:15

The word "tar" in this verse is *kopher*, a word used throughout the Old Testament that also means "atonement." Noah was told to seal (literally, "atone") the ark as a symbol of Christ's blood that preserves us from judgment.

Jesus has placed his seal upon our hearts, and we are joyfully his for eternity. Nothing can separate us from his love—not pain, the storms of suffering, or even death. Our yielded life calls forth his merciful hand, and he locks out the intruders who seek to vandalize our souls. He is the faithful One who has redeemed us and encases our hearts with the fiery seal of divine love. It isn't our achievements, the number of verses we've memorized, or the way we discipline our flesh that fastens us to him. It is his grace alone.

Father, let your divine love be the seal that irrevocably fastens me to you. Hold me close so I might not sin against you. I want to remain aware of your Holy Spirit in and around me at all times. Wrap me in a cocoon of your presence everywhere I go. Nothing will separate me from your love!

Hidden Treasure

"Construct a door on the side of the ark,
and design it with lower, middle, and upper decks."

GENESIS 6:16

Woven into the stories of our lives are mysteries of divine making.
We meet someone and think it's a meaningless encounter until,
years later, we realize the meeting was pivotal to the course of our
life. A random conversation launches a career; a book opens us up
to new revelation. Situations that at first seem insignificant are life
altering.

The story of Noah's ark has hidden treasures neatly planted into it.
The ark was made of cypress wood, which speaks of the humanity
of Jesus. With one door leading in, we recognize Jesus as the only
way to God. And this same door, set in the ark's side, reminds us
of the pierced side of Jesus on the cross. The three levels of the ark
remind us that Jesus provides salvation for our body, soul, and spirit.
It's so exciting to walk with a God who gives us daily opportunities
to uncover the gifts he has tucked away for us in both the Scriptures
and throughout our lives.

*Father, forgive me for the times I've thought my life is boring and
mundane. Each day is a gift. Every conversation is teeming with
life when I listen for you in the midst of it. When my life is wholly
yielded to you, every thought, choice, and random act can become
something magnificent.*

The Safety of His Love

> "I am going to release a great flood that will destroy all life upon the earth, and every breathing thing under heaven will perish—everything on earth will die."
>
> GENESIS 6:17

In one of the darkest times of history, the same God who judged mankind also wrapped his chosen ones in protection. Noah's ark wasn't a prison but a shelter from the punishing storm, just as the Lord Jesus Christ is our place of refuge. He is our safety when the pounding rains of difficulty fall like torrents.

God saw Noah as a man of integrity. Noah didn't have to jump up and down to get God to notice him. His heart had the Lord's attention, and so does yours. He knows all who are his. All who keep themselves pure in times of wickedness. And he will keep them safe in days of judgment. This God who was moved with compassion and soon provided a Redeemer for all of humanity is willing to receive all who come to him.

Father, thank you for the compassion and mercy that have saved me. Thank you for the love that has marked my life and awakened my soul. Wrap me in the safety of your love. Keep me close and be the light that guides me every day. I'm honored that you would notice me. Blessed that you call me your own.

The Ark of His Presence

"I will establish my covenant of friendship,
and you will escape destruction by coming into the ark,
you and your wife, your sons and their wives."

GENESIS 6:18

Friendship with God draws us into a place of confidence and safety. When trust, even in trials, becomes our anchor, God in his mercy provides an ark. The ark is a symbol of Jesus, the One whose love has saved us. The ark endured the fury of the flood, just as Christ endured the wrath of God for us. Jesus is the sinner's provision as the ark was provision for Noah and his family.

The beauty of symbolism hidden in the account of the ark reminds us that there is always more to the story than we see at first. As time passes and our friendship with the Lord becomes sweeter, he reveals secrets. So often we want to understand every tiny detail in times of testing, but God asks us to trust him. To step onto the rising waters with him as our only refuge. And as we do, we discover that he is more than enough.

Father, establish your covenant of friendship with me. Teach me your ways as I relinquish the right to understand what can only be accepted by faith. You are my ark of provision—my place of safety. You are my future, and my destiny is safe in your hands.

Say Yes

Noah completed all these preparations
and did everything exactly as God had commanded him.

GENESIS 6:22

Sometimes obedience to God stings. It often carries a lofty price
tag that only we can pay. The decision to bow low is one we make
repeatedly. It crucifies our selfish desires while breathing life into
the deepest parts of our souls. Obedience to God is our honor and
ultimately our joy.

The more we get to know the Lord, the easier it is to say yes.
Year after year, we learn that his faithfulness is greater than we've
imagined. Our Father extends the invitation to take a risk so he can
show us how exciting it is to adventure with him. Faith becomes the
substance we walk upon. Love answers the incessant questions of
unbelief. Mercy proves to us how trustworthy he is.

*Father, I say yes to you! Yes to following your lead. Yes to laying
down my will to experience the thrill of discovering yours. Living in
obedience to you is my delight. You are the King of my heart and
the wise Counselor who guides my decisions. Let selfishness die
and holy devotion take root.*

Come Closer

The day came when Yahweh said to Noah,
"Come into the ark."

GENESIS 7:1

This is your invitation. Today is your day to draw closer to the lover of your soul. Don't let your fears or busyness stop you. Resist the temptation to put it off until later. Do you feel him wooing your heart? Come closer. Drink from the well of Living Water. Taste and see that he is good!

Jesus is the answer to every prayer you've prayed. His presence is the crux of everything you need. He is the starting point, the end, and everything in between. Grace, wisdom, favor, and blessing will saturate every situation you face if you walk through it with him. Even painful circumstances are different when you face them with the Lord. Don't stand afar off, racking your brain, trying to figure this out on your own. Come to him! Stay in the place of grace.

Father, thank you for removing the veil that once separated me from your presence. Now I can come as close as I want. You have accepted me. Your scepter is extended toward me, and you have invited me into your holy presence. Jesus, thank you for clearing the way for me to stand face-to-face with you.

It Is Well

Noah obeyed all that Yahweh had commanded him. ...
Then seven days later, massive floodwaters covered the earth.

GENESIS 7:5, 10

It's hard to comprehend what Noah went through as he prepared for the flood. Imagine how he must have felt knowing that as much as he warned people to turn their hearts to the Lord, they wouldn't listen. The wondrous joy he may have felt watching the animals gather to enter the ark. The gratefulness that swelled in his heart because God was merciful to him and his family. The overwhelming sorrow of knowing that those who scorned would be swept away.

This ebbing, flowing, living relationship with the Lord stirs every emotion our Creator has given us. Truthfully, not everything makes sense. All we know is that we sense him in every fiber of our being. We experience the indwelling of his Spirit and know he's alive within us. He speaks in ways we find difficult to explain. And though many don't understand, we continue because through every doubt, the Lord is the most unshakable reality of our lives.

Father, at times I cannot fathom how you'll do what you say you will, yet you have proven your faithfulness. I'm learning to be okay with mystery. Learning that it's safe to feel the tension of faith and emotion. Confident that, in the end, it will be well with my soul because it is held in your hands.

Open Floodgates

All the fountains of the subterranean deep
cracked open and burst up through the ground.
Heaven's floodgates were opened.

GENESIS 7:11

The heavens are open over your life. Bursting with glory rain, ready to saturate every crevice of your dry ground. You don't have to collapse by the streams of his presence, using shaking hands to lift drops of water to parched lips. Just turn your attention to him, and his presence will rise as an ever-flowing fountain within you, quenching your thirsty soul.

Nothing can stop God's desire for you. The forces of hell cannot hinder his love. He has chosen you. God has seen your steadfast heart and heard every cry of holy resolve. The waters of his love are cascading over your soul and healing every wound. Drink deeply. Swim in the deepest oceans of sacred bliss. Dive in!

Father, saturate me with the awareness of your presence so I can tap into its life-giving waters at any time. Drench me in your love. Refine every longing. Rise within me and quench my thirst for happiness and true love. Submerge every thought in your cleansing flow. My heart is wide open.

Our Refuge

Yahweh himself shut them in.

GENESIS 7:16

We've done everything God has asked us to do. Despite the crowded questions trying to push the faith from our hearts, we remain true. As the waters rise and it seems the entire earth is shifting beneath us, we fix our eyes on him and cling to his promises. He will not forget us. God himself will protect us.

God himself shut the door of the ark. He sealed Noah, his family, and the animals for his purposes, just as he encloses you in the sanctuary of his love. Yes, at times clouds swirl, and we want to question the validity of his promises. We'd rather hide than keep believing. But as we turn to our Father—again and again and again—he watches. He takes note of the way we say yes through tear-filled eyes and nearly exhausted faith. We are his, and though we sometimes falter, we don't give up. And in this place of total dependency on God, he comes. The Lord shuts the door and pulls us into the refuge of his presence.

Father, when I'm weary and troubled, come to my rescue. Enclose me in the beauty of your tangible presence. I don't have the strength to face trials without you. There are some doors only you can shut. I can only rely on your mercy and compassion. Here is my surrendered heart. Protect it.

Safe above the Waters

The swelling floodwaters lifted up the ark
until it rose high above the ground.

GENESIS 7:17

Higher and higher, above the raging seas of adversity. This is your safe place. This is where you find peace in the middle of turmoil. Your Father in heaven is your fierce Protector. The One who scoops you up in his strong arms and offers you a place to rest.

As much as you would rather sail on calm waters, storms are inevitable. But the Lord's presence isn't blown away by the opposing winds. He's there. Immovable. Unflinching. Undefeated. He's Emmanuel—with you right now. When all you hear are the bellowing winds, the whispers of his voice will rise from within. Fold yourself into this love, and it will carry you to the place of safety. He will heal your tattered heart. His presence will guide you home.

Father, draw close to me. Wrap your arms around me and carry me to safety. The storms of life have made me seasick, and I need your grace. You're here. I feel you now, gifting me with peace. The sun is rising, and the clouds are dissipating. I can breathe again. Slowly. Steadily. All because you love me.

At the Top

...until the highest mountains were completely submerged beneath the rising waters.

GENESIS 7:19

Mountains of opposition are no match for the splendor of God. Everything that stands in your way will bow to his lordship in your life. It will serve to strengthen you as you climb its heights with Jesus. You were made for this!

Don't get sucked into a mental battle. Stop trying to figure this out in your own wisdom. The Lord has already claimed this land, and you are his inheritance. It's time to rise above the clutter of unruly thoughts and look at them from his point of view. Keep climbing. Keep going! Don't let go of the Lord's hand. He's got you. He won't let you stumble. At the top of this mountain, you'll see clearly.

Father, thank you for your encouragement. I'm not going to stop pressing into you. You don't want me to be sidetracked by the hike but to remain in step with you as we climb out of this pit. And when I don't have the strength to keep going, you will impart your strength. At the top of this mountain, I will shout your victory!

A Holy Life

All life on earth was blotted out—all that he had made, animals large and small, wild and domesticated, birds and reptiles, including humanity, was wiped off the face of the earth.

GENESIS 7:23

Our Father, Lord, friend, and Savior is also our righteous judge. He isn't impatient and cruel. He extended divine revelation to those who despised and rejected it at every turn. They deliberately persisted in wickedness, and when their sins stacked up to the heavens, God stepped in. His judgment would cleanse the earth of its wickedness and give it a fresh start.

This Holy One requires more than lip service. He sees our hearts, calls us to righteousness, and graciously empowers us. On our own, we are frail, weak, and easily led astray. But through our acceptance of his love and desperate reliance on him, we are made strong. Each day we choose who we'll live for—ourselves or the One whose love paves the way. When we bow low, we're filled with the very glory of God, able to effortlessly live a holy life.

Father, let the fire of your love burn brightly in me. May I walk before you in the righteousness you have provided. And if I ever forget who I am, remind me. By your grace, keep my heart soft and pliable in your hands. I yield my life and will to you.

Set Apart

God's heart was moved with compassion as he remembered Noah
and all the animals, large and small, that were with him in the ark.

GENESIS 8:1

While Noah and the others were shut away in the ark, God was
watching. Though they were sealed away in a floating box, God
never left. From the day the waters rose until the day they settled on
dry ground, the Father's plan remained intact.

Many of us can relate. We experience times when we feel boxed in
and alone. God shuts us in a situation that sucks us dry. The waiting
doesn't make sense. But if we trust his love, we discover that God
uses everything for his glory. Our darkened surroundings become
illuminated by a single source of light: Jesus, just as the ark's only light
was its solitary window. It's in these places of confinement, in these
boxes, that God prepares us for promotion and power. We cling to
him like never before. When we feel alone, he whispers that we have
not been *set aside* but *set apart* for the blessings he has in store.

*Father, in this place of solitude when I feel trapped and unable
to move forward, I will embrace you. I will yield the desires of my
heart to your cleansing fire. Purify me. Refine my motives, fine-tune
my ideas, and set me on a firm foundation that cannot be shaken.
Here in the stillness, I wait.*

The Curse Is Reversed

The ark came to rest on the highest peak in Ararat.

GENESIS 8:4

One of the meanings of *Ararat* is "the curse is reversed." Just as the ark rested after the season of suffering, we, too, rest because of the suffering love of Jesus. The cross and empty tomb have reversed the curse that once held us in bondage. The Father has offered us a place close to his heart, where peace reigns.

Now in the high and holy land of the heavenly realm, we are seated with Christ. We are not victims. We are royalty. Our King has conquered every curse. In this place of victory, we do not strive to prove our authority. Peace is the evidence of our faith. Grace is the bond that secures us to him even when we struggle.

Father, you have paid a high price to set me free. Thank you. Sometimes I forget that I'm seated with you in heavenly places. I get distracted by the sound of the enemy's pebbles being hurled in my direction and overlook my powerful shield of faith. You are the champion who has taught me to stand. You have reversed the curse and brought me into your family.

April

My Dove

Noah put out his hand and grasped the dove
and put it back into the ark.

GENESIS 8:9

The dove, a symbol of the Holy Spirit, has come to rest inside of you. You are his home. His dwelling. The one who flows with the oil of glorious anointing. Through you, his purposes are released, and the world witnesses his love, mercy, and power. You are destined to soar with him.

One of the most powerful statements of Jesus' heart is revealed when he calls you his dove (Song of Songs 2:14). By comparing you to the Holy Spirit, he confirms your identity as a vessel of purity and perfection. Even when you botch things up and disappoint everyone, including yourself, God sees himself inside of you. He sees your devotion, even when you make a mess. Instead of punishing you for your immature faith, he comes with gentleness and offers you an olive leaf as a reminder that you have a destiny. When you're crushed, oil flows out, just as it does from the olive leaf. God's mercy is limitless. His grace defines you.

Father, thank you for encouraging me even when I struggle. Help me to remain single-minded with my heart fixed on you. Rise within me and lift me so close that I see you face-to-face. I want to fly with you. To soar above my doubts. To release your glory on the earth.

The Olive Leaf

Before evening, the dove came back to him—
and there in its beak was a freshly plucked olive leaf!

GENESIS 8:11

Inside of you is a vat of heavenly oil ready to share. It is the anointing of God—alive and fresh. It is the presence of his Spirit, which soothes, heals, and releases peace. It flows from Jesus, the branch, into us—his vines. The olive branch speaks of the Spirit of God bringing life and peace to the soul. It also speaks of the anointing—the oil within.

Every time the Dove of God comes, he brings fresh oil. The Holy Spirit has a freshly plucked olive leaf (a gift of anointing) specifically created just for you. Never doubt the power you carry. Release it whenever you feel his gentle nudge. The anointing rises from within and flows from your lips as words of encouragement, prayers of faith, and testimonies of God's goodness. Don't hold back.

Father, I want to flourish like an olive tree full of sacred oil. Let the glory of your presence seep into every crevice of my being. Leave nothing untouched by your tangible love. As I keep my affection set on you, pour out the anointing of your Spirit through my life so others will know this love as well.

Look Up

Noah lifted the hatch,
looked out,
and saw the dry ground.

GENESIS 8:13

Sometimes when we've been in a long season of adversity, it's easy to mentally get stuck there. We get so used to the way trials feel that we anticipate the worst. If we're not careful, we can become cynical and negative in our outlook on life. We doubt the validity of good news and question everything. We allow reasoning to take the lead instead of faith.

Seasons don't last forever. Wounds heal. Circumstances change. Wisdom overtakes foolishness. Doors that once slammed in your face open with favor. But you may not notice if you're not paying attention. Lift your weary head and look around. Like they did for Noah, the waters of adversity are drying up, and God is placing you on dry ground. Rid yourself of that negativity and believe again!

Father, I shake off everything that's been trying to bring me down. Breathe upon me—spirit, soul, and body—and give me back my zest for life. Ignite my faith afresh. I'm ready to see with new eyes and believe again. I repent for living in the shadows when your glory beckons me into the light.

Waiting

God said to Noah, "Come out of the ark,
you and your wife, your sons, and their wives."

GENESIS 8:15–16

Can you imagine spending a year on a boat with smelly animals? That's how long Noah and his family waited for God's permission to disembark. Five months floating and seven months on the mountain. We hear no record of Noah complaining. We don't read that he argued with the Lord or tried to leave the ark prematurely. He was patient. A man fully resigned to the will of God. Obedience saved his life.

Waiting can be hard. You want to run and *do*, but God says to stay and *wait*, instructing you to rest. If you're feeling antsy, finding it difficult to be at peace in a season of waiting, stop and take a breath. You're here for a reason. Press into these moments God has provided—they are meant to be refreshing. These quiet times are preparing you. Don't waste them. As you defer to his wisdom, you're growing in maturity. Rest and listen. Be still and know.

Father, sometimes I feel I'm at the cusp of something magnificent, and instead of being patient, I feel anxious. Give me the grace to wait with peace. To trust your ability to speak to me more than my inability to hear you. I will wait. I will rest. I will trust.

A New Beginning

Noah and his family left the ark;
and every animal large and small,
every bird and crawling thing
came out of the ark by families.

GENESIS 8:18–19

No matter what has happened in your life, regardless of the disappointments and seemingly lost dreams, God can give you a new beginning. He can breathe substance out of nothing other than the glory that exists within him. He doesn't need help. He doesn't need advice. He only asks for your faith. And when your faith feels like it's lying in a coma, you can ask him to awaken it with a holy kiss.

To step into something new, you first leave the old behind. You connect your heart to the Lord's heart. His desire to bless you and your acceptance of that truth must meet. Lay your doubt at his feet as an offering. The Lord isn't limited. He has all you need and then some. When you've come to the end of yourself, he has a new beginning for you!

Father, my own doubts have held me back for too long. Take my hand and lead me to the new thing you have for me. Whether it's what I've prayed for or something better, I'll let you decide. But from now on, I'll leave the unbelief behind and trust your loving heart.

An Altar of Worship

Noah erected an altar dedicated to Yahweh.

GENESIS 8:20

Worship is the safest place to begin any leg of our journey. Whether we've stepped into victory or had the rug pulled out from under us, setting our hearts on the Lord is a foundation he can build upon. When we offer him our tears, praise, questions, or our excitement, he sees. When we whisper declarations of love and proclaim his goodness in circumstances that feel far from good (or are a mixed bag like they were for Noah), we're worshiping in spirit and truth. True worship is an expression of love from someone who knows that God alone is in control.

The first thing Noah did when he stepped off the boat was to worship God. He didn't scout the land or build a house. Knowing that he and his family were the only people alive on the earth, he quite possibly had a lot going through his mind. Yet worship was his starting point.

Father, I want my life to be a pleasing offering, rising to bless you. I long to be known as a worshiper—one who seeks you in every situation. With absolute sincerity, I dedicate myself to you afresh. With unashamed devotion, I lift my hands and declare you are good. May every breath be a declaration of my love.

Faith over Fear

> When Yahweh smelled the sweet fragrance of Noah's offerings, his heart was stirred.
>
> GENESIS 8:21

Noah's worship captured God's attention. He had a lot to be thankful for—the Lord had spared his life and the lives of those he loved most. But it also must have been heartbreaking to witness such destruction. Still, he offered a sacrifice to the Lord that stirred God's heart, causing him to make a covenant with Noah.

There are times in our lives when everything around us feels chaotic. We experience both the faithfulness of God and the inexplicable times when he doesn't make sense. Yet we choose to trust the One who has made himself real to us. We cannot explain what is both mysterious and invisibly tangible, but our hearts are stirred to worship. We sacrifice the doubts, questions, and fears and embrace faith. And every time we do, each moment we choose faith over fear, God takes notice. He sees you, beloved. Your worship has his attention.

Father, I'm fully convinced that you are perfect in all your ways. Holy. Judging all things rightly. Let my worship and my confessions of trust be louder than the questions screaming for my attention. I am yours without reservation. All of me honors the beauty of all you are.

The Constant One

> "As long as earth exists there will always be seasons of planting and harvest, cold and heat, summer and winter, day and night."
>
> GENESIS 8:22

Life carries with it the promise of change. It is continually ebbing and flowing with the certainty of the unexpected. The highs and lows of life have one thing in common—God can be found in their midst.

No matter what we face, our Father is available to face it with us. He is the constant One. His love is our life-source, and it's always available. It infuses us with courage and strength. The presence of the Holy Spirit is our home. Our safe place. The ultimate reality that keeps us grounded and secure when hell rages against our souls. His joy isn't dependent upon the changing seasons. And, regardless of how happy or unhappy our circumstances make us, our deepest joy remains when it is found in him.

Father, walk with me today. Let me smell the blooming fragrance of your love everywhere I go. When the cold winds of adversity blow against me, tuck me into the warmth of your constant care. In the ups and downs of life, whisper the reassuring melody of our holy union.

Value Others

> "To kill a person is to kill one
> made in God's own beautiful image."
>
> GENESIS 9:6

God made each of us a reflection of his beauty. We are worthy of love and acceptance, regardless of our social status, language, color of skin, or political and social viewpoints. Every life is both precious and powerful in God's eyes. When he started over with Noah and his family, he made it clear: do not murder. In this portion of Scripture, God speaks explicitly of murder, but Jesus brings clarification in Matthew 5:22 when he tells us that holding anger in our hearts subjects us to the same judgment as a murderer.

Learning to honor and value others are keys to healing the trauma in our world. So is forgiveness. We must do more than give lip service to this vital subject. We must be willing to look into the eyes of another—even those we don't agree with—and remember that we are looking at someone who is loved by God and is made in his image.

Father, teach me to love. Help me to forgive. Guide me with wisdom so I understand how to walk with my brother, friend, and even those I consider to be enemies. You have equipped me to bring healing to our land. Grant me the ability to love unconditionally and purely and to see everyone through your eyes.

The Beauty of Promise

"I have placed my rainbow among the clouds,
and it will be a sign of my loving covenant
between me and the earth."

GENESIS 9:13

Look into the sky on a cloud-filled day, one ripe for rain yet holding on to a few scattered rays of sunlight, and you may see a rainbow. This sweet message of promise has not ceased. Notice that this bow arching now and then in our sky is mercifully missing one thing—an arrow. God's unstrung bow is a sign of peace that he paints over the human race. A token of a new relationship.

God turned judgment into grace, and every time he sees the rainbow, he remembers his covenant with us. Now we have a covenant more precious than a rainbow—the eternal promises of Christ! Mercy rushes into the storm clouds turning them into arches of triumph. Salvation turns our tears of repentance into glorious jewels, each one shining and valuable. Mercy has colored in the areas of our lives that once were void of meaning. When God sees the rainbow, he remembers. We might forget him, but he will never forget us.

Father, thank you for mercy. Thank you for the beauty of your unbreakable covenant with us. Every time I see a rainbow, I'm reminded that you have not forgotten about mankind. You, in perfect wisdom and unmatched power, hold our destiny in your hands. Your love is astounding. Your glory will be revealed.

He Remembers

"I will remember my covenant with you."

GENESIS 9:15

God has not forgotten you. He has not forsaken the promises he's made. Even when things don't turn out the way you anticipated, he is in control. There is always more to the story.

When everything is shaking and you cannot see the manifestation of his promise, don't anxiously strive to find an answer. Be still and seek his face. Trust his heart that desires to bless you with wisdom and peace. He will not fail or disappoint. His promises are rainbows of hope and declarations of truth for your life. Soak in their beauty. Remind him of the ones you're holding onto. Allow yourself to rest in the wonder of his faithfulness, even when unexpected shifts fight to make you nervous. Trust him. He will never turn his back to you. He will remember his covenant.

Father, sometimes things feel out of control, and I scramble for answers. I look outside of your presence for direction when I know it is only found in the quiet place of surrender. Thank you for reminding me to be still. To resign myself to the simplicity of trusting your love. You haven't forgotten me.

Mercy and Intercession

Noah...drank so much of the wine he made that he got drunk and passed out naked inside his tent. And Ham, the father of Canaan, went into the tent and gazed on his shamefully exposed father. Then he went out and informed his brothers.

GENESIS 9:20–22

In the first garden, Adam fell, and in the second, Noah did. His sin was not just that he got drunk and forgot to put clothes on. The Hebrew text infers that it was a deliberate act of nudity. Interestingly, Moses, the author of Genesis, seems to keep the details of this sin private, and this is the lesson we should take to heart.

As much as we esteem our leaders, they're not perfect. Their failures test *our* hearts, revealing more about us than those we criticize. Ham sinned by not covering his naked father. It isn't our duty to shame anyone, to gossip, or to cast judgment. In their moments of disgrace, those who fall need our prayers. Let's tap into the flow of mercy and cover them with intercession, the same way we'd want someone to pray for us. It is only by grace that we stand.

Father, you have poured your mercy and saved me in moments of weakness and shame. Forgive me for casting judgment over those who reveal their human nature as if I am above reproach. Thank you for teaching me about compassion. Teach me to pray by the leading of your Spirit.

Pride

> They said, "Come, let's begin work to build ourselves a city
> with a lofty tower that rises into the heavens.
> We'll make a name for ourselves, a monument to us."
>
> GENESIS 11:4

God alone lifts man from one level of glory to the next. When he opens the doors to favor, we should step into its halls with humility. If there comes a time when fame or recognition is entrusted to us, it's vital we understand that God has a greater purpose. God gives gifts, anointings, talents, titles, and recognition as a way to bless, encourage, and strengthen others.

Pride is a tragic tower that will eventually topple with us inside of it. It tricks us into forgetting that God is the bestower of gifts, and we are the receivers. It isn't sin to become great. It's sin when we become Babel-builders: those with impure motives who seek their own greatness without thought of the Lord. Let us leave behind our spiritual Babylon by rejecting pride and refusing to do things our own way and for our own purposes. Let's embrace our strengths with humility and make a name for the Lord.

Father, all that I am, have, and know come from you. Every perfect and beautiful gift is meant to remind me of your love and help others. I want you at the center of all I do, and I want to represent you well. Help me remember that when no one else is watching, you see it all.

Unity

That is why the city was called Babel—
because it was there that Yahweh
confused the language of the whole world.

GENESIS 11:9

God's original intention wasn't to divide us by language. Unity in the Spirit has always been his idea. It wasn't until pride rooted itself in the hearts of man that God made this drastic division. But on the day of Pentecost, we saw this judgment reversed. The nations of the earth each heard the apostles speaking in his own language as the Holy Spirit enabled them (Acts 2). And one day, all languages will gather around the Lamb on the throne in glorified praise to him.

We don't have to wait until we get to heaven to walk in unity. It begins by positioning our hearts in humility, honoring God in submission, and esteeming others. God calls us to treat others the way we'd like to be treated, despite cultural, sexual, religious, or political differences. He is the Light of the World, and when we let his light shine, it will illuminate every dark crevice with truth.

Father, give me your heart for the masses. Show me the way you see others, especially those I strongly disagree with. Give me the grace to talk through differences with respect. Teach me the ways of your Spirit—in humility, courage, and truth.

The Voice of Love

Yahweh said to Abram...

GENESIS 12:1

Abram wasn't inspired by a burning bush. He didn't have pastors to pray for him, prophets to prophesy over him, or priests to counsel him. He didn't even have a temple to worship in or a Bible to read. Abram had one thing—a divine encounter with Yahweh. And that was enough. His obedience to the leading of God established his future and legacy.

All too often, we encounter the Lord but shrink away from his instructions when doubt rears its ugly head. At times, we lean so heavily upon the wisdom and counsel of others that we reason away his will. Instead, let's stand on truth. Let's bravely walk upon the path that love's voice has paved. Let's be humble enough to heed the counsel and wisdom of those we trust but ultimately yield to him alone.

Father, in the stillness I feel your peace and know that you are with me. You alone guide me day by day. In every season, in front of each fork in the road, you are the compass for my life. You are the voice of love that leads me forward. So lead me. Surround me with wise counsel but teach me to notice your instructions nestled in the words I hear. Take me by the hand and make my steps sure.

Diving In

> Yahweh said to Abram, "Leave it all behind—
> your native land, your people, your father's household,
> and go to the land that I will show you."
>
> GENESIS 12:1

Leave it all behind! Nothing must stand in the way of your pursuit to be wholly his. Every mindset that contradicts the truth of who you are and who God is must be surrendered. Forgotten. Laid at his feet as an offering of your fully yielded heart. It's time for something new. Time for something that stretches you and causes you to depend on him alone.

There are times when the Lord requires a sacrifice that feels too great. Too difficult to trust him with. But buried beneath our questions, we sense seeds of peace and faith pushing through the ground with forceful life. We may not understand, but we know God has our best interests at heart. We leave behind the comfortable and predictable for what he has promised. With sometimes-shaky hands, we release control and dive into the waters of abandon. We are his. We are ready to forsake the good for the best. We will trust.

Father, life with you is an adventure. You lead me through waters that are refreshing, invigorating, and, if I'm honest, a bit scary. But I wouldn't have it any other way! I hear you calling my name and inviting me to discover what I've only dreamed of finding. I yield it all to follow the leading of your voice.

A Lifestyle of Faith

"Go to the land that I will show you."

GENESIS 12:1

God's promises fill our hearts, but often that is all we have to go on—a promise. We may be holding on to words from the Lord about spouses, ministry, children, careers, and more, but we seldom foreknow the journey these promises will take us on. Like Abram, we step out on nothing more than the foundation of God's Word. Our relationship with him fuels our faith and becomes our source of confidence. Our Father is worth trusting.

A life of obedience is lived moment by moment. In simple trust and absolute devotion, the Holy Spirit's guidance leads us. And this guidance is unmistakable when our hearts are fixed on him. The gentle nudges, random desires, dreams in the night, and open doors help guide us toward our destiny. May we never be afraid of following the Lord's prompting, even when we have no idea how the details will unfold.

Father, sometimes the ideas that arise in my heart feel unobtainable. I'm not always confident that my dreams will come to pass. I see the promises in the distance, often dancing like a mirage. Forgive me for doubting. Increase my faith. I will run the race you've set before me, knowing you'll cheer me on the entire time.

He Will

"Follow me, and I will make you..."

GENESIS 12:2

Sometimes we complicate the very things God has made simple. We strive to understand every tiny detail of his instructions before he's ready to unveil them. We want to know that the platform he's asking us to stand on is safe, strong, and immovable. We question and analyze when all he's asked us to do is follow.

When all we receive is an exciting invitation to trust and move with him, it should be enough. Instead of asking him for a map, let's look in his eyes and see the joyful anticipation he has for the journey. It isn't our job to figure it all out. He said, "*I will make you.*" Not "*You will make yourself.*" Our only part is to follow with a willing heart. To trust that he knows the plan and that it is good.

Father, I release control. You are worth believing in. Your love isn't complicated, but it is beautifully precise in its unveiling. Instead of trying to understand every detail of my life, I'll trust this love. My main job is to follow you and enjoy the journey. I'll put my faith in you and believe.

A Pure Heart

"Follow me, and I will make you into a great nation.
I will exceedingly bless and prosper you."

GENESIS 12:2

God looks for those whose hearts are toward him. Those who know that if there is any cause for greatness, any mark of fame, it is all by the grace of God. Those who desire to bring glory to his name and to serve others with their gifts.

God's promises are much too grand for our limited understanding. He promised Abram that he would become a great nation though his wife was barren. Talk about having your faith stretched! Yet he believed, and it was accounted to him as righteousness. God would exceedingly bless Abram, who would become Abraham, because he chose to follow the Lord.

It takes humility to choose God's way of doing things. To follow *him* and not our selfish drive to be rich or famous, even if those things have been promised. Let's examine our hearts and honor, love, and give our all for him with joyful surrender.

Father, you stir my heart with your promises, but they are not my focus. You have captured my full attention. You are the One I long for. It's your presence I crave. I want you more than the promise of fame, riches, or recognition. I want my unhindered devotion to bring you joy. May the intentions of my heart bless you. May my overflowing love be pure.

A Posture of Humility

"I will make you famous, so that you will be
a tremendous source of blessing for others."

GENESIS 12:2

When our hearts are toward the Lord and we are determined to bring him honor ahead of ourselves, we are setting ourselves up for blessings. It is this posture of obedience and deference that set Abraham up not only for the blessings of God but also to be a man through whom generations of blessings would flow.

God seeks those whose desire for him rises above every other pursuit. Humility and understanding of our absolute dependence upon the Lord actually position us for greatness. When we recognize that God has bestowed every success, achievement, and talent, he can trust us to manage more of it. Each time we bow low and offer him glory, our character is refined. Both a stance of pride and a posture of humility are contagious and passed down to our family and those we've been entrusted with. Let's choose wisely.

Father, I'm reminded today of the power of your Spirit inside of me. You lead me to places I never dreamed I would go when everything I do starts and ends with you. You are the great One—the source of my wisdom and creativity. Give me the grace to continue in humility and demonstrate what a lifestyle of unconditional trust and devotion to you can do.

Responding to the Lord

Abram erected an altar there to Yahweh,
who had appeared before him.

GENESIS 12:7

Every encounter with the Lord is meant to fuel our faith, stir our thankfulness, and remind us of his love. Like Abram, who built an altar each time God appeared to him, we cannot overlook the importance and power of our response. Abram presented God with a burnt offering—an offering of himself to God.

Most of us haven't had the Lord appear to us as Abram did, but we do have something he didn't. We have the Spirit of God inside of us. Each day we are invited into divine encounters with the One who loves to meet with us. What a privilege! The blessing of his nearness should cause our souls to sing and our spirits to rejoice. May we never take his presence for granted but learn from Abram about the power of responding to God's presence. We are the gift God longs for. Our response of love, appreciation, and surrender moves his heart.

Father, forgive me for being too busy to acknowledge you when you greet me with your presence. Sometimes I allow my circumstances to dictate my focus. Help me to slow down and recognize the many ways you try to get my attention. You're such a beautiful Father and friend, and I never want to take your presence for granted.

In Sync

> He journeyed on toward the hill country east of Bethel and pitched his tent. ... Then Abram journeyed from there by stages.
>
> GENESIS 12:8–9

When we pitch our tents in the presence of God, he inhabits them. We are transformed—these beautiful and complex bodies becoming even more impressive when we're open to him. Our lives are best enjoyed when they're fully surrendered to the One who is faithful and true. When we align every movement and decision with the will of God, he sets us on the right path.

We must submit every desire to control our future to the Lord. This perfect Father will order our lives as we yield them to him. Once we make this shift in our mindset, it frees us to enjoy his leading, even when it contradicts our own desires or understanding. We find ourselves moving forward into unexpected blessings, encounters with the Lord, and peace that we cannot explain. Obeying his voice is the key to walking in our destiny and experiencing the joy and peace he wants us to have.

Father, your presence is my land of promise. All my hopes, dreams, and desires start with you. I fix my eyes on the fullness of your kingdom within me. Your Spirit leads me more perfectly than I could ever lead myself. Whether big or small, help me to remember to submit every decision I make to you.

The Place of Safety

A severe famine struck the land of Canaan,
forcing Abram to travel down to Egypt
and live there as a foreigner.

GENESIS 12:10

Canaan was the promised land. A land flowing with milk and honey. A land that God had led him to. Yet that is where Abram experienced a famine that tested his faith. In a place where he expected to taste the richness of God's blessing, Abram faced great difficulty. And it was this unexpected trial that pushed him to run to Egypt for help instead of to the Lord.

One of the hardest tests is when the anticipated place of blessing becomes a swamp of adversity. Smack-dab in the center of God's will, our faith is tested. During these times, we fix our gaze upon the Lord. We quiet our racing thoughts by handing them over to him. We give ourselves permission to sink deep, past the chaos, into the stillness of his love. Here we wait for his guidance. This is the place of utter dependence upon him. This is the place of safety.

Father, I offer my confusion and frustration to you as an offering. See my heart. I don't want to sin against you by leaning on my own understanding or by doing things my way. Show me your way. Lead me by your Spirit. Strengthen my resolve. I will not move until your peace settles my soul.

Worry

"Look, I'm worried because..."

GENESIS 12:11

Worry is written in our minds with a pen of fear. It runs through a rational list of reasons why it's a good idea to freak out and take matters into our own hands. It doesn't play fair. It tells us we're smart to understand every single way this situation could go wrong. After all, if we don't take action and fix things, who will?

Lay those questions, rushes of anxiety, and analyzation skills at the feet of Jesus. Take a deep breath and find the presence of God. He's there, ready to envelop you with fiery love that incinerates fear. In his presence, you'll discover the peace that passes understanding. You'll receive his wisdom that comforts your soul and is far easier to implement than anything you can conjure on your own.

Father, forgive me for getting drawn into a rational debate with the spirit of fear. You have called me to live on a higher level—one that taps into the person of love and only moves when he moves. You have given me your Holy Spirit to guide me on paths of peace that often serve as bridges over rational thinking.

Merciful God

"Why did you lie to me by saying, 'She's my sister,'
so that I took her as my wife?"

GENESIS 12:19

Abram's sin could have derailed the promises of God. But God's grace was exceptional. His love was and is always more powerful than our greatest act of defiance. Though we often get tunnel vision—only seeing what is directly in front of us and often not realizing the magnitude of our choices, God's wisdom sees the entire picture. And in his mercy and wisdom, God knows how to get us back on track.

What a merciful Father we have! When compromise and sin drag us away from God's will, he runs ahead of us and stands on our littered path wooing us to himself. His love becomes a merciful detour leading us back to truth. Sin cannot restrain us if we humbly fall into the arms of grace.

Father, I'm astounded by your love. Held captive by your grace. You are so kind. So patient with me when I mess up and sin against you. Forgive me for the times I've ignored your whispers and yielded to my flesh. Wash me clean. Purify my heart. Draw me closer to your heart than ever before and hold me there.

Returning

He returned to the place between Bethel and Ai where he had pitched his tent at the beginning. This was the place he had first built an altar to pray and worship Yahweh.

GENESIS 13:3–4

Distractions, sin, compromise, and laziness can cause our hearts to drift away from the sweetness of God's presence, but mercy invites us home again. Grace softens our hearts and reminds us that there is a better way.

When we've been enticed by trivial things, the Holy Spirit draws us back to first-love intimacy. It's humbling to think that God, who possesses everything in creation, desires us. In our messy, distracted state, he pursues us. He blows upon the embers of our hearts and reminds us of his love. Abram knew where to find God again, and so do we. This revelation of first-love communion is ours to return to again and again and again. God in his compassion and mercy will not turn us away.

Father, forgive me for allowing distraction to cover my heart like a smokescreen. Being with you and enjoying your presence are the true longings of my heart. You pursued me with passion stronger than the grave. Now I'll walk with you in the cool of the day. I'll run alongside you. I'll seek you and find you because you are gracious.

Humility Leads to Blessing

Abram said to Lot, "Let's not quarrel with each other,
or between our herdsmen, since we are relatives. ...
If you choose the land on the left, then I'll go right,
and if you want land on the right, then I'll go left."

GENESIS 13:8–9

When we choose to walk with God, the way of peace is easy to find. Abram demonstrated this when, instead of waring with his family, he trusted God for his inheritance. Instead of fighting for the land God had promised, he waited for God's perfect timing. He chose the way of peace—a road that we cannot find outside of trusting the Father.

When we become more satisfied with our relationship with God than the promise of his blessing, we set ourselves up for something far greater. No sacrifice will ever outweigh the glory of remaining close to him. Holding our promises loosely, knowing that God is ultimately in control, frees us to rest and enjoy him. Otherwise, we get fixated on temporal desires and are willing to fight and strive to get them. Let's posture our hearts before the Lord in humble faith. Humility is the precursor for his richest blessings.

Father, I want to reflect your nature and demonstrate your patience and kindness. I long to be Christlike in the way I pursue what you've promised. Forgive me for pushing to make things happen and not trusting your timing. Help me to live above reproach by walking in humility and temperance as I wait patiently for you.

Compromise

It looked beautiful, like the garden of Yahweh, or like Egypt.
So Lot chose to settle in the Jordan Valley.

GENESIS 13:10–11

The enemy entices us with what appeals to our flesh. He wants our worldly appetites to lure us away from the promises of God. Just because something looks, sounds, and seems exciting doesn't mean it's a blessing from God. Extravagant gifts, favors, and opportunities will reveal our truest intentions and devotions.

Lot looked over the land and chose Sodom, the place destined for judgment. He chose the world. He walked by sight, what looked good to the eyes, and didn't ask for the Lord's direction. Ultimately, Lot left the place of blessing and entered the place of judgment. Let's take this lesson to heart and always seek God's counsel in every decision.

Father, lead me by your wisdom and help me not to be led astray by the enemy's temptations. I set my heart on you. Direct every step, every relationship, and each decision. Be my center—the truth that anchors my life. I want to live aware of every nudge of your Spirit. I long to follow you forever.

Our Greatest Desire

Abram settled in the land of Canaan
while Lot settled in the cities of the lowlands,
at a place near Sodom.

GENESIS 13:12

The blessings of the Lord follow those who pursue him. Very often, they also splash onto those nearby. Lot was blessed because he walked closely with Abram and not as a result of his relationship with the Lord. Satisfied with the blessings but seemingly having no desire to know God for himself, Lot eventually fell in Sodom.

It's not enough to follow in the tracks of someone who is blessed. God created us for much more than *borrowed* blessings. Though God leads us to people who will encourage and mentor us, we must be careful not to put them in our God-spot. It's vital that we seek God for ourselves. Anytime we depend more on people than the Lord, we are settling for much less than God has for us. Let's be cautious in our pursuit of earthly favor and an unhealthy desire to please man. Nothing should ever take the place of God in our lives.

Father, forgive me when I get sidetracked. No one can take your place. No amount of favor, riches, and applause are worth sacrificing my relationship with you. You are my reward. Being near you fills me with depths of joy that cannot be found in any other source. You are my greatest desire.

No Sacrifice Too Great

After Lot separated from him, Yahweh spoke to Abram,
"Lift up your eyes and look around you
to the north, the south, the east, and the west."

GENESIS 13:14

God is so patient with us. He so tenderly and skillfully leads us through life, teaching us what's important and what is not. For Abram to finally realize the magnitude of God's desire to bless him, he had to let go of every earthly hindrance. Once he did, his life was immeasurably blessed.

The deep work of God that takes place within us isn't always enjoyable. The sacrifices we make may feel too great, too difficult, too costly. But as we yield, we begin to see clearly. This is what happened with Abram, and this is what happens with us. Our desire to walk with the Lord in wholehearted devotion sets us on a beautiful journey. Every price we pay becomes insignificant compared to the glory of holy intimacy. And soon, we lift our eyes and see that we are surrounded by the goodness and faithfulness of God. Nothing compares to bliss of his nearness.

Father, forgive me for focusing more on the cost of obedience than on the joy it brings. Being near you and tasting the sweetness of your love are the true longings of my heart. They far outweigh the sacrifice of surrender. Have your way in me until I am wholly yours.

May

Dreaming with God

"As far as you can see in every direction
is the land that I will give to you forever—
to you and your seed."

GENESIS 13:15

God's plans often seem too lofty. Too extravagant. Our souls stir
with dreams and goals, and if we're honest, at times, it scares us.
Reasoning fights to limit what we'll do with what is in our hearts.
*What if these things don't come to pass? What if I fail? What if I'm
disappointed? What if...*

It's time we allow ourselves to dream big. To do what we can to
partner with these desires by preparing and working hard while
recognizing that, ultimately, God is the only One who can pull it
all together. It takes courage to allow ourselves to dream, but it's
essential that we do, or we may miss what he has in store. God
wants us to live with bold faith. To embrace his promises with a
joyful heart and to seek his counsel regarding every step.

*Father, you have placed extravagant dreams in my heart.
Sometimes, I try to figure out how I can push to make them
happen instead of lifting my eyes higher—to you. When I look at
you, I'm not afraid to dream. I'm not afraid to cast reason aside,
risk it all, and run with you!*

He Is Extravagant

"I will multiply them until they are as numerous
as the specks of dust on the earth. ...
All the land you walk upon will be my gift to you!"

GENESIS 13:16–17

Some of us have drawn an invisible line that restricts the miraculous in our lives. We've put limits on our faith. We say God can do anything, but when it comes down to it, we don't actually believe it. Too often we cower away from radical prayers and outrageous dreams, not because God isn't able to answer but because we're afraid that he won't.

But what if we decided, over and over again, to ask for the extravagant? To take him at his word. To put ourselves out there, as many times as it takes, and risk believing. The One who held oceans in the palm of his hand and breathed substance into the wind is also our Father. The miracle worker who spoke to Abram hasn't changed. And he loves to bless us!

Father, forgive me for doubting. I've tried to understand the incomprehensible instead of allowing my faith to soar. You may not always say yes to my prayers, but I'm going to be bolder. To believe for more than I ever have before. I want to please you with my faith instead of hindering your blessings because of my unbelief.

Settling In

Abram moved his camp and settled by the oaks of Mamre, which are at Hebron, and there he built another altar to Yahweh.

GENESIS 13:18

After Abram received the magnificent promises of God, he responded. We're told he moved his camp to the place of strength (signified by the oak trees) and settled into the anointing (Mamre signifies fatness and anointing). We aren't told he analyzed God's promises or dismissed them as wishful thinking. No, he got up and pressed into the strength of God's anointing.

How often do we start out excited over God's promises then fall prey to fear? We scrutinize what he's said instead of accepting the blessing and holding on to faith. Doubt creeps in because, rather than settling into the anointing, we analyze. Beloved, we're allowed to respond with zeal even when things look bleak. He is our strength, and we can take him at his word. It's okay to run into his presence with undiluted hope and remain there with unshakable faith.

Father, I'm shaking off every hindrance of doubt and surrendering myself to your presence. I'm not afraid to settle into the comfort of faith. I'm ready to zealously pursue all you've promised. This is what you created me for—to believe in your love. To live each day with zeal, joy, and expectancy.

Overcoming the Enemy

They faced off against Kedorlaomer, king of Elam;
Tidal, king of Goyim; Amraphel, king of Babylon;
and Arioch, king of Ellasar—four kings against five.

GENESIS 14:9

The enemy has many names, but he is always easy to spot. He is the one who lies, kills, steals, and destroys. He is the one who seeks to draw our attention away from God. He is the one who wants us to fear and forget who we are. But we will not forget! We are more than conquerors through Jesus.

Yes, we have an enemy. But more importantly, we have a victorious Savior! We're aware of the enemy's schemes and aren't ignorant of them, but we must refuse to get sucked into a frenzy of fear and anxiety. One of the most powerful ways to overcome the enemy is to keep our eyes on the Lord. To worship despite what we see or feel. To declare God's promises. To find things to be thankful for and to remind ourselves of God's goodness. Though the storms may rage, we choose where to set our focus.

Father, sometimes it takes all of my effort to keep my gaze on you. But by your grace, I will. In the storm, I will set my heart on your faithfulness. I am not a victim. I am powerful because you are with me. I may feel the winds of adversity, but you are the anchor that steadies my soul.

Walking in Compassion

When Abram heard that his nephew Lot had been taken captive
by the four kings, he mobilized all the men in his camp.

GENESIS 14:14

Character is formed in situations just like this—when we choose
between reacting with our spirits or our flesh. Abram could have
shrugged his shoulders and said, "Lot's paying the price for his
bad decisions. Hopefully, this will teach him a lesson." Instead,
compassion moved Abram to rescue Lot and the others whom the
kings had taken captive. We should also respond like this.

It's easier to pass judgment on those suffering the consequences
of sin than it is to restore them. But when we remember the way
mercy has marked our lives, it helps keep our hearts pliable so we
can extend that compassion to others. Let's display the character
of God and not mimic the ways of the world by finger-pointing and
criticizing. When we lean into the heart of God, it changes us and
the way we respond to the world around us.

*Father, I want to be led by mercy and compassion. Show me how
to restore those who have fallen. Teach me how to extend a helping
hand in a way that softens a hardened heart. And when I'm prone
to criticism, gently remind me of the many ways you've been
gracious to me.*

Victorious

He recovered all the stolen possessions and brought back his
nephew Lot, together with the women and all the prisoners.

GENESIS 14:16

Sometimes life slams a fist in our face and threatens our resolve.
The enemy hopes we'll be so shaken by what he's stolen that we'll
lose our dauntless determination to find God's presence. More than
any physical loss, the enemy is after our faith and hope. But despite
his best efforts, he cannot steal our awareness of the Lord if we
don't let him.

Where you set your focus is up to you. In trials and suffering,
God's presence can be sweet. Healing. He will gently wipe away
every tear and breathe life back into your soul. He is the God of
restoration. The cross was not the end. It was the precursor to
resurrection. It was the victory that recovered everything the enemy
could ever steal from then on. Even in your pain, you are victorious!

*Father, I don't always feel victorious. Life really does throw me off
course sometimes. Trials feel like they suck me dry. But even in my
pain, I can lean into your embrace. In times of uncertainty, I can
count on the sweetness of your presence. And that reality, more
significant than any loss, makes me victorious. I am yours, and
nothing can ever change that.*

The Blessing of God

Melchizedek...spoke over him a special blessing...
Then the king of Sodom said to Abram,
"Just give me the people you rescued;
keep all the spoils for yourself."

GENESIS 14:18–19, 21

Directly after our greatest triumphs, temptations often come. This was the case for Abram, who was offered great wealth to satisfy his fleshly nature or the blessing of God through Melchizedek. Abram, unwilling to allow a worldly system to take the credit for his good fortune, accepted the blessing of God.

There is nothing wrong with receiving gifts or wealth through the hands of man when God orchestrates it. More than anything else, God is concerned with the condition of our hearts. The beauty of a surrendered heart shows in our behavior and the things we strive for. When the Lord means everything to us and we aim for every decision to honor him, *he* blesses us. And nothing can compare. No sacrifice will outweigh the great reward of God's favor, love, and protection. God sees every choice we make. Let's aim for each one to reflect our fully yielded hearts.

Father, with every decision, with each longing of my soul, I want to esteem and honor you. Give me the wisdom to choose wisely. To discern between a potentially dangerous yet seemingly amazing gift and a true blessing from you. May the desires of my heart be established in your Word and in the reality of our relationship.

Paying Attention

Afterwards, the word of Yahweh
came to Abram in a vision.

GENESIS 15:1

Quiet now. Listen to the healing words of the Lord stirring inside of you. He is there. His loving kindness and tender mercy have never lifted from your life, even if it seems that way. After every battle, every victory, yes, even in the crumbling center of it all, the Lord's presence speaks.

Sometimes he speaks in obvious ways—through Scripture, dreams, an encouraging word from someone he sends across your path. But other times, the Lord confirms his love in the warmth of a sunrise, a gentle breeze, a washing rain, or the white of snow. He'll slide an email, book, or an encouraging video in front of you because he knows you need to see it. But rest assured, when God wants to get your attention and remind you of his love, he will. You only need to pay attention.

Father, thank you for this reminder. I'm going to pay attention. I'll lean into the quiet and notice your presence. I'll enjoy the sound of birds singing and remember your faithfulness to provide. I'll pause and notice the encouragements you scatter along my path just to let me know you're thinking of me. Each day is a gift—a reminder of your love.

His Peace

"Abram, don't yield to fear,
for I am your Faithful Shield
and your Abundant Reward."

GENESIS 15:1

Allow God's encouragement to Abram to become your own. All you need is found in the One who taught your heart to beat. And he knows exactly how to get it to you. When you choose him over the many temptations that come your way, he notices. Though no one else may see, God does, and he is so thrilled with your desire toward him.

Beautiful one, fear is not your friend, so don't embrace it. Turn your full attention to the One who faithfully comes to your rescue. Don't sink into despair or allow it to steal your identity. Grasp the hand of the Lord, and he will pull you safely into his presence. Into his love. Into his peace that contradicts every trial. You're allowed to say no to fear. To reject the temptation to overthink, be anxious and overwhelmed. To laugh in the face of adversity. To choose the path that keeps you close to him.

Father, when I'm tempted to fear, come with your love and wrap me tight. Pour out the peace that washes away anxiety. In your presence, I remember that you love me. You are my reward. My friend. My Savior. And the tears that sought to drown my faith have become tears of thankfulness.

Change Your Perspective

Abram replied, "I'm about to die without a son, and my servant,
Eliezer of Damascus, will inherit all my wealth."
Then Yahweh brought him outside his tent and said...

GENESIS 15:2, 5

God doesn't get mad when we express what we're thinking.
After all, he already knows what's on our mind. The questions,
frustrations, and doubts don't scare him away. He doesn't shake
his head, sigh deeply, and cross his arms with a disapproving look,
wondering what to do with us. Instead, with loving patience, he
offers us another point of view.

Our courage to be brave and honest with the Lord should be
accompanied by a willingness to hear his answer. To accept
his mindset by letting him lead us outside of our own. To
quiet ourselves and listen. To humbly accept the answers and
encouragement that so often come in ways we don't anticipate. In
order to change our perspective, we must allow the Lord to give
us his. What an incredible privilege it is to lay our hearts before the
Lord, who knows how to direct our attention where it needs to be.

*Father, thank you for inviting me into a relationship with you that
is real, open, and honest. For being patient with me when I'm
distracted by what I don't understand and for never giving up on
me. When questions have wearied my soul, you lift my eyes so I
can see straight into your heart.*

The Timing of God

"Gaze into the night sky. Go ahead and try to count the stars."
He continued, "Your seed will be as numerous as the stars!"

GENESIS 15:5

Delay is not the same thing as denial. When the promises of God feel just out of reach, it's time to settle our questions with the infallibility of his Word. Remaining close to him and reminding ourselves of his faithfulness is vital. He loves to bless us. Longs to bestow far greater gifts than we've ever had.

It's time to believe it. Time to let hope arise! To dream great big dreams that can only be accomplished by the power and wisdom of our loving Father. Dreams that seem too good to be true. Dreams that both excite and scare us. It's okay to run after his promises with the carefree joy of a child who's never known defeat. The wisdom we've gained from being with God stabilizes us and guides our steps. The closer we get to the Lord, the more we trust his timing. We understand that love holds our promises in the safety of his hands.

Father, sometimes your promises feel as if they're taking too long to come pass. Doubt creeps in, and I wonder if you've forgotten. I need your grace to steady my faith. Help me to trust. To remember that my days are orchestrated by your wisdom and that all I have to do is tune into the harmony of your love.

Trust Every Word

Abram trusted every word Yahweh had spoken!

GENESIS 15:6

What an incredible testimony! Imagine God writing highlights from your life and letting everyone know that you trusted every word he said to you. Since he's a forgiving, wash-away-the-past kind of Father, we still have a chance for this to happen. Each day we get to start again.

When we decide to part with unbelief, God wipes it away. With a smile on his face, he extends his promises again and waits for us to grab hold and take them to heart. Radical faith swallows partial faith. It's not enough to believe some of his words and not others. Let's trust *every* word! This is the legacy we can leave behind.

Father, I've been ruled by my emotions and have believed what fit into my limited understanding for too long. I'm ready to change! Ready to trust you in ways I never have before. I know the boundaries of my faith will continue to be tested, but as long as you are with me, we'll conquer every doubt together.

In Tune with Him

> Because of his faith,
> Yahweh credited it to him as righteousness.
>
> GENESIS 15:6

One encounter with God can change our lives forever. We aren't told if Abram heard God's audible voice or interacted with the still, small voice within. All we know is that Abram believed. And because Abram believed the seemingly impossible promises he was given, God was pleased.

We mustn't dismiss the thoughts, gentle whispers, or reminders of Scripture that rise inside of us when we live in tune with the Lord. As we get to know him and his Word, we become more confident in discerning his voice. Will we make mistakes? Yes. But our willingness to take a chance and trust opens the door to deeper understanding and revelation. We learn what God sounds like when we spend time listening. Faith wouldn't be necessary if the things we hear and see in the quiet of our hearts were easy to believe.

Father, I want to live with radical faith that defines my life. I want to have faith that is deeply rooted in your love—knowing you always want what's best for me. Teach me the difference between my great ideas and the greater ones you've breathed into my heart. Help me to slow down and notice when you're trying to get my attention. I want to live in tune with you.

Remember

> "I am Yahweh, who brought you out of the Babylonian city of Ur, to give you all this land to possess."
>
> GENESIS 15:7

He is Yahweh. He is the faithful One. Our hero, Savior, and way maker. It's imperative we remember who God is to us and what he's done in the past. In the safety of recollection, we keep ourselves from falling into fear and doubt. In the strength of thankfulness, we stand encouraged and hopeful.

We all forget from time to time. We have an unpleasant tendency to lose sight of the greatness of our Father. We slip into autopilot—that mindless place where prayer and Bible reading become habitual. When we lose our sense of awestruck wonder at the privilege we have of knowing the Lord, it's easy to forget how magnificent he is. Let's remember. Let's practice mindful gratitude. When there seems to be no way, the One who taught the stars to dance and the seas to roar will make a way.

Father, forgive me for succumbing to frustration and forgetting all of the wonderful ways you've come through in the past. You are good. You have always been good. This is what I will focus on. I will choose to recall the many ways you've shown yourself strong on my behalf, and I will be thankful.

Certainty

Abram said, "Lord Yahweh,
how can I be sure that I can possess this land for myself?"

GENESIS 15:8

Even Abram, the man recorded in Scripture as having trusted every word God said, wanted assurances. Isn't it comforting to know that God didn't hold this against him? And he doesn't hold it against us either. What a merciful Father we have!

Often, we try to wrap our minds around the miraculous before diving in and accepting the validity of God's extravagant promises. We reason and examine every detail as if we can figure out how God will do what he's said he will do. It sure would be nice to have certainty before taking a risk! But the only guarantee we have is that God will be with us. Even if we misconstrue what he's said, he knows how to get us back on track. The mercy, love, and compassion of God are our safety net in every decision.

Father, I'll be honest—taking a leap of faith is scary. As if I'm about to jump from a diving board one hundred feet in the air into your open arms. My feet feel glued in place. I've wanted confirmations that everything will turn out all right. The truth is your love and faithfulness are the only assurances I have. And they are enough.

Stand Your Ground

Vultures swooped down upon the carcasses,
but Abram stood there and drove the vultures away.

Genesis 15:11

When the enemy comes to steal from you, drive him away. Stand your ground by keeping your eyes on the Lord. Don't entertain the enemy's lies! They only lead to doubt and confusion. Protect your faith by holding the promises of the Lord close to your heart.

Receiving God's promises doesn't mean we won't deal with doubts and conflicting thoughts. We must respond as Abram did—driving away the circling buzzards that try to steal our faith. We must reject every fear. We must drench each question in worshipful surrender. We don't need to yell and scream. It is our attitude of worship and praise that repels the enemy and strengthens our faith. Waiting can be difficult, but we mustn't give up! The longer we entertain thoughts of disappointment and impatience, the more they grow. Let's pay attention to what we're thinking and line up our thoughts with what is true and praiseworthy.

Father, as I wait for your promises to come to pass, I will set my mind on you. I will praise you for what is to come before I ever see it manifest. I won't worry about tomorrow. You've got it under control. I'll focus on this moment because you are here. Your presence gives me the confidence I need.

The Darkness of Delay

A great dreadful darkness surrounded him
and he was filled with fear.

GENESIS 15:12

What an accurate picture of waiting on God! We believe his promise but then find ourselves passing through the darkness of delay. The timing of God is out of our control. The flesh withers, our strength evaporates, doubts clog the flow of faith, and we wonder when or if he'll come through.

For those of you holding on to prophetic promises yet to be fulfilled, be encouraged: delay and denial are not the same thing. In seasons of dreadful darkness, face your fears and invite God into them. Don't be afraid to deal with your doubts, knowing they're rising to the surface for a reason. Use the darkness as a launching pad into your most significant breakthrough ever. Your faithful God will not disappoint you.

Father, it's quiet in the darkness of delay. Some days I don't hear you say a word. But I feel your presence, and I know you are here. Fears are rising to the surface, but I won't push them back down. I'll lay them at your feet so you can squash each one. In the safety of your love, I will wait. I will trust your timing.

The Fiery One

When the sun had set, and it was very dark,
there suddenly appeared a smoking firepot
and a blazing torch.

GENESIS 15:17

In every dark trial, the believer has a blazing torch—the glory of Jesus that illuminates every dark and lonely place. Suddenly, and often when we least expect it, he chases away the shadows so we can see clearly. God, who faithfully turns every night into day, shines brightly upon our paths. Peace replaces anxiety, and all is well with our souls.

God calls us to walk in the light of this blazing torch. To taste, see, and understand his goodness that manifests even in our darkest night. And the day will come when this fire blazes within us. When suffering, sorrow, and pain will not quench our faith and trust. His Spirit rested as fire upon the heads of his disciples but now lives inside of us.

Father, you are a wildfire of passion and power, and you have set my heart ablaze. Just when it feels that all hope is gone and I cannot see the light, you come. You illuminate the shadows when you draw near. Thank you for showing me the way. For drenching my path in glory and causing my soul to sing. Fiery One, I love you.

The Good Fight

"I have given this land to your descendants...
the entire land of the Kenites, the Kenizzites,
the Kadmonites, the Hittites, the Perizzites..."

GENESIS 15:18–20

The promises of God are yours to hold on to. Fight the good fight of faith and take the land (your spiritual inheritance) he's declared is yours. Don't give in to discouragement. Stop looking at what isn't going right, and let God's Word frame your world. Speak his truth and take it to heart.

It's time to stop allowing the "-ites" (symbolic of demonic powers) from dictating your course and talking you out of faith. Don't be tricked by the lies. Don't worry about what it looks like. Keep your eyes on God. If he has given you a promise, don't let it go. Overcome doubt by the testimony of your faith, and don't stop believing! It's time for you to fully inherit the promises of God.

Father, in your presence, my faith soars! So here is where I will remain. I will fix my gaze on you and hold tightly to every word you've said. Together we will laugh and dream. We will plan for a future filled with hope. We will take the mountains one step at a time, walking in the victory you have won! And more than anything else, we will enjoy each other along the way.

Waiting with Grace

Sarai said to Abram, "Please listen. Since Yahweh has kept me childless, go sleep with my maidservant. Perhaps through her I can build you a family." Abram listened and did what Sarai asked.

GENESIS 16:2

Too often, in the discomfort of delay, we look for the quickest exit instead of allowing patience to shape our character. The pressure of waiting causes the murky waters of impatience to rise, and in desperation, we react. We reason and try to find a solution that sounds good without consulting the Lord. We can use these situations to refine us if we let them.

God wants us to be content in the waiting. To trust him instead of needing an explanation that satisfies our impatience. To use the discomfort as a launching pad into new heights of surrender. The moment we allow our emotions to lead us, we are in danger of stepping out of the will of God. And it is only in his will that we will taste the sweetness of breakthrough the way he has ordained it.

Father, I lay every unfulfilled desire at your feet. I will not fight to have my way. I give you the many ideas floating through my mind, and I will not force things to happen outside of your timetable. I resign myself entirely to you and trust your plans. May I honor you by taking my hands off and waiting with grace.

In the Wilderness

The angel of Yahweh encountered Hagar
by a spring in the wilderness,
the spring on the way to Shur.

GENESIS 16:7

It's easy to despise the wilderness seasons of our souls. These are the times we feel isolated and alone. When we're surrounded by trouble and cannot find our way out. These seasons threaten our joy, faith, and steadfast devotion. But the wilderness can also become our place of encounter.

It's here in the place of shadows that we recognize the light is still shining. It's our decision whether we will sink into the darkness or turn to the One who wraps us in hope. These desert seasons activate our deepest hunger and most feverish thirst. We long for the necessities of life and discover that the nearness of God is our lifeline. He is the only One who can satisfy our souls.

Father, I never thought my wilderness seasons could be filled with such tangible encounters of your love. But now that I know, I won't be satisfied with anything less. I may not have the strength to do more than whisper your name, but if my heart is turned toward you, I know you will come.

He Sees

After her encounter with Yahweh,
Hagar called him by a special name,
"You are the God of My Seeing," for she said,
"Oh my, did I just see God and live to talk about it?"

GENESIS 16:13

Our encounters with Yahweh shift the course of our lives. When we realize that he sees into the deepest parts of our souls—the areas hidden to others and sometimes ourselves—and still loves us, we're undone. Gloriously wrecked. Forever marked by his benevolence.

This holy One doesn't keep us at a distance. His compassion doesn't come with restrictions. He brings us close enough to look into his eyes. To see and be seen. He encourages us to run with boldness, tempered in humility and seasoned with gratefulness, straight into his presence. To open ourselves to his holy gaze. We never need to fear rejection because even in our mess, his love for us is stable.

Father, thank you for seeing me through the eyes of love. For providing the healing my soul needs and encouraging me not to hide. When I'm with you, I feel celebrated, known, accepted. It gives me the courage to open myself to your searching gaze. Knowing you love me makes me want to know you more.

Rest in Truth

> When Abram was ninety-nine years old,
> Yahweh appeared to him again and said,
> "I am the God who is more than enough.
> Live your life in my presence and be blameless."

GENESIS 17:1

Before *the God who is more than enough* displays his power, we first come to terms with our own insufficiency. It wasn't until Abraham's body was as good as dead that God fulfilled his promise and gave him a son. God's sense of timing is related to our character formation. Every delay has a purpose. And it is often when we give up that God is ready to act.

Don't despair when everything around you screams of impossibility. Hold tightly to what you know to be true, especially when it contradicts the realities staring you in the face. God is more than able to turn things around. When you don't have natural answers or enough strength, he steps in as your *more than enough God*. All he asks is that you stay with him. And if it feels as though he's left, rest in the truth. Lean into his invisible hands.

Father, you are the all-sufficient One, the source of perfect wisdom. I have no desire to live outside of your grace. I am absolutely dependent upon you for every aspect of my life. I need your presence. I worship you amid my weakness and cry out for you to show yourself strong on my behalf.

Reverence

Abram fell on his face in awe before God.

GENESIS 17:3

When man bows in humility, God comes in grace. This is the posture of someone who is beginning to understand the wonder of abiding close to God's heart. We don't drop our heads and stare at the floor as if we're unworthy or full of shame. The weighty presence of love leaves us no other choice than to prostrate ourselves in surrender. His magnificence is more than we can handle. Its waves crash upon us in cleansing flow.

The profound revelation of God's power strips us of excuses. We come as we are, knowing his love never pushes us away. He is the Father we've always needed. He is the Savior who rescues us—over and over again. Held by grace, we give ourselves as an offering of love. Unable to resist. Unwilling to compromise. Overtaken by the glory of his grace. Comfortable with his searching gaze.

Father, come. Rise within me. Pour down upon me. Let every fiber of my being sense the glory of your presence. Nothing in me wants to resist. And if some part of me does resist, I invite you to cleanse that area. I want to be wholly yours. Fully surrendered. Dependent upon you for everything.

A Humble Heart

"You will no longer be named Abram
because I am changing your name to Abraham,
for I have made you a father of many nations."

GENESIS 17:5

When we finally recognize our pride and humble ourselves before the Lord, our life takes a radical turn. This is what happened to Abram. It was when he came to the end of himself and was completely dependent upon the Lord that God entrusted him with a blessing that would have previously crushed him.

With his face to the ground, he gained perspective and a new name. No longer would he be *Abram*—"exalted father"—but *Abraham*—"father of a multitude." It takes absolute surrender, holding no part of our lives back from the Lord, for God to entrust us with the hearts of others. We no longer see ourselves through the eyes of exaltation and fame, but with fresh perspective, we understand our position of partnership with God. For Abram to become Abraham, he needed to carry a father's heart instead of a self-indulgent one.

Father, show me my heart. Reveal tainted motives, self seeking, or any other mindsets that keep me from walking in the fullness you have for me. I want my desires to be in line with yours. I long for a pure heart. I'm beginning to understand that the talents, favor, and anointing you've entrusted me with are gifts for others that must be tended with a humble heart.

Surprisingly More

"I will make you abundantly fruitful,
more than you expect."

GENESIS 17:6

God loves to do exceedingly more than we ask, hope, or imagine. The ways he can answer are unlimited. His generosity is surprising and unmatched. He is extravagant—far exceeding our most lavish ideas. He absolutely outdoes us in every way. Our most astounding dreams are incomparable to his desires. Our most enormous requests, the ones that seem over the top and unrealistic, don't make him flinch. He cheers us on when we run toward our future with faith.

Disappointment wants to wear us down. The enemy wants us to tone down our zealousness, but God wants us to get excited again. To run with undiluted hope toward promises that feel just out of reach. To go after goals that are too high to achieve on our own. Our outrageously good and extravagant God wants to bless us with surprisingly more, so let's not be satisfied with anything but his best!

Father, though I've felt the drain of disappointment, I feel the breath of faith pushing me forward again. I've decided not to be satisfied with the average or mundane when you've promised me so much more. I'm going for the blessing of your glory. I'm chasing after you, knowing that in you is everything I need.

Covenant of Love

"Yes, I will establish my eternal covenant of love between me and you, and it will extend to your descendants throughout their generations."

GENESIS 17:7

God's covenant of love reaches out to us today. It is eternal. Unbreakable. A bond of unending devotion meant to establish us in our identity and purpose. A blessing of inexplicable value sent straight from a loving Father.

The beauty of our merciful connection is that it extends to the generations that come after us. Our relationship with the Lord overflows its banks and soaks into the deep heart crevices of those we love. Love is contagious. The joy others see in this mysterious yet very real exchange imparts longing to them. Nothing speaks louder than a heart on fire. This is what we release to future generations— the glory of knowing him. This is the blessing of covenant that God has promised. A covenant of love and all that it contains.

Father, you are my promise of life, love, joy, and peace. My relationship with you becomes a gift passed down to those I love. Nothing I could possibly give compares to the beauty of knowing you. Let my life, lived in your presence, pave the way for future generations. You are the One I long for.

He Will Be Their God

> "I will be your children's God,
> just as I am your God."
>
> GENESIS 17:7

If you have children, whether those you mentor or those who are a part of your family, this is a fantastic Scripture to declare over them. It doesn't matter their ages or whether they are wholeheartedly following the Lord right now. God's Word slices through every lie and cuts the enemy's plan into pieces.

In all of our well-planned parenting, we can only go so deep. The heart of the matter, the nitty-gritty of what truly impacts their relationship with the Lord, is personal. Eventually it's between them and God. He cannot be forced, only presented. The real act of faith is when we lay our children before the Lord and choose to trust that he alone will win their hearts. We stand on his promises, like the one above, and know that he loves them even more than we do.

Father, I pray your blessing upon my children. Pour out your Spirit and draw them close to you. Make yourself real to them so they always have a foundation of your presence to stand on. May their experience of you be one of tenderness, joy, and unshakable confidence. Be their Lord, friend, and wise Counselor.

A Change in Season

God also said to Abraham: "Concerning your wife Sarai,
you are not to call her Sarai anymore,
but Sarah, 'My Princess,' will be her name."

GENESIS 17:15

You may not experience a time on earth when God gives you
a new name. But there are seasons of life when you may notice
you've stepped into a new dimension of God's blessing. Doors
of favor open wider, the wells of wisdom seem deeper, and the
breakthrough you dreamed about finally manifests.

We are all growing from glory to glory. All created to know the God
whose love exceeds expectation. And we are all acquainted with
seasons of hardship and seasons of joy. It's important to pay attention
to every season. To learn from the ones we'd rather skip over, enjoy
the sweetness of others, and to praise him during them all. In all things
and in every moment, we must find God. We must approach new
assignments and seasons with hearts finely tuned to him.

*Father, I want to mature into the person you've created me to be. To
speak from a heart that's saturated with your wisdom. To recognize
your hand in every season and rise with praise for each one. I
want to remain in tune with your Spirit in times of barrenness and
seasons of bliss. To find your face no matter what comes.*

Dare to Believe

He spoke out loud:
"O, that Ishmael might prosper with your blessing!"

GENESIS 17:18

After laughing so hard he fell to the ground, questioning how God could possibly bless him and his wife with children at such an old age, Abraham came up with a solution. He took what felt like an impossible promise of God and whittled it down to something more reasonable.

Have you ever caught yourself dismissing the random thoughts that go through your mind during prayer or even throughout the day? Those ideas, gentle whispers, or a general sense that God is speaking to us often seem too good to be true. But we need to pay attention to what God is saying, even if it doesn't make sense. How many blessings have we declined because we couldn't figure out how they could happen? How many times have we settled for something less than God's best because we reasoned it away? God is more powerful than we sometimes dare to believe. Let's be willing to take a risk and believe the promises coming alive in our hearts.

Father, teach me to discern your voice. I sense you encouraging me to go after the great big promises I've been too afraid to take to heart. I've allowed fear of the unknown to steal my blessings, but I won't any longer. I offer you my questions and doubts. Show me what to do next.

Ready to Run

During the hottest part of the day, as Abraham sat at his tent door, he looked up and suddenly saw three men standing nearby. As soon as he saw them, he ran from his tent to welcome them.

GENESIS 18:1–2

In the heat of the day, when the pressure is on and the enemy fights to capture your attention, look up. Keep your heart tender toward the Lord. His blessings come in all shapes and sizes, especially ones we don't anticipate. At times, the Lord himself will come wrapped in human flesh—reaching through the words, actions, and hearts of others.

When you're sitting, waiting for your day of visitation, don't get stuck in discontentment. Anticipate the moment of breakthrough. Even when the only thing left to do is to be patient and believe, don't become indifferent or calloused. Be ready to run when the Lord comes with his hands full!

Father, I'm looking with faith toward my day of visitation. I'm going to allow myself to imagine what it will be like, trusting it will be a thousand times better. I shake off weariness. Forgive me for becoming detached and aloof. I feel hope rising. I sense faith awakening within me. You are coming. You will meet with me, and I will never be the same.

June

Stay a While

> He bowed down to the ground and said,
> "My Lord, if I have found favor in your sight, don't pass me by.
> Stay for a while with your servant."
>
> GENESIS 18:2–3

You have found favor with the Lord. At this very moment, God is extending an invitation into blissful encounter. He is your friend. Your Creator. Your patient, merciful Father, who is absolutely in love with you and wants to spend time with you. Don't rush through this devotion without noticing the gentle tug of God's Spirit. Take a few moments to quiet yourself in his embrace. Stay awhile.

Be content, even if you don't hear him say a word. Be still. Notice what it feels like to be washed in the beauty of God's presence. Sink deep into an ocean of peace. He's with you right now. He's pouring out all you need for today. Gracing you with the glory of holy intimacy that is reserved for those who are willing to stay and enjoy.

Father, every breath is a reminder of your faithfulness. Each heartbeat designed to point me to your love. May an awareness of you drench my thoughts. May encounters of your nearness eclipse my busy moments. You are all I need. You are the experience I've longed for all of my life.

Our Friend

Yahweh appeared once again to Abraham…
"I'll have some water brought to you all
so that you can wash your feet.
Rest here a while under the tree."

GENESIS 18:1, 4

What an incredible scene! God, who previously appeared to Abraham in his glory, now comes to him as a mortal man—a friend. He sits with him under a shady tree, and they enjoy each other's company. Long before Mary of Bethany washed the Lord's feet with her tears, Abraham washed Jesus' feet by his tent door.

These are the days of sweet intimacy. When Jesus reveals himself as our friend, we get a glimpse of his kindness in ways we previously hadn't noticed. He sees us—our real, sometimes great, other times not so great, selves. He's comfortable sitting beside us, listening, talking, laughing, and enjoying the day that our Father has made. These are the moments that awaken our hearts.

Jesus, what an honor it is to know you as friend. To sit in fellowship with you as if you are my equal, and then to hear you say that I am. You leave me breathless. I am overcome. It is my joy to know you. To enjoy your company as I go about my day. To join my faith with what burns in your heart.

Increasing Faith

Sarah laughed to herself with disbelief, saying,
"A woman my age—have a baby?"

GENESIS 18:12

Have you ever laughed at people who have audacious faith? You know the ones—those who cross the invisible boundaries we've drawn for God. Those who excitedly declare the miracle they're believing for. Maybe you didn't laugh aloud, but inside you couldn't help but think how ridiculous they sounded. Of course, God can do anything in a very general sense, but let's be reasonable! Miracles are few and far between.

But what if we decided to throw caution to the wind and to believe with childlike expectancy? What if the only things holding back our miracles are our disbelief and fear? Will every prayer be answered? Probably not. At least not in the way we imagine. But we've played it safe for too long! We've allowed the fear of disappointment to guide our prayers instead of God's Word and directive. It's time to awaken our slumbering faith! Time to be known as *believers* again!

Father, forgive me. I've played it safe, only believing for things that make sense and fit into my God-box. I know you can do anything, but I've been afraid to apply this truth to certain situations. Open your Word to me. Speak to my heart and show me where I've been ruled by unbelief. Increase my faith.

His Searching Gaze

Yahweh knew her thoughts...
Sarah was afraid, so she denied it.

GENESIS 18:13, 15

The loving conviction of the Lord is meant to empower us. Given as a means of freeing us from the masks of perfectionism and pretense that hinder us. It is intended to draw us closer to him by revealing the areas that need his grace and mercy. His searching gaze shouldn't scare us; it should be something we long for. Something we welcome and invite.

The Lord knows our thoughts and deepest intentions, and he wants us to become aware of them as well. When our behavior could potentially cause our hearts to grow cold and indifferent, we need his correction. We need to be reminded who we are in him. True conviction is freeing when we accept it. It draws us closer to him where he provides the grace to overcome. Let's lean into his loving-kindness and resign ourselves to those eyes that blaze with zealous love.

Father, peer into my heart. I open myself to you completely. No area of my life is restricted. Show me anything I've believed that has limited your hand in my life or impeded my growth. I want nothing to hold me back from following you unreservedly. Thank you for seeing me—the real me—and loving me still.

Loved

> "It is true; I have singled him out as my own."
>
> GENESIS 18:19

Imagine hearing the Lord talk about you with such delight. To know he not only sees you but that you've also captured his heart. You've been singled out as his own—one of his favorites. How would it make you feel to know he thinks of you that way?

The truth is that you are the joy of heaven! You are the one the Father chose as a gift for his Son. You are the love he longed for. The one Jesus laid down his life for. And now that you are his, he cannot, *will not,* take his eyes off of you. Right now, you have his undivided attention. Perhaps it's time for an identity adjustment. If you have heard this said for years but it hasn't felt personal or touched you at the core of your being, stop. Reflect. Let this truth sink in. As it does, it will shift the atmosphere of your life, attracting favor, blessings, and joy-filled relationships.

Father, you're speaking to me today. Letting me know that your love isn't only a general love for all mankind but also a very personal one. You love me. Jesus died for me. Before I was born, you knew me and made provision for my life. Accepting this truth and pondering it every day is changing me.

Friendship and Intercession

Yahweh explained to Abraham, "The outcry for justice against
Sodom and Gomorrah is so great and their sin so blatant..."
So Abraham came forward to present his case before Yahweh.

GENESIS 18:20, 23

God shares his secrets with his closest friends. He brings them close
and lets them in on his process. And as Abraham demonstrated,
friends of God shouldn't be afraid of having brave communication.
It's in the moments when we seek to understand God's ways that
we delve deeper into his heart. What did Abraham do with these
divine secrets? He considered the information and pleaded for the
city. He became an intercessor!

God reveals his plans to those he trusts. It seems ludicrous that the
all-knowing God would care what we think, but he apparently does!
He takes friendship seriously. Perhaps he wants us to do as Abraham
did—to stand in the gap for those who are lost and cry out for God's
mercy. When the hand of justice falls on the unrighteous, instead of
nodding in agreement because they deserve it, let's remember this
story of Abraham. Let's pray for those who need mercy.

*Father, I set myself in agreement with your mercy and ask you to
awaken the hearts of those who have grown cold. Let your promise
of restoration chase down the lost with irresistible love. May grace
cause others to see their condition through your eyes and create a
holy desire for purity.*

Identity and Confidence

Abraham spoke up again and said,
"I am just a man formed from earth's dust and ashes
but allow me to be so bold as to ask you, my Lord."

GENESIS 18:27

Humility and confidence go together. Humility because if not for the mercy and kindness of our heavenly Father, we could not stand before him. Confidence because by accepting our position as sons and daughters of God, we honor Jesus' sacrifice.

His radical love defines us and gives us identity. It keeps us safe by reminding us how dependent upon him we really are. Anything praiseworthy about our lives, character, or actions is a gift meant to bless others. Love encourages us to remain close to him. To enjoy the freedom of friendship and the honor of kinship. We come boldly before him, unafraid of being honest because we've grown to trust his love. Fulfilling our purpose on earth begins by discovering our identity in the Lord. It opens the way for us to walk in continual communion with Christ and release his will upon the earth.

Father, your love fills me with confidence. As I walk with you and learn your ways, I trust you more. I depend upon your grace. Grace that empowers me to stand with confidence and make the world around me a better place. May my confidence in our relationship keep me humble—safe in the knowledge of your love.

Looking Ahead

Lot's wife turned and gazed longingly on the city
and turned into a pillar of salt.

GENESIS 19:26

Don't look back. Don't hold on to what was when God is calling you into something new. The fear of the unknown will grip you and try to hold you back if you don't keep yourself saturated in God's presence. Love is the antidote for a doubting heart.

The truth is that we usually don't understand the finite details of things we're told will turn out for our good. But when we freefall into the deep waters of faith, we become stronger. The less we understand, the more we depend on God, who is our strength. It can be scary moving forward into the unknown. This doesn't mean we jump at every crazy idea. We pray. We submit ourselves to the Lord and invite his wisdom and counsel. We follow peace that settles our souls, even if it doesn't make sense to our minds.

Father, lead me by your Spirit. Take me by the hand, and I will follow you into the unknown. You are worthy of my trust. Though at times I remember the past with fondness, my heart is set on you. I'm excited about the path you've set before me. Prepare me for the blessings you have in store. I look to you with joy-filled anticipation.

The Beauty of Surrender

Abraham answered, "Because I thought,
'There's no one here that fears God.
They will kill me to get to my wife.'"

GENESIS 20:11

It had been about twenty-five years since Abraham had committed this same sin—he lied about Sarah being his sister in order to protect himself. After countless encounters with God, Abraham was still in need of mercy. The man who would become the father of nations was still an imperfect vessel in need of a perfect God. How relevant this is to our lives today!

God, in his mercy, confronts our sin. He allows the murky waters of faithlessness and doubt to rise to the surface for us to realize they're still there. It may surprise us when old reactions or ways of thinking pop up, but it shouldn't discourage us. We're all growing in the Lord, and when our fleshly ways show up, it is an opportunity to bow in prayer. To cry out for purity and resign ourselves to the beauty of surrender.

Father, with each passing day, I want to become more like you. More intentional with my love and commitment to you. Growing from glory to glory, leaving behind everything that doesn't reflect your beauty. I long to live before you in holiness and complete surrender. Fill me with the desire to please you always so I never stray.

Pray for Others

Abraham prayed to God; and God healed Abimelech! He also healed Abimelech's wife and female servants of their infertility.

GENESIS 20:17

This first account of healing prayer in the Bible is especially compelling since Abraham believed for a fertility miracle for his own wife. He didn't reserve his faith for *his* breakthrough; he prayed the blessing of what he desired over someone else. When God healed Abimelech's household, it was a catalyst for faith in Abraham's family.

When we're waiting for answers to prayer, it takes compassion to stand with someone else. It takes integrity and proper perspective to see others blessed with what we want. These unselfish prayers become seed for our own breakthroughs. A strong foundation for our character. When we allow ourselves to understand someone else's position, it's easier to rejoice with those who rejoice. It softens our hearts, gets our minds off of ourselves, and builds our faith.

Father, thank you for reminding me that as I sow into others, I am becoming more like you. Though your timetable is often a mystery, I won't stare in jealousy at the blessings of others. I will celebrate your faithfulness, knowing you love me just the same.

Believe for the Extravagant

> Yahweh visited Sarah, just as he said he would,
> and fulfilled his promise to her.
> Abraham was one hundred years old
> when his son Isaac was born.
>
> GENESIS 21:1, 5

Why do we pick and choose what we think God can or can't, will or won't do? Why do we limit him based on what we decide is a miracle we can wrap our brains around and accept? Nothing is too hard for our miracle-working God, who is waiting for us to believe he is who he says he is.

It's time we let our faith arise! Time for us to dig out those promises we've given up on, no matter how long we've been waiting. Time to shake off discouragement and complacency and get excited! If he can set the oceans within their borders, care enough to number the hairs on our head, and hold the sun in place, he most certainly can answer our most extravagant prayers. On our own, we can do nothing, but with him, when we connect our faith and allow ourselves to believe for the extravagant and outrageous promises, miracles flow.

Father, I repent for giving up on some of the promises you've made. I've examined them under a microscope of doubt when they should be planted in the ground of faith. Now I will water them with the Scriptures you place in my heart and thank you in advance for bringing them to pass.

Enjoy Life

Sarah said, "God has brought me laughter."

GENESIS 21:6

God isn't a stodgy, hard-faced, boring Father. The One who paints the sky every day also brings color to our lives. He is fun, creative, the author of laughter and joy. He gave us bodies that dance, voices that sing, minds that chime with brilliant ideas.

God has filled each of us with a personal list of things that make us happy, and it's time we honored that list. Some of us get so caught up in duties, work, goals, and the future that we forget to enjoy the now. To play and have fun. To laugh. Joy feels good because he has created us for it. Our lives may not be perfect, but they're ours. They are gifts from a good, good Father. And it's time we honored the Lord and ourselves by enjoying every moment.

Father, forgive me for getting sucked into the busyness of life or mundane attitudes. I'm going to pay attention to the beauty around me. The people surrounding me. The silly things. I'm going to intentionally look for the good, and I'm going to learn to laugh more. I'm going to accept this gift of life and enjoy it!

Do It Again

> "Everyone who hears about this will laugh with me."
>
> GENESIS 21:6

Your testimony of breakthrough isn't meant for you alone. This history of God's faithfulness is yours to share. It releases faith in the heart of those who hear. It encourages. Extends a lifeline to those who have fallen into despair. Your testimony releases substance into those whose hopes have melted from the heat of fiery trials.

The very word *testimony* comes from a root word that means "to do again." When we share with joyful conviction what God has done in our lives, we're creating a platform for others to stand on with us. We're partnering with the Lord by giving living examples of how he's moved. Our words become like refreshing breezes, blowing away the dry, crusty remains of doubt. Our testimonies are full of life that is meant to be shared.

Father, I want to be a voice of encouragement. Bring to my attention those who would be helped by stories of your faithfulness. In the various conversations, remind me of situations where I've seen you move. Let my words carry life. May my testimonies infuse hearers with faith and joy.

Lean Upon Our Beloved

Hagar and her son Ishmael departed
and wandered off into the wilderness of Beersheba.

GENESIS 21:14

Times of trial and difficulty, these wilderness seasons of the soul, can actually contain some of our most profound encounters with the Lord. In our pain and desperation, when we're bowed low and can scarcely utter a word, Jesus makes himself known to us like never before. In Hebrew, the word for *wilderness* literally means "the place of speaking or the place of communing." Hagar was forced to wander into this wilderness. Desperation took her deep into the place of hearing the voice of God.

When we understand that our exhausting, dry, desert seasons are opportunities to experience our most profound and refreshing moments with the Lord, we stop fighting them. Instead, we lean upon our beloved and learn what it means to be emptied of self. We stand in our darkness, only to discover the Light that never dims. We hear the whispers of his voice that we hadn't heard before.

Father, I am desperate for you, but I will not clamor to find you. I will rest. I will resist the urge to fight and claw my way out of this painful cage and, instead, find you in it. I will still my soul and listen. You are with me. I will sink into your arms of love and wait for you to carry me out.

Shine with His Light

King Abimelech and Phicol, his army commander, came to
Abraham and said, "It is obvious that God is with you and blesses
everything you do."

GENESIS 21:22

The world teaches that fame and fortune are worth striving for. It
convinces us that we are accepted and appreciated in relation to
our level of success. It tells us that we must be better, richer, thinner,
and more beautiful to be happy. But we have found peace in the
simplicity of trusting God. We believe we're significant because
our omnipotent Father affirms us. We experience joy because we
are thankful. We are comfortable being ourselves because, in our
uniqueness, we shine with a facet of God's glory.

Agreeing with who Jesus says we are sets us up to experience our
best life. The blessings of God make us rich in a much different way
than the world comprehends. We may not have all we desire, but
we carry the profound understanding that we are enough. When we
believe that God loves us, we live differently, and others will notice.

*Father, I want to shine with your light. I don't want to be different
just for the sake of being controversial but to attract others to the
glory within me. I want people to recognize the peace and hope I
carry so I can point them to you.*

A Surrendered Life

God said, "Please take your son, your only son, Isaac, whom I know you dearly love, and go to the land of Moriah. Offer him up to me."

GENESIS 22:2

God knows when our affections become tainted. He sees when our pursuits sidetrack us. In his mercy, he asks us for anything that has taken the place of our first love. He wants every part of us, and we are only truly free when nothing in this world holds us more tightly than Jesus. When we lay our lives on the altar over and over again and call for God's refining fire. When we want nothing—no dream, blessing, or promise—to consume our hearts more than he does.

Few dare to lay their will on the altar. It's rare to find someone who has absolutely resigned his or her self to live fully for the Lord. These precious treasures, these dedicated ones who have wholly devoted themselves to Jesus, have discovered the joyous recompense of a surrendered life.

Father, I have tasted your glory. I have seen that you are good. I know that when you ask me to give you something I care about, it's because you either have something better or are showing me my own divided affections. Give me the grace to live with holy resignation, knowing a surrendered life is a life ripe for your loving intervention.

Costly Worship

"Stay here with the donkey," Abraham told the young men.
"Isaac and I will go up and worship; then we will return to you."

GENESIS 22:5

Worship costs us something. It requires us to lay aside our idols, sacrifice, or time and recognize our need for a Savior. Worshiping in spirit and in truth means giving God our dearest treasure and calling it our delight. It causes an internal shift, allowing us to see not what we give up but the beauty of the One we worship.

Our sacrifice of love is beautiful to the Lord. We cannot compare the ways he meets with us, as we prostrate ourselves before him, to anything on earth. Jesus held nothing back to prove his love for us, and now we have the honor of loving him back. Wholeheartedly. Unreservedly. Without conditions. It seems too simple to believe that what we really yearn for is found in his presence, but until we live this way, we will never truly know.

Father, all that I am I lay before you as an offering. May I be so completely yielded to you that my life rises as a costly fragrance before you. I want my worship to capture your attention. I want to lavish you with my love and my truest, most heartfelt praise. May my love be without conditions.

Set Free by the Lamb

Abraham answered,
"My son, God himself will provide
the lamb for an offering."

GENESIS 22:8

God provided a lamb for Isaac and a Lamb for you. Jesus was the pure and spotless Lamb who forever took away your sin. He is the offering God made on your behalf. He is the reason you stand before the Lord, blameless and whole. Nothing you've done testifies against you because the blood of the Lamb has washed away your painful past.

Jesus has paid the price to set you free in every area of life. His love defines you. You don't have to revert to sin or slip back into habits of unrighteousness. You are his beautiful beloved. You are wanted, fearless, and valuable. You are not your past. Not required to answer the door when sin comes knocking. Jesus has set you free. Called you to rule and reign at his side with honor. Remember who you are.

Father, help me to remember who I am when temptation lurks nearby. You have redeemed me with your kindness and pierced me with the revelation of your love. I bow before you, knowing mercy has placed this crown upon my head and removed my cloak of shame. Thank you for your unfathomable love. For the Lamb who has set me free.

Step Out and Trust

Abraham took the knife in his hand to plunge it into his son,
but the angel of Yahweh called to him from heaven.

GENESIS 22:10–11

Have you ever been concerned that you've missed God? You think
you know his heart, but the burden of being wrong is very real.
*What if this decision messes everything up? What if I'm wrong? What
if I ruin my life or the lives of others? Am I deceiving myself? What
will others think? What if...What if...*

Abraham didn't miss God. But one can't help but wonder if he
experienced a great internal struggle. Would God stop him if he
was making a huge mistake? In the end, God did stop him. But not
because he was wrong. This was a matter of the heart. And this is
the truth we must hold on to: God sees our desire to honor him. He
doesn't punish us for choosing wrongly if we sincerely seek his will.
And if he needs to stop us or get us back on track, he knows exactly
how to do that.

*Father, sometimes I'm so afraid of missing you that I don't do
anything at all. I get frozen in place, unsure if I hear your voice or
my own desires. But it's time for me to step out. I've sought your
will, and now I will trust that my life is in your hands.*

Led by His Spirit

"Because you have obeyed me,
the entire world will be blessed through your seed."

GENESIS 22:18

Your obedience contains seed powerful enough to change the world around you! One decision to follow what God has placed in your heart may result in thousands of lives touched by the reality of God. Or it may transform one person. The important thing is to heed his voice and let the Lord decide how many are reached.

Fear and rationalization often hold us back and limit what God wants to do. We assess the calling on our lives based on our ability, connections, wisdom, and finances instead of diving in with noteworthy faith. God doesn't usually give us each step of the plan ahead of time. He simply awakens desire then waits for our *yes*. Agreement opens the way for greater things. Once we agree to follow his leading and seek his wisdom, he unveils the next step.

Father, the beauty of what you've placed inside of me seems too extravagant. Sometimes I have no idea how these things will come to pass, but I say, "Yes." Have your way in me and through me. Breathe upon these dreams. Show me what to do next. I don't need to understand all of your plans. I simply ask that you lead me by your Spirit.

Bridal Love

Abraham called for his trusted head servant,
who was in charge of all that he had.
"Find a wife among them for my son Isaac."

GENESIS 24:2, 4

In allegorical form, this chapter points to the Father releasing the Holy Spirit to seek a bride for his Son, Jesus. The Holy Spirit is searching the earth, gathering the church, his bride, the wife of the Lamb. Love is not demanded of us. It is offered. Eternal bliss is given as a gift for us to unwrap now as we enter into heavenly union with Jesus. With arms outstretched, he welcomed us into the family.

An awakening of bridal love carries the commission to rouse the hearts of others. Undeniable love is ours to share. Transformed by our encounters with his glory, the Lord invites us to let our lives shine so others may find their way. We don't need a title or anyone's permission to partner with the Holy Spirit. All we need is a tender and obedient heart willing to share his love.

Father, I am beside myself. Amazed that you would invite me into this holy union with your Son. My entire life has been transformed by love. Now I want to emit the fragrance of your presence everywhere I go. To carry your presence with grace and see others awakened by your holy kiss.

Angels

"I know he will send his angel before you."

Genesis 24:7

Though most of us don't see the spiritual realm with our natural eyes, it is there. It's interesting to think what life would be like if we could see our angels clearly and continuously without any hindrances. Seeing their care and protection would help dispel our fears. Witnessing how they lead us and draw our attention to various situations, people, and items would increase our confidence.

But this is the life of faith. This is the mystery of believing what we know to be true but cannot always see. God could have kept our angels a secret, only revealing them in heaven. But he wanted us to know they're with us. When we accept what the Scriptures say about our angels, we can engage our faith and connect our prayers with heaven's help. We don't worship these messengers, but we certainly should be thankful for them!

Father, may my songs of love and heart of adoration draw your presence and invite angelic protection. I want the atmosphere around me to be saturated with your glory. For every room I enter to become a chamber of angelic activity. Thank you for these heavenly helpers who faithfully serve your children.

The Attitude of Our Hearts

> After she had finished giving him a drink, she added, "I will also draw water for your camels until they have finished drinking."
>
> GENESIS 24:19

Rebekah's act of kindness toward a stranger opened the door for her to become Isaac's bride. Our humble acts of service often bring surprising promotion. When we live with humility and a desire to represent the Lord in all we do, others take notice.

Eliezer had simply asked Rebekah for a drink of water, but she had a spirit of excellence and offered to do more than what he asked. Her generosity reflected a compassionate heart. It invited the blessing of God. The Lord notices the attitude of our hearts when doing menial tasks. He hears the musings of our souls that are hidden from others. When we have the heart to help, God will reward us. When the true bridal spirit comes upon us, we love to serve in the same way that Jesus loves to serve. God looks at our hearts.

Father, forgive me for the times I've been selfish, felt inconvenienced, or served with a bad attitude. I repent for the times I've done things with arrogant pride, hoping others would notice. I want every motive of my heart to be pure. To serve with generosity when no one else sees but you.

Divine Setups

"This was all planned by Yahweh!
If this is his plan, what can we say?"

GENESIS 24:50

Spend some time in this chapter, and you will be amazed at the way
God answered Eliezer's prayer. Not only had the Lord given him a
wife for Isaac, but he also led Eliezer to precisely the type of woman
Abraham sent him to find for his son.

Many times, we chalk up chance meetings or random conversations
as nothing more than happenstance. We dismiss them quickly and
therefore miss one of God's divine setups. When we're only looking
for answers to prayer to come in expected ways, we risk missing the
opportunities that present themselves. We stand back, scratching our
heads, wondering why breakthrough hasn't happened when all along
God has been trying to get our attention, and we didn't notice. Let's
keep our eyes open and our spirits in tune with the Spirit of God so
we don't miss the blessings that are right in front of us.

*Father, teach me to live in tune with your Spirit. Lead me. Don't let
me miss out on a single thing. Too often, I miss the opportunities
you create for me, but I'm learning to be sensitive, to pay attention,
and to not overlook your blessings. Grace me with the ability to
become more aware.*

Into the Unknown

They called for Rebekah and asked her,
"Will you go with this man?"
"I will gladly go with him," she answered.

GENESIS 24:58

Stepping into the beautiful expanse of our destiny often means letting go of control. When we've grown comfortable with the way life has been, there's a chance of becoming complacent. Of succumbing to convenience and ease because we fear the unknown.

The One who beckons us to his peace-filled chamber also leads us to the edge of adventure. His smile lights up the room as he extends his hand and invites us into something new. Something we've never done before. Something we have always desired but never thought we'd be brave enough to do. When we say yes to going with Jesus into the unknown, it may be scary at first. It may take every ounce of resolve, but it will be worth it. And it may possibly be the fulfillment of a dream.

Father, sometimes it feels as if you're asking me to jump off a cliff when really you're just asking me to trust you and take one small (sometimes big) step. So today, I say yes to the unknown. To taking that step, no matter how big. Yes to doing what I don't feel qualified to do. Yes to the new things that await. Yes to following you.

Meditate on the Lord

Isaac went out in the evening into the field to meditate.
He looked up, and saw camels coming in the distance.

GENESIS 24:63

When we meditate—turn off our racing thoughts and focus on nothing more than the awareness of God—we put ourselves in a position to see what we hadn't seen before. Stillness is one of the places where we receive vision. It's where peace introduces itself as the antidote for anxiety. Where hope dismisses discouragement.

We've grown so accustomed to busyness that many are unable to be still. If this sounds like you, don't give up! Make time in your day for quiet, even if it's only for five minutes. Schedule it. Practice being still until it feels natural and you can easily go for much longer. Close your eyes and whisper his name—*Jesus*. See his beautiful face. Believe that he is with you because he is.

Father, I long for the peace that is rooted in your presence. Show me how to take advantage of moments throughout the day when I can center my attention on you. Teach me how to turn off my racing thoughts and be still. Truly still, focused on nothing but the beauty of your presence.

Close to His Heart

Isaac settled near the well named
the Well of the Living One Who Watches Over Me.

GENESIS 25:11

Settle yourself in the knowledge that your Father is watching over you. As a loving mother who broods over her young, God is brooding over you. Every morning, before you open your eyes, the Holy Spirit hovers over you. He anticipates your waking and avails himself to you first thing. When night falls and sleep comes, he wraps you in his arms and whispers reminders of his love.

Drink deeply of this remarkable revelation: God takes time to know every thought, each breath, and every movement of your soul. It is his delight to watch over you. To fix his loving gaze upon you, even when you're not gazing upon him. You are his delight. The one whom he gave everything to be with. He has an unobstructed view straight into your soul.

Father, I'm undone by your attentiveness. In awe that I am worthy of your constant focus. The revelation of your love settles my soul. To know you are with me and always available is mind-boggling. Thank you for reminding me how loved, cared for, and valued I am. I am always close to your heart.

Serve the Younger Generation

"The older will serve the younger."

GENESIS 25:23

Oh, that we would take this message to heart! Imagine what could happen in the church today if the "older" would serve the "younger." If they would see the value of fathering and mothering a generation of radical Jesus lovers and future world-changers. Too often, church leaders *require* the young to serve the leaders' vision and forsake their own. But what would happen if a new breed of leadership arose to say, "I see the call on your life and want to bless you and help you fulfill *your* vision." A generational transfer must take place for the church to receive the fullness of her inheritance.

Let's make way for the new thing God desires to do. If you're one of the older ones, pour into those who God has placed in your care. Let your ceiling be their floor. Encourage and mentor them. Consider it an honor to be entrusted with such tender and zealous hearts.

Father, as the years pass, I want to spend my days representing you well. I want my life to be an example for all to follow. To make people feel known, loved, and championed. To be excited about what I can pass down and to do for others what I'd like them to do for me.

Patient Trust

Isaac was sixty when the twins were born.

GENESIS 25:26

Isaac and Rebekah waited twenty years for children, and when God opened her womb, he blessed them with twins. There is no mention in Scripture that Isaac had children with his handmaid. Patient trust brought about a double blessing!

There are only two ways to wait for God's promises to manifest: in peace or in stress. The choice is ours. Fear that he won't come through forces us to act impulsively, as Abraham did by fathering a child with Hagar. Sometimes, like Abraham, we want something so badly we take matters into our own hands. But when we present ourselves to the Lord, impatience and all, we can tap into his presence. Living in this atmosphere of love settles our questions and brings us peace.

Father, sometimes waiting is hard. Anxiety and impatience nip at my heels and peace feels a million miles away. But I know that you have perfect wisdom. You know precisely when to manifest the promises you've made. Bless me with the grace to remain steadfast and immovable. Help me to stay focused on your love—the place where fear cannot exist.

Resist Temptation

"Can't you see I'm dying of hunger," Esau said,
"What good is the birthright if I'm dead?"
So, Esau swore an oath and surrendered his birthright to Jacob.

GENESIS 25:32–33

This is a somber picture of what we look like when we say yes to sin and no to God. We forget that we've been crucified to the flesh and our bodies have been given over to the Spirit of God. Everything in us must give way to the increase of Jesus in our inner man. But Esau chose to live without blessing.

How easily we trade our privileges in God for the things of this world. As his children, we are destined to be like Christ and reign with him in glory. We've been blessed with eternal treasures that we must hold dear. We do not have to yield to temptation and sin. We are more than conquerors! Stronger than these fleshly cravings. We have power over our enemies, and we are called to enjoy our godly inheritance.

Father, highlight the areas that haven't yet bowed in submission to you. Set me free from temptation, pride, and lethargy. Remind me who I am when I am distracted by the lure of sin. Give me grace and strength to say no to the lesser things of this world and yes to the beautiful blessings of life with you.

July

Go Deeper

Isaac reopened and restored the wells his father Abraham had originally dug—the wells the Philistines had stopped up after Abraham's death.

GENESIS 26:18

Wells speak of our life in the Spirit, a source of refreshing and satisfaction. In seasons when you feel spiritually dry or emotionally spent, it's time to dig deeper. To draw from the waters of his love and allow them to stream into every dry and dusty place. Like the parched ground that doesn't readily absorb the refreshing rain, an anxious soul may need more time to soak in his love before it penetrates. As you go deeper, the presence of the Holy Spirit will quench your thirsty soul.

We can easily tap into the refreshing waters of his love. Jesus has already broken open the way for you. Be still. Drink deeply. Set aside time each day to saturate yourself in his refreshing love. He's ready to create streams within you that you will be able to drink from for years to come.

Father, take me deeper. Saturate me with the awareness of your presence so every part of me is drenched in your love. My deepest desires and my thirst for unspeakable joy are satisfied when I'm submerged in your living waters. Let not one dry or contrary thought remain.

The Well of Refreshment

One day, when Isaac's servants dug in the valley,
they uncovered a spring-fed well.

GENESIS 26:19

In our valleys—these prolonged spaces filled with mundane and stuffy days—we long for something more. These foggy, hard-to-move-a-step seasons when we scarcely remember the heights of victory are invitations to dig deep. To press into the Lord and uncover the well within.

If this is you, if it seems as though those glory days of his presence have slipped away, don't despair!

God is leading you to a place of refreshment. He is offering you the chance to go deeper than you ever have before. To mature in your identity as his beloved and find the peace that stabilizes you in every season. This is why you've been led to the valley: not to punish or confuse you but to help you discover the depth of spirit you've been longing for.

Father, thank you for reminding me that in every season, I can find your presence. When you seem far away, you've only stepped back to extend your hand in invitation. Together we will dance into a deeper reality of your love. You are the well of refreshment for which my soul thirsts.

Trust His Love

"You will never need to fear a thing for I am with you."

GENESIS 26:24

There is no one like our God. None as holy, compassionate, and mighty. None who loves so passionately and redeems so fiercely. All that he has done through the cross reminds us of his untamable desire for us. He wants us to trust this love that encompasses every aspect of our life.

When we completely trust his love and get a glimpse of how powerful it is, fear begins to melt away. We stop trying to force ourselves to have faith and find the posture of rest. We're able to believe because we've finally allowed love to quiet our minds and silence the questions. Fear loses its grip when our need to comprehend facts bows its knees. Love holds us securely so we are no longer moved by what we don't understand.

Father, thank you for directing my attention to the power of your love. I offer you my need to understand what doesn't make sense. I know that facts are only temporary circumstances ready to line up to the truth of your Word. You will not forsake me. You haven't forgotten the promises you've made.

Your Children Will Succeed

"Your children will flourish and succeed."

GENESIS 26:24

Who are you pouring into? Whom has the Lord entrusted you with during this season of your life? If you have children of your own, are raising someone else's, or are mentoring spiritual children, this is a promise you can take to heart. Your children will flourish and succeed.

Whether you are witnessing the manifestation of this promise or haven't seen it come to pass yet, let it flood your heart and encourage your faith. Declare this powerful truth over those in your care: God desires your offspring to be blessed! He has called you to know his will and to pray with settled conviction—no matter what you see happening with your children, God's Word is true. He will give you the wisdom to pray for them and the understanding about what to impart.

Father, I lift my children (spiritual or natural) to your remembrance. You have promised that they would flourish and succeed. Draw them close to you now and make yourself real to them in ways they have yet to experience. Give them wisdom. Direct their steps. May they know the glories of life with you.

Crush Fear

"You will never need to fear a thing
for I am with you and I will greatly bless you."

GENESIS 26:24

If you find yourself repeatedly tormented by fear, today can be your day of breakthrough. Fear and love will always be at odds with each other, but love has already won. And the peace you desire is found in the acceptance of that love. It is a truth that must be embraced, not with polite acceptance that makes you appear reverent and holy, but with the grip of a desperate heart.

It's time you crushed fear by allowing yourself to freefall into love. Give yourself permission to completely let go. To put your life unreservedly in the hands of your Father who loves you. To roar with resolve as you take a risk and release control. Even the worst-case scenarios still include his presence. No matter what happens, God won't leave you.

Father, instead of living in my head and trying to figure everything out, I'm going to relax. I give myself permission not to worry. I've already done everything I know to do, and if there's anything I missed, you'll tell me. But I won't be able to hear your instructions unless I find my peace. So that will be my new life's mission—to live from the place of peace.

Live with Authenticity

Isaac asked them, "Why have you come to me now,
since you hated me and sent me away?"
They answered, "We have witnessed firsthand
how powerfully Yahweh's favor has been with you."

GENESIS 26:27–28

Our testimony, the way we carry ourselves both publicly and
privately, is powerful. Even when we don't think people are
watching, they are. Especially when we declare before the world
that we are Christians. How we behave in times of crisis, the way
we react to criticism, and how we navigate favor are all compelling
examples of what we really believe.

Living with authenticity, allowing people to see our struggles and
triumphs, gives them a real taste of what life with Christ is all about.
Skeptics don't want to hear how life-transforming walking with
the Lord is. They want to see it. They want *you* to be so convinced
of it yourself that it infiltrates every aspect of your life. When you
demonstrate peace in times of stress, compassion instead of anger,
or joy when things aren't going your way, people will be drawn to
what you carry.

*Father, may what I believe be reflected in the way I speak and
behave. May I demonstrate the beauty of your Spirit within me with
authenticity and humility. Let others see the blessing, favor, and
reality of you in my life. May I live above reproach with you as my
chief defender.*

Release Mercy

Isaac prepared a wonderful feast for them,
and they all ate and drank together.

GENESIS 26:30

This was a feast enjoyed with those who previously harassed and spoke ill of Isaac. He could have dismissed them and rejected their proposal to make peace, but he didn't. He invited them to his table.

God watches not only the way we respond to our enemies but also the inner musing of our hearts in times of gossip and criticism. It is our Father's will that we become people who are quick to forgive, just as Christ has forgiven us. Anger fights to keep mercy in a vice so we won't enjoy the liberties forgiveness releases to us. Often, we miss opportunities for surprising friendships because we want to hold on to our *right* to stay mad.

Father, I want to walk upon paths of mercy and grace. To not only receive and enjoy forgiveness but also to release it readily. I don't want a self-righteous attitude to hinder my intimacy with you. I refuse to remain angry. Unbind my soul from entanglements of hatred or unforgiveness. I need mercy just as much as those who have sinned against me.

Lavish Rewards

Isaac's servants came with wonderful news
about the well they had dug, saying, "We've just found water!"

GENESIS 26:32

After Isaac released forgiveness to his enemies, God blessed him.
He didn't quarrel and fight with them about the wells they had
stopped up, and he didn't withhold forgiveness until they agreed
to give him back what was his. He trusted God to take care of his
needs, and God did just that.

Our decision to walk in integrity captures the Father's attention
and sets us up to be blessed. There will come a time when every
wrongful thing will be made right, but it is not our job to dish out
judgment. When we choose to walk in righteousness, God repays
us in lavish ways. Trusting the Lord with what has been stolen puts
us in position to receive as a gift what we couldn't have obtained on
our own. He is skilled at resurrecting good from bad situations.

*Father, turn every plan of the enemy into a victory celebration. I will
not focus on the wrongs done to me but instead release each one
as an offering to you. I trust you to turn everything around for my
good. I forgive my enemies and ask you to draw them closer to you.*

The Power of Words

Esau pleaded with his father,
"Is that the only blessing you have to give?
Bless me too, my father!"
Esau could not hold back his tears and he wept loudly.

GENESIS 27:38

This was Esau's reaction when he heard Isaac had given Jacob his blessing. Notice that they didn't act as though the words could be overridden by the fact that it was done in error. Isaac didn't say, "Well, I meant to bless you, so I'll tell Jacob to forget everything I said, and I'll bless you instead." They understood the power of words.

Oh, that we would treat our speech with such attention. That we would believe that the way we speak to those we love has the power to frame their entire future. Our words either agree or disagree with God's desire. They either attract or repel the blessing of God. We were created to walk in the authority of God, and with that position comes the responsibility to use our words wisely.

Father, I repent for being unaware of the idle words I speak. Holy Spirit, help me to notice when I'm inadvertently speaking curses over people. Anoint my lips to declare what is true, holy, and empowering to those who hear. Declarations that agree with your desire. May I never doubt the authority and power of my words.

True Riches

"May the God who is always more than enough
bless you abundantly."

GENESIS 28:3

Jesus came to give you an abundant life. A life dripping with favor, joy, and peace that contradicts every trial. Everything you need flows from the reality of his presence in your life. The more you're aware of this heavenly union, the more blessed you realize you are.

He is more than enough. More than able to meet every need. He wants you to live under an open heaven of his blessing. To dream big and expect the best. To understand that while he sometimes holds things back, it's only because he's waiting for the perfect timing. When you live in tune with his Spirit in you, your whole attitude about life changes. Situations that once left you nervous and fearful suddenly seem small in comparison to his glory.

Father, you know my needs, wants, and dreams. As I lay them before you today and focus on you, I know you'll take care of every one. I'm going to start focusing more on the things I have to be thankful for than the problems that have weighed heavily on my mind. I want nothing to consume my heart more than my desire for you. The true riches of your kingdom are found in life with you.

A Dry Place

Jacob left Beersheba and journeyed toward Haran.
He encountered a certain place at sunset
and camped there for the night.

GENESIS 28:10–11

Jacob was alone, fleeing his brother. You can almost imagine his thoughts as he journeyed. Perhaps he realized the sinfulness of his deception or was grieved over leaving his mother behind. Whatever his feelings, Jacob was at the end of himself. This was when he *encountered a certain place*. A location that God had designed to get his attention. This ordinary place was Haran, which means "a dry or parched place."

It's amazing how smack-dab in the middle of our dry and life-draining deserts we might be on our way to our greatest awakening. When we don't dismiss the pain of trials but cry out for mercy, God redirects our desert paths so they lead to him. Every painful season carries the potential for some of our most beautiful interactions with the Lord. When we come to the end of ourselves, we are in the perfect position for a life-altering encounter.

Father, when I'm dry and feel emotionally and spiritually undone, come and refresh me. Infuse these weary bones with life. Let your strong love carry me through difficult seasons, straight into my greatest awakening. Thank you for your inexhaustible patience.

The Anointed Stone

He took a stone from there, made it his pillow,
and lay down to sleep.

GENESIS 28:11

As night fell, Jacob was weary, having walked for many days. In his helpless, lonely, exhausted condition, he laid his head on a rock and slept. Some believe Jacob may have used one of the same stones his grandfather Abraham used to erect an altar to God. Little did he know he was about to have a dream that would change his life.

Jesus is the anointed stone where we must lay our heads. He is the perfect place to rest our minds and soothe our heavy hearts. He is the Rock beneath us—the One who steadies us in the storms. When we rest our minds on his faithfulness, peace is the result. And in this place of peace, we're in position to see what he wants us to see.

Father, I choose to unite my thoughts to yours. To rest my anxious thoughts and receive the gift of peace. You are my safe place. Your presence is where I see things from a proper perspective. Give me the grace to set my mind on you, over and over and over again.

Dreams

He had a dream.

GENESIS 28:12

Jacob laid his head on a stone pillow and had a dream. God, in his wisdom and mercy, knew exactly how to bypass the questions, fears, and sadness. He waited until Jacob was asleep and spoke to him in a way that captured his full attention.

Before you fall asleep, ask the Lord for dreams that reveal his heart. When you lay your head down, expect the Lord to bless you with divine encounters. Fill your mind with thoughts of him. Focus on his love for you. Let your heart move closer. Your beloved longs to share his wisdom and unveil his mysteries while you sleep. Your pillow will become a pillar of glory and your bedroom a chamber of angelic activity.

Father, your presence kisses my soul, even while I sleep. As I release my cares and rest in your love tonight, bless me with heavenly dreams. Unveil your secrets; impart wisdom and understanding. My bedroom is the very doorway to your presence. I will sleep in total peace because I know you're with me. My spirit meditates on your love. Speak to me.

Reach into Heaven

He had a dream of a stairway securely fixed on the earth
and reaching into heaven. In his dream, messengers of God
were ascending and descending on the stairway.

GENESIS 28:12

Jesus is the ladder that leads from earth to heaven. Through him,
we climb into the heavenly realm and leave behind the lower life of
anxiety, stress, and fear. In this realm, the Father speaks to our hearts,
and we receive spiritual revelation. As we ascend this *Jesus-ladder*,
we step into glory encounters that influence every area of life.

Jesus is the only valid entry into the spirit realm. He is the true way
into the heavenlies. In him, we experience life in fullness. All other
ladders fall short, never reaching the sky. Church attendance can
only take you so far, but Jesus himself has bridged the gap. Now
glorious encounters with the Lord can fill our prayer time. We touch
the eternal and release it back to the earth.

*Father, I want to ascend into the heavenly realities of your glory
every day. I want to see things that are too magnificent for words.
To have all my spiritual senses awakened by your perfect love. To
experience holy encounters that change my life. To be closer to you
than anyone ever has been before.*

Enclosed in His Love

> "Never forget—I am always with you
> and will protect you wherever you go."
>
> GENESIS 28:15

You are set apart—royal and beautiful. Protected by God's holy angels and chosen for an incredible purpose. Never belittle your calling or compare it to others. This promise is yours to hold on to. To remind him of and to declare when the enemy looms. Whether you're pouring out love to a houseful of children, doing business with the elite, or encouraging those around you, you are his beloved. Your call is important to him.

His love encloses you. The safety of his strong arms happily steadies you. Profoundly protected, your destiny will be released in its ordained season. God and angels alike care for it. Your willingness to trust him despite opposition tends it. Your faith empowers it. Never forget—he is with you always.

Father, you have surrounded me with yourself. You are my protection from the power of the enemy. My strong tower and place of safety. All that you have destined me to do will come to pass as I allow your Spirit to lead. You are with me, wrapping me in the safety of your love.

Always Near

When Jacob awoke from his dream, he said,
"Yahweh is here! He is in this place and I didn't realize it!"

GENESIS 28:16

One of the most influential times of our life is when we stand on the other side of adversity and realize how profound God's nearness actually was. In times of difficulty, we often don't see clearly. It's as if we're in a mental fog, unable to see, hear, and even feel his nearness when he's right beside us.

An important thing to do during trials is to journal what we are feeling, hearing, dreaming, reading, etc. It's an incredible tool to use when future difficulties arise. We often think what we're experiencing is tiny or insignificant. We get so desperate for relief and breakthrough that we dismiss some of the gentle ways that he lets us know he's with us. Looking back, we recognize the strength that carried us, the presence that washed us, and the way he spoke through friends, books, articles, and more.

Father, in every trial, you are here. Even though I don't realize it until later, you never leave. Your faithfulness transcends time. You always find a way to heal my pain no matter how long it takes. Now I can look at my past and laugh. I am more than a conqueror! You have proven your love.

His Presence Is a Portal

"This place is a portal,
the very gate of heaven!"

GENESIS 28:17

Once you have experienced the manifest glory of God, you realize how surprisingly accessible it is. Your faith paves the way for you to return to the awareness of his presence whenever you want. Everywhere you go, the Spirit of God goes with you. In essence, the Holy Spirit in you has become a type of portal into the very gate of heaven. He has become your entryway.

You are the place where God dwells. You have already received all that you need to access heaven. Instead of mentally striving to get there, lean back in his presence. By faith, by simply accepting the truth that you are already with him, you become aware of the glory. It's as easy as closing your eyes and fixing your heart on the Lord.

Father, now I understand that your Spirit in me is the entryway to bliss. Your presence is like a portal into the beauty of heaven. You beckon me to come. You provide the way. And you even escort me into your chambers. Take my hand and lead me into your eternal joys that begin right now.

Pause and Ponder

Jacob took the stone he had under his head,
set it up as a pillar and anointed it
by pouring oil over the top of it.

GENESIS 28:18

When Jacob woke from his dream, he didn't rush off to start his day. He didn't let the impact of the dream slip away. He stayed with it and took time to carefully honor what God had shown him by memorializing the moment. Jacob counted the experience as holy—worth poring over. He displayed his gratitude.

This is such a beautiful lesson for us. Often, God speaks to us in our dreams (or through a prophetic word, email, or devotion), and we may only give it a minute or two of our attention. His encouragement, wisdom, or direction slips our minds. Before we know it, we're feeling desperate to hear him, having forgotten what he's already said. Rather than allowing that to happen, let's pause and ponder. Let's write down what speaks to us and pray into it. Let's remember.

Father, forgive me for not always giving your voice the attention it deserves. Sometimes, I react with excitement but don't write down what you've said. I forget because I haven't honored the subtle (sometimes enormous) ways you speak. I repent, and I ask the Holy Spirit to help me change that.

The House of God

He named that place Bethel;
though the city was once called Luz.

GENESIS 28:19

Jacob's encounter with God prompted him to change the name of the city. Instead of calling it *Luz*, which means "separation," he named it *Bethel*, meaning "the house of God." This was also a divine revelation for Jacob. He understood that it was God's grace that brought him near the Lord. And as a result, Jacob distanced himself from the fleshly desires that had ruled him.

As we become the house of God, we, too, break away from worldly entanglements. We choose to put behind us our old lifestyles, mindsets, and sins that once separated us from God. We gratefully accept the invitation to live as a child in the house of God. Now, nothing will separate us from his love. Our vessels of flesh and bone become *Bethel*—the house of God.

Father, thank you for lifting the veil of separation that was once between us. For leading me by the hand and bringing me into the courts of your love. I want to be a vessel of honor and unyielding devotion. I'm ever grateful to be your dwelling—the place you call home.

Divine Love

As soon as Jacob took one good look at Rachel, the beautiful daughter of his uncle Laban, he quickly went over to the mouth of the well and single-handedly rolled away the stone and watered all the flock of his uncle Laban!

GENESIS 29:10

Reread this verse and think of Jesus. When he looks at you, he is overcome with love. You are the one he died to save. He rose from the dead, rolled away a heavy stone, and has been "romancing" your soul ever since (see Song of Songs). He drew you to faith in him and then offered you a drink from the well of life.

This is your story of divine love. It isn't a fairytale. It isn't a dream come true. It's more significant than that. More beautiful than anything you could imagine. And it is real. It is love that chased you down and rescued you. Love that will last for eternity. Love that overflows from the inside out. Love that you are invited to partake of every day. Take this to heart—you are the object of his affection. You are loved.

Father, I'm overcome by your divine love. Awestruck. Undone. My doubts are silenced in the stillness of your peace. My fears are drowning in your presence. I pray they never rise again. I know that I will never be the same. You have come. You have made your love real.

Holy Passion

Immediately, he walked up to Rachel and kissed her!
Unable to hold back his tears, Jacob wept aloud.

GENESIS 29:11

Jacob's passionate response to seeing Rachel is unrivaled in
Scripture. He became incredibly strong, rolled a heavy stone away,
swept Rachel into his arms, kissed her passionately, and cried out
loud! What an emotional and passionate scene!

Did you know that Jesus responds similarly to you? With one glance
of your lovesick eyes, you have conquered him (Song of Songs
4:9). Jesus rolled away the stone and awakened you with a holy
kiss. You have left the King of kings undone. This revelation is much
too high for us to grasp with our minds; our hearts must embrace it.
His depths of holy passion span every generation into eternity. You,
despite your human frailty, have ravished the heart of God.

*Lord, your love crashes upon me in waves of never-ending wonder.
How can it be that my love does the same to you? Yet knowing it
does, I will worship you and love you with every fiber of my being.
I long to bring you the love that touches your heart. You are worthy
of this and so much more.*

Reignite Your Heart

Rachel had a lovely figure and was gorgeous,
but Leah's eyes were weak.
Jacob had fallen in love with Rachel.

GENESIS 29:17–18

When we view the story of Jacob, Leah, and Rachel as a parable, we see a picture of the church. Two distinct characteristics set some apart from others within the bride of Christ. One ravishes the heart of the Bridegroom with her beauty (the beauty of a lovesick heart), and the other has a weak view of her beloved.

For those who feel their faith is weak or who deal with doubts and fears, humility is the cure. We cannot manufacture a lovesick heart. Cannot force ourselves to yearn for him when we feel dry and weak. But we can bow low and invite the Holy Spirit to purify our hearts and make himself real to us. He doesn't mind stirring our hearts. We only need to ask.

Father, I know your love for me isn't based on how I see you. You love me, regardless. But I don't want to offer you weak love. I want to live with holy passion and unquenchable zeal. Reignite my heart. Draw me into face-to-face encounters so I can see again. Let my love for you become contagious.

A Glorious Exchange

He confronted Laban and said,
"What have you done to me?
Didn't I serve you these seven years for Rachel?
Why have you tricked me?"

GENESIS 29:25

Jacob had cheated his father and brother, and now Laban tricks Jacob. God often uses the actions of others to bring us to the end of our cleverness. He knows how to wake us up. The Lord faithfully confronts our old nature and invites us to partake of the nature of Christ.

Our character, integrity, and the way we deal with others matters to God. In his wisdom, he will do whatever is necessary for us to see the flaws in our character. He'll even lead us into uncomfortable environments where we can witness our own ungodly reactions. Then he invites us to exchange our weakness for his strength. A glorious exchange! Unless we yield our selfishness and need for control, we won't truly enjoy the benefits of a fully surrendered life. A life of true freedom.

Father, you have created me to live in joyous abandon. I open myself up to you and invite your cleansing fire. When I'm annoyed by character traits in others, help me to pause and ask you if those are present in me. When I react, help me to notice so I can submit my thoughts to you. Help me not to run from your correction but to embrace your grace.

Lay Your Heart before Him

Leah conceived the third time,
gave birth to a son, and named him Levi,
saying, "This time my husband will be joined to me,
because now I've given him three sons!"

GENESIS 29:34

Leah named her son Levi in hopes that Jacob's heart would be joined to hers. It was as if the Lord had prophetically given her the name to point Leah to God's desire for her. She was busy trying to win Jacob's love, but the Lord was working to win hers. She was so desperate for love, not realizing that the Man who *is* love was offering what no one else could give.

How often have we found ourselves in similar situations? We become consumed with our need to be loved and aim it at one particular person (even someone who has rejected us) as if it's his or her responsibility to fill our void. No one belongs in our *God-spot*—the place in our heart that is meant for him alone. Human love is vital, but it will always fall short in comparison to his divine love.

Father, draw me into the secret chambers of your love. Past the limits of natural understanding and beyond my need for human acceptance. I'm all in. Willing to lay my heart before you, knowing no one cares for me the way you do. I'm ready to experience your fathomless love.

The One We Love

Once again, Leah conceived and gave birth to a son.
She named him Judah, saying,
"This time I will praise the Lord!"

GENESIS 29:35

After years of struggling with the pain of being unloved, Leah finally opened her heart to the Lord, and grace touched her. Through the struggles and disappointments of her marriage, God tenderly wooed her to himself. When she gave birth to her fourth son, she resolved to praise the Lord no matter what. Leah became a worshiper. She finally found fulfillment in God, so she named her son Judah (praise) and declared, "This time I will praise the Lord!"

Every struggle has the potential of opening our hearts to a greater awakening. Pain can be used as a catapult, launching us into the strong arms of the Father who is waiting to catch us. We can use every trial as an opportunity to find the Lord, who is worthy of our praise. When we release our disappointments to him, we discover that our most profound sense of fulfillment comes from the One we love.

Father, I welcome you into my struggles. Heal my deepest wounds. Infuse yourself into every hurtful memory until they hold no more pain. Be the Lord of every thought. You are the One I love. My truest sense of fulfillment. The One who has loved me from the beginning. The One who deserves my unreserved praise.

God's Timing

Rachel gave her servant Bilhah to Jacob as another wife, and Jacob slept with her. And Bilhah conceived and bore Jacob a son, and Rachel named him Dan, saying, "God has vindicated me. He heard my voice and gave me a son."

GENESIS 30:4–6

Impatience enjoys pushing us to make things happen out of God's timing. Succumbing to our restlessness, we settle for immediate gratification instead of waiting for his best. Then we declare that his blessing brought it about when it was actually the fruit of fear—fear that God wouldn't come through. More than anything, this should reveal our need for greater intimacy with the Lord.

When we're convinced of God's love, we believe he has our best interests at heart. We know he enjoys blessing us, and though we may eagerly (sometimes anxiously) anticipate his gifts, we are willing to wait. Trust becomes easier when we live inside the framework of God's love. Though we may be tempted to control the outcome and birth something prematurely, we submit each day to him.

Father, I believe you love me and that your hands measure my days and seasons. Fear will not dictate my actions. I will not be moved to take control when I feel restless and impatient. Peace will be my indicator. Love will be my driving force. Take control. I submit my dreams to you.

Walk in Victory

Rachel named him Naphtali, saying,
"I have wrestled mightily."

GENESIS 30:8

Jesus is the One who wrestled the forces of darkness on our behalf and gave us an example to follow. He is the champion who lives in us and teaches us how to war from the seat of victory.

When we're facing our most significant challenges and can only trust that the roots of our faith will anchor us, we're in battle. When we have no strength but press ourselves tightly into the Lord's arms, we're overcoming. When our shouts of praise turn to silent tears of unconditional devotion, we're at war. These moments make us shine. When we have nothing to offer but the yes that rises from our hearts, we are walking in victory.

Father, thank you for reminding me that I don't have to yell and beat the air to overcome. I am victorious when I keep my heart fixed on you. You are a brilliant example of complete surrender. This posture of love awakens a faith that knows how to rest. And here in your arms, where I don't worry about a thing, I receive my greatest breakthroughs.

Our Joyful Provision

Leah named him Asher, saying, "Oh happy day!"

GENESIS 30:13

Asher means "happy." And no one grants us happiness like Jesus does! He is the source of our most authentic joy. A deep-seated well that never runs dry. Even in our trials, his presence heals our tattered hearts and leads us to the rivers of refreshing. No sorrow is too profound that the love of God cannot find its way in.

Jesus wants to fill you with such delight that you cannot contain it. As you lay hold of this promise, don't be surprised when unexpected laughter bubbles from within. Joy contradicts every reason for negativity. Laughter is freeing and delightful. Giggles of contentment crack open your heart and shift your paradigm. Allow it. It's okay to be happy. Rejoice in him, and he will be your joyful provision every day.

Father, may the refreshing winds of your glory blow away every lifeless and stagnant emotion. Here in your presence, I come alive! Your love invigorates me and causes me to sing. I can't help but laugh in joyous anticipation of all you will do. You make me truly happy.

Always More

She conceived, and bore a son,
and named him Joseph.

GENESIS 30:23

The name Joseph means "may he add." This is God's desire—to daily increase the glory and blessing of his presence in your life. To overwhelm everything that steals, kills, and destroys as you sink deeper and deeper into this divine love.

Your relationship with the Lord is the foundation upon which these blessings rest. In him is everything you need for your spirit, soul, and body. As you make yourself aware of the reality of his presence each day, you will see his eternal provision manifest. He becomes more real than the superficial desires of the soul. He satisfies yet stirs your appetite for *more*. There is always more love, peace, joy, creativity, wisdom—whatever you need. It's all found in endless supply in the glory of knowing him.

Father, each day I bow before you in pure, untainted, unflinching devotion. I seek the glory of your face. I long to pour my love out to you as a blessing. Your presence adds more to me than I could ever grab on my own. Your love is the fountain that never runs dry.

Behold

As they lowered their heads to drink, they saw the stripped branches in front of their eyes. Miraculously they gave birth to streaked, speckled, and spotted young.

GENESIS 30:39

God wanted to bless Jacob with the streaked, speckled, and spotted goats, which he would then take as wages from Laban. Through a heavenly dream, the Lord downloaded an incredible revelation that applies to us today—what the goats set their eyes on would affect what they would birth. What we fix our eyes (heart, desire, and focus) on will determine what manifests in our lives.

When our desire is toward the Lord and we set him before us, we reap the blessing. What we focus on either empowers or weakens us. If we're fixated on what can go wrong, it often does. If Jesus is our focal point and his Word our meditation, blessings follow. To have the fruitful life Jesus died to give us, we keep him as the object of our desire. As we bow our heads to drink of his love, we see the man who was stripped of his dignity in order to bless us extraordinarily.

Father, I hold you as the object of my desire. I turn from the crowded thoughts that seek to drown my faith and set my gaze on you. You are good, beautiful, and want the best for me. As I fix my gaze on you, I will bear fruit that honors your name.

Miraculous Wisdom

He produced his own special flocks,
which he didn't allow to mingle with Laban's.

GENESIS 30:40

God's wisdom often seems miraculous. It confounds the wisest of men and often makes no logical sense. It is unearthly. Superior to natural wisdom in every way.

Too often, in our need for direction, we search for something reasonable. Something that we can figure out if we think hard enough. But the wisdom we need isn't found in books, articles, or universities. It is found in Jesus. So let's ask, seek, and set aside the efforts that will only take us so far, and be still. Let's tune into the frequency of heaven so we can hear clearly. If we will lay aside distractions when we are in dire need of wisdom and allow our minds to rest in his presence, we will be surprised at the brilliance God will share.

Father, I don't want to trip over my interpretation of the way things should be. Take my hand and lead me with your perfect, miraculous, and life-giving wisdom. Give me the grace to rest my thoughts so I can hear yours. Come and reveal your surprising ideas to me.

August

Protected

"I could harm you, but the God of your father spoke to me in a dream last night, saying, 'Be careful that you neither harm nor threaten Jacob.'"

GENESIS 31:29

The Lord is our fierce protector. When we're tucked into the safe embrace of our Father, the enemy cannot reach us, and his plans will backfire. If necessary, God will speak to those who are intent on our destruction and warn them not to harm us.

It's time to be bold and stop letting fear keep us from our destiny. To trust that when we're following the leading of the Lord, he will make our enemies be at peace with us, or he will move them out of our way. To believe that, in times of danger, God gives his angels to protect us. My friends, let's realize that Jesus is adamant about our calling, and when we partner with him, we can trust him, even when he leads us through the camp of the enemy.

Father, when the road ahead seems bumpy, I will lean back in your strong embrace and trust you. It doesn't matter how difficult the journey or how dangerous the call because you will never fail to protect me. You're faithful, and I believe you're working behind the scenes on my behalf right now!

He Takes Notice

"God in his mercy took notice of how much I've suffered
and how hard I've worked—and that's why he rebuked you
last night in your dream!"

GENESIS 31:42

God notices everything you do. Every movement of your heart,
each time you've said yes to him despite the questions. All that
you've sown, sacrificed, and wept over has caught his attention.
Don't despair, beloved, for he has seen it all.

All that you've poured into others, the work that goes
unappreciated and feels overlooked, hasn't gone unnoticed by him.
He will turn things around for you in ways you don't anticipate.
Jacob had no idea that God had spoken to Laban in a dream. He
didn't know what God was doing behind the scenes, and most of
the time, we don't either. In his mercy, when it feels like he doesn't
see and nothing will change, he speaks to others on our behalf.
Don't lose heart, God hasn't forgotten you!

*Father, may all I do become an offering of love. You not only see all
that I've done to be faithful, but you also know the struggles. You
know the times I've said yes and fought the fear. You know that
although sometimes I falter, I genuinely want to live an honorable
life before you. I will not despair; you're working behind the scenes
on my behalf.*

Honor Our Vows

"Come now, let's form a covenant between you and me."

GENESIS 31:44

In the days of the Old Testament, promises meant something. When someone made a verbal pledge, it carried value. People seemed to believe their covenants were trustworthy. Today even legally binding agreements aren't always honored. But that is not the way of the kingdom. God wants us to be people of integrity whose promises are sure. To consult with heaven before opening our mouths. To be those whose vows aren't flippantly tossed about.

Every part of our lives should honor God. Even the promises we make, no matter how insignificant they may seem. If we commit to something, let's carry it through. And let's not commit to something unless we've checked with the Lord first. Let's become people whose integrity is reflected in every area of life.

Father, I want my life to reflect you in every way. I want my words to be seasoned with your anointing, so I will seek to honor you with everything I say. Thank you for reminding me that you don't take promises lightly, even the small ones, and I shouldn't either.

Angel Armies

As Jacob continued toward Canaan,
the angels of God came to meet him!
When he saw them, he exclaimed,
"This is God's military camp!"

GENESIS 32:1–2

On his way to fulfill his destiny, Jacob's eyes were open to see the angels of God protecting him and his family. They must have been very impressive, perhaps warring angels, because he compares them to a military camp. Seeing what was usually hidden from view was a blessing given to encourage Jacob. God, the Commander of Angel Armies (see Isaiah 6:3) was with him, and God is with you!

We aren't told anything more about Jacob's encounter, only that they came to meet him. God loves to stir our curiosity! He wants us to know that angels are an integral part of our lives. It seems evident that he wants to awaken our awareness of the invisible. To believe what we cannot see. To be thankful for the angels whom he's given to assist and protect us.

Father, you are the Commander of Angel Armies. You are the magnificent One who merits praise from humans and angels alike. Thank you for these protectors, guardians, messengers, and keepers of those you love. Thank you for the angels surrounding me even now.

The Beauty of His Love

"I am so unworthy of all the loving-kindness and faithfulness
that you have showered upon me, your servant."

GENESIS 32:10

Allow this verse to resonate deep within you. Nothing you can
ever accomplish, no height of holy living, will ever qualify you for
the treasures of heaven. All that God has given you is a gift, simply
because he loves you, exactly the way you are.

It is by grace and mercy that we stand before our magnificent
King. Jesus has made us worthy, and it is our greatest delight to
live before him with open hearts and surrendered lives. It is our
pleasure to lavish him with our thankfulness. May we spend the rest
of our lives undone by the beauty of his love. Stand in constant,
reverent awe of the blessings he has showered upon us. We do not
deserve his loving-kindness, yet he faithfully pours it out each day.

*Father, I bow before you. Awed by your unmerited love. Humbled
by your patience with me. You have freed me from shame and
revealed my worth. Your glory is my delight. I am overcome by the
beauty of your presence. Thank you for this life of grace. Even my
desire to please you is a gift.*

Powerful Prayers

Save me, I pray, from...
for I'm afraid...
You said to me...

GENESIS 32:11–12

Jacob's honest prayer sounds much like many of our own. He was afraid, cried out to God for protection, and reminded of what God had promised. These honest prayers become some of our most powerful ones when we combine them with declarations of God's Word. He wants us to remind him of his promises—not because he has forgotten them but because when we infuse them with our faith, they become fragrant offerings.

Our prayers move the heart of God. He enjoys our commitment to see his will come to pass in our lives. He loves when we communicate with him, expecting him to respond! He isn't looking for forced prayers that sound holy. He wants our hearts. He longs for us to mingle our deepest, most vulnerable conversations with our trust in him.

Father, I'm not going to wear a mask in your presence. You already know what's on my mind. I come before you, knowing I'm desperate for what only you can give. Your Word anchors me to your heart. I will stand on your truth, speak it forth, and find you in the middle of every situation. You alone sustain me.

Solitude

Jacob was left all alone.

GENESIS 32:24

For some, solitude is torturous. For others, it's something they crave. For everyone, it is a place where stillness and the divine collide. Quiet has a purpose. If we lean into the discomfort of boredom and seek to find the Lord in the layers beneath it, we set ourselves up for breathtaking encounters.

So many cry out for more of God. We yearn for him to make himself real. We long to touch the divine. To see the invisible and know the unknowable. Yet few are willing to fight for it by pushing aside distractions. We've become a society addicted to the stimulation of trivial things. Let's go deeper. Let's schedule quiet time where we reach for nothing more than the tangible presence of our beloved.

Father, I've prayed that you would take me deeper into your presence. Now I see that the decision to dive into the waters of holy encounter is mine. Holy Spirit, help me to make alone time with you a habit. Teach me how to embrace solitude. Saturate my crowded thoughts with the glory of your abiding love.

Relinquish Control

Suddenly, out of nowhere,
a man appeared and wrestled with him until daybreak.

GENESIS 32:24

God knows how to get our attention. He knows that sometimes, in order to drain us of our self-power, he must appear out of nowhere and confront our sin. Our tendency to control things and make sense of them without his insight is dangerous. It will lead us down a perilous path of self-righteousness, where we believe we are the master of our own life.

More than likely, you've wrestled with him yourself. Perhaps you were surprisingly humbled. Maybe you stepped in front of God and tried to do things your way only to come face-to-face with pride. Relinquishing control can be painful. It hurts when we fight against the will of God. But once we yield, a new season of blessing is released.

Father, you have my attention. I'm sorry I've fought to have my own way. I'm done wrestling against your will. I'm weary and tired. Take control. Forgive my pride. I have no idea what will happen, and to be honest, it scares me a little. But I'd rather walk with you into the unknown than to continue wrestling with the One I love.

The Power of Confession

"What is your name?" asked the man.
"Jacob," he replied.

GENESIS 32:27

When the Lord asked Jacob his name, it wasn't because God didn't know it. He was getting Jacob to acknowledge his past so he could walk in the freedom of the future. Jacob had once lied and told his father that he was Esau to get what he wanted. It was time for him to find a new identity—one the Lord wanted him to have.

Crossing the threshold from the old to the new starts with a choice to leave the past behind. God doesn't want us to carry the weight of our sins, but first we must let repentance do a deep work. The power of confession lies in the way our hearts respond. When we are willing to embrace correction, ask for and receive forgiveness, we step into a new season of our life.

Father, your mercy is so tender toward me. Thank you for never leaving me to wallow in my failure. For always offering me the chance to see myself the way you do and run with you to freedom. Highlight the areas of my life that hinder me from stepping into all you have. May I remain humble and teachable in your sight.

Know Him

Jacob named the place Penuel, saying,
"I have seen God face-to-face,
yet my life has been spared!"

GENESIS 32:30

If Jacob could meet God face-to-face and live, how much more can Spirit-filled believers? We were created to live in awestruck wonder. To taste and see that he is good. To believe that our Father wants us to know him even more intimately than generations before us.

Let's not become complacent in our walk. Let's believe for the outrageous, radical, and miraculous. Let's come before the Lord with hearts on fire—not willing to leave his presence without encountering the beauty of his face. Relationship is about knowing and being known. When we press in to discover God's heart, he reveals it in quiet whispers. When we yearn to know him, we see him, hear him, and feel his nearness. There is always more glory to discover. Always deeper places of his presence to enjoy.

Father, the more I know you, the more I want to know you. I can scarcely voice my songs of devotion when I feel the glory of your presence—it leaves me speechless. Unveil your face. I want to see the fiery passion for your bride blazing from your eyes. Your love astounds me. Holy One, let me see your face.

Reconciliation

Esau ran to Jacob and hugged him! He threw his arms around Jacob's neck, he kissed him, and they wept in each other's arms.

GENESIS 33:4

God is in the business of reconciliation, especially between loved ones. Hurtful words, actions, and misunderstandings are often challenging to get past when they've left wounds. But nothing is impossible for God! He can heal any trauma. He's more than capable of doing what seems unlikely when it comes to matters of the heart.

If you're holding unforgiveness, today is your opportunity to release it to the Lord. While you cannot change others, you can be in charge of your own heart. You can take the stance of mercy and choose to forgive (sometimes more than once, while God heals your heart). If you have wronged someone, ask them and the Lord for forgiveness. Love always reaches out, so do your part to initiate reconciliation. If you feel the Holy Spirit tugging on your heart while reading this, ask him to lead you in the ways of restoration.

Father, I lift (name the person) before you. I pray you would reveal the truth and bring every lie to the light. Soften the hearts of everyone involved and bring restoration to our lives. I forgive (name) and ask for forgiveness on my part. Heal our relationship and our hearts.

Unlikely Places

"Seeing your face after all these years,
it's like looking upon the face of God!"

GENESIS 33:10

Jacob, who had just seen the face of God, now sees that same glorious face through the mending of this relationship with his brother. This is what happens when mercy and forgiveness kiss our lives. When we choose to walk in humility, we notice God's face shining through the most unlikely places.

We will see God most clearly when our lives flow in harmony, forgiveness, and Christlikeness. When our hearts are pure—nothing intentionally and blatantly standing between God and us—we find him. When we've embraced a lifestyle of humility and loving abandon, we tend to notice what others don't: the somewhat covert ways God moves in each of our lives. He is there. Always. All we need to do is pay attention. To look with a humble and loving heart that isn't offended with where and with whom God chooses to dwell.

Father, I want to live in purity before you. To notice you moving in the lives of sinners. To see you quietly stirring with compassion in movements, cultural beliefs, and societal norms that I don't agree with. You want to be found, so shine your light into the depths of shadows where sinners dwell.

First-Love Devotion

"Arise, go at once to Bethel,
and settle there."

GENESIS 35:1

Bethel was the place Jacob encountered the Lord and witnessed the stairway to heaven. Now the Lord is telling him to go back there. To return to the place of first-love devotion. God is wooing all of us to this place. Stirring our hearts for the love the world cannot offer.

Breathing upon this yearning of our souls for the deeper, more meaningful, and most significant encounters of our lives. This is not a time for visitation. It is time for habitation. To become continually aware of the One who lives within. To be so consumed with sacred passion that our lives revolve around the reality of his love. This is where God has called us to dwell: in the safety and bliss of first-love devotion.

Father, I feel you stirring my longing for you. You're awakening the deepest part of me that I didn't realize had become sluggish. Blow upon the embers of my heart. Let me burn with first-love devotion. I don't want to have occasional brushes with glory. I want to remain there forever.

Idols

"Get rid of every foreign god you have,
purify yourselves, and change your clothes."

GENESIS 35:2

Let nothing stand in the way of becoming all that God intends you to be. You must deal with anything that consumes your attention more than he does. The enemy wants to lull you into complacency and lure you into temptation. Beware of idols of the heart—things that hold your attention and desire more than God does.

Plenty of subtle distractions dull our relationship with the Lord. Pay attention to the time stealers that cause your connection with him to feel dry. Jesus wants us to enjoy life, and he isn't against fun and entertainment. But when outward things consume our inward focus and steal our hearts, they've become idols. We must guard ourselves against spiritual laziness and cultivate the most beautiful relationship of all. Nothing must hold our hearts more than he does.

Father, how easily I can ignore you and turn to frivolous things. Highlight any areas of complacency or laziness that have held me back from living my best life with you. May worldly idols and temptations no longer divert my attention. Show me any idols that have stolen my heart.

Your Life Is an Altar

"Then come with me; let us go up to Bethel. I will build an altar there to God who answered my prayer when I was in distress and whose presence has been with me wherever I have gone."

GENESIS 35:3

You are Bethel, the house of God. Your life has become an altar of devotion. All that you are becomes a reflection of what you carry inside of you. Your thoughts, deeds, and desires are purified when each day you surrender to the holiness surging through your being.

This revelation isn't meant for you alone. When you live in the awareness of God's presence and grace upon your life, others feel it too. Your life becomes a testimony, inviting others to join with you. You don't need to shout it from the rooftops. Your countenance, response to opposition, and the joy and peace you release will draw others to want to know more. Embrace the astounding truth that you are a vessel of God and then let his presence splash on everyone you come near.

Father, all that I am, I surrender to you. I invite you to take up residence upon the altar of my heart. To be my overwhelming passion and desire. To remind me of your faithfulness in times of distress so others may see the way you change me. May my life become a testimony.

Powerfully Connected

A tremendous fear of God fell upon all the cities around them,
and no one dared pursue them.

GENESIS 35:5

Nothing terrifies the enemy like a child of God walking in purity and
wholehearted devotion. When we cast aside our idols, shake off
distractions, and set our hearts on the Lord, a powerful anointing is
released. Loving Jesus always leads to a revelation of our condition.
And when we confess our humble need for the Lord, we become
empowered with his might.

Humility keeps us powerfully connected to the Lord. Knowing
our great need for mercy and grace ensures pride will not come
between us. We cry out for all of him to consume all of us and
soon realize that a sanctified life is a dynamic and authoritative
one. Instead of fighting the enemy, our clean hearts repel him! The
wraparound presence of God becomes our shield, and those who
come against us find their hearts pierced with conviction.

*Father, purify my soul. Highlight the areas that aren't entirely yours.
Others may judge, but your opinion is the only one that matters.
I submit myself to your holy gaze. Search me and reveal the
thoughts that don't align with yours. As I seek to walk in holiness,
you will protect me from reproach.*

The Unveiling

It was the place that God had unveiled himself
when Jacob was running from his brother.

GENESIS 35:7

Sometimes we just need God to step in and unveil himself. In our weariness, when it feels like all we're doing is running from one trial after the other, we need to stop. We need to plant our feet in the truths of mercy and trust that God knows exactly how to reach us. He will not deny a yearning heart.

Trials are meant to wear us down. The enemy knows that if we fix our attention on our problems, eventually distractions will consume us. Oh, but the love of God is more powerful still! And when we reach for the Lord, even with shaky hands and tired faith, he will not deny us. He knows precisely how to reveal himself to us again.

Father, your faithfulness never fails me. You know how to reach past the confusion and straight into my heart. I long for face-to-face encounters that change the course of my life. My heart says, "yes!" I believe that I should fill every day with the glory of communing with you. Come, unveil yourself to me.

The One We Need

Rebekah's nurse Deborah died. They buried her under an oak tree near Bethel, and they named the place Weeping Oak.

GENESIS 35:8

The place of the weeping oak is where we surrender all to the Lord. Where we lay every idol, unhealthy relationship, and distraction at the feet of Jesus, our strong *oak tree*. It's always painful to our flesh when we abandon all to God, but it is here that we begin to truly flourish.

We often turn to friends and loved ones to sympathize with us, to soothe and comfort our weary hearts. But the day will come when all our nursing mothers will be gone. In due time, our *Deborahs* will be removed, and the God of Bethel will be all to us. He'll be there to bring us into a deeper relationship with him. We won't need sympathy or "nursing" because we will have the One we really need!

Father, you're teaching me what it's like to be fully dependent upon you. How to find comfort and counsel in the safety of your presence. To seek your wisdom before I pull on anyone else. To not just say you're my best friend but to also allow you to be it. You are the One I've always needed.

Remember Who You Are

God appeared to him once again and blessed him, saying,
"Your name was once Jacob, but no longer.
Your new name is Israel!"

GENESIS 35:9–10

This was the second time that God told Jacob he had given him
a new name. It sounds as though Jacob Israel needed reminding!
Sound familiar? How often has the Lord stepped in and reminded
you who you are?

In his patience, the Lord will speak to your identity over and over
again. He will open the eyes of your understanding so you can
embrace the truth of who you are to him. He will remind you of
your beauty, worth, power, and anointing until you believe it. The
Lord believes in your calling and wants you to remember who you
are. You are his beautiful bride. You are royalty. You are sought
after, desired, and important. Worth the price of sacred love. This is
your identity.

*Father, I'm so affected by the way you see me. By the care you take
to remind me because you want me to believe it. I position myself
before you with humble confidence—teach me to embrace my
identity and to be all that you say I am. Place a guard over my mind
and words so I only think and speak about myself in line with your
Word. I am yours. I am worthy of this love.*

Do the Impossible

"I am the God who is more than enough."

GENESIS 35:11

God often asks us to do impossible things. He's not setting us up for failure; he's laying the groundwork for a life of radical faith. When we are aware of our inability, it causes us to depend on him. He is the God of more than enough. He is the One who works through us to do what we cannot do on our own.

Jesus loves to turn inadequacy into abundance. Our obedience and willingness pave the way for miracles. When we're aware of our insufficiency but choose to partner with the all-sufficient One, our faith becomes a magnet for miracles. When the Lord asks us to do something impossible, it isn't to deter us. It's so that when he comes through, we'll know exactly who deserves the glory.

Father, you are the God who is more than enough. More than able to turn every hopeless, lifeless situation into a glorious victory. Every promise is true and full of life—rewiring the way I think and uniting my heart to yours. May I always be known as one who dares to believe the impossible is possible with you.

Be Fruitful

"Go and have many children, and they will multiply.
A nation and a gathering of many nations will come from you;
and you will be the ancestor of kings."

GENESIS 35:11

Your life is meant to be a blessing. God has called you to multiply yourself, and that includes spiritual children as well as natural. He wants you to reproduce yourself in the lives of others. To sow into the spiritual children he is asking you to mentor.

The Lord is calling you to pour into those who are drawn to what you carry. He trusts you with the people he loves. Impart the wisdom and revelations he's given you. Pray with them, teach them, encourage them, and disciple them so they, in turn, can nurture others. Champion their dreams and anointing. Look for ways to bring the reality of God's presence into their lives. Encourage them to grow closer to the Lord and to become all that their hearts desire.

Father, I want to inspire others the same way you inspire me. Give me grace and wisdom to lead others in their pursuit of you. Help me to represent you well. Thank you for entrusting me with your cherished ones. May my love for you be contagious, always leading them to you.

Honor Your Encounters

Jacob set up a stone pillar to memorialize
the place where he had met with God.

GENESIS 35:14

While most of us don't create memorials when we hear from God,
it's a good idea to honor the times of connection that stand out.
One of the ways we do this is by journaling what he has said, what
we've seen, and what we've experienced in the glory.

We memorialize these sacred times by keeping track of them and
reminding ourselves what the Lord spoke to our hearts through his
Word or during encounter. We esteem every *rhema*, or "spoken,"
word as vital because it is. When we reread our experiences, we
often reconnect with the glory and wisdom that was first released.
Often, the Lord will breathe fresh revelation as we revisit these
golden nuggets of truth we have chosen to count as significant.

*Father, every encounter with you is worth remembering. Thank
you for reminding me to keep track of the lessons you teach. Not
only will I preserve these treasures safely in my heart, but I will also
write them down and refer to them as you lead. I want to honor
you by safeguarding every word you say.*

Woven throughout Our Lives

With her dying breath, Rachel said,
"His name is Son of My Sorrow,"
but his father called him Son of My Right Hand.

GENESIS 35:18

Throughout the Old Testament, we find glimpses of Jesus. Both of the two aspects referred to in the verse above are found in Christ. He is described as "the Man of sorrows" in Isaiah, and the book of Acts tells us that he has been "exalted to the right hand of God." When we get to heaven, we'll be amazed at the brilliant ways he infused himself into Scripture without us realizing it.

This is true in our day-to-day as well. It's easy to miss the subtle ways God weaves himself into our lives. We often overlook a gentle nudge as he directs our attention to a passerby. We ask him to speak, yet when we read an email, article, or hear a song that causes our hearts to leap, we don't pause to acknowledge his voice coming through. God speaks in a multitude of ways—a calming sunset, a random thought, a conversation with a friend, just to name a few. We mustn't dismiss the subtle ways he tries to get our attention.

Father, teach me to recognize the many ways you infiltrate my life. I want to know your voice more intimately than any other. Teach me to recognize your faintest whisper as it brushes my subconscious. I tune myself into you.

Even in the Night

One night Joseph had a dream,
and when he shared it with his brothers,
they hated him even more!

GENESIS 37:5

Your beloved longs to share his heart and unveil mysteries to you, even while you sleep. As you lay your head down to rest, your bedroom becomes a doorway to God's presence. Your pillow becomes a pillar of glory and your bedroom a chamber of angelic activity. The Lord will give you answers to prayer and entrust you with secrets.

Each night before you fall asleep, ask him for dreams that give you wisdom and strategy and reveal his desire for your life. But be cautious about running to others and sharing what he's said before seeking the Lord's interpretation and guidance. Not everyone will be as enthusiastic about the blessing of God in your life. Write down your dreams and pray over their meaning. Sometimes their mysteries aren't revealed instantaneously, and other times their treasures are meant for you alone.

Father, reveal yourself in my dreams tonight. I expect to receive beautiful dreams, to have sweet and refreshing sleep, and to wake with wisdom for tomorrow. My mind is filled with thoughts of you, and my spirit meditates upon your love. Speak to me, and I will honor the treasures you entrust me with.

In Him Alone

When his father and brothers heard it, his father scolded him,
"What kind of dream is that? Do you really think that I, and your
mother, and your brothers are going to come and bow to the
ground before you?"

GENESIS 37:10

When God sparks your heart with a dream for your future, not
everyone will cheer you on. One of the hardest things to walk
through is when those you expected to champion your calling
judge and misunderstand it. These are the seasons when you learn
to lean on God more than anyone else.

It hurts when we're misjudged and misunderstood, but these are
also some of our most significant times of discovery. We learn that
God's love satisfies us in ways no one else's can. He teaches us to
lean into his counsel and depend on his guidance more than any
other. And when the light of all other support grows dim, we behold
the brightness of his countenance. In Christ, we discover who the
Lord created us to be and forge ahead with him by our side.

*Father, wash away the sting of rejection and heal the wounds
of misunderstanding. You have awakened me to experience the
adventure of life with you. To depend on you more than any others.
To be satisfied in your love alone. Thank you for encouraging me
today. In the deepest darkness of conflict, you provide the light.*

Slow to Judge

His brothers grew more jealous of him,
but his father kept pondering Joseph's dream.

GENESIS 37:11

It's easy for us to cast judgment on others when we react in our flesh instead of responding from our stance in the Lord. We have much more patience with ourselves than we do with others. We are quick to require mercy but, at times, slow to give it. But as we grow in character and love, we understand that wisdom is slow to judge.

It is often the broken ones, those whom God's goodness has restored, who have an easier time extending grace. We realize that things aren't always the way they appear, and to get the Lord's perspective, we must be willing to seek it. Jacob pondered Joseph's dream and tucked the matter safely away in his heart, where he could hear from the Lord. Remember, just because we don't understand something doesn't mean God is not involved.

Father, promotions, favor, and increase sometimes come to those who I don't think deserve it. Forgive me for judging instead of praying and seeking your thoughts. I want to hear your viewpoint over the clamor of my own. And when I want to jump to conclusions, help me to slow down and remember grace.

Critics

They said to each other,
"Here comes this dream expert.
Let's kill him."

GENESIS 37:19

Your anointing sets you apart, but it also draws the attention of critics and haters. No matter how hard you work at getting people to like you, there will always be those who misunderstand you and the calling on your life. If you're going to make a difference in the world around you, rest assured, you will have opposition.

It's not fun to face criticism or be unappreciated, especially when you're doing what you know God wants you to do. But ultimately, promotion comes from the Lord, and if he is the one leading, it is his job to get you where you need to be. All you need to do is keep your heart right and your eyes fixed on the Lord. Don't worry about the haters and don't bother defending yourself. Pray for those who persecute you and bless everyone who gets in your way. More than anything else, you are called to love.

Father, no man on earth can stop your call on my life from coming to pass. Infuse me with the courage and faith to fully embrace the destiny burning in my heart. I will not live in fear of those who oppose me. I will fix my thoughts on you and trust you to bring these things to pass.

Let Him Shine Through

They seized him, stripped him of his ornamented robe,
his beautiful full-length robe,
and threw him into the dry, empty pit.

GENESIS 37:23–24

There will always be a time of testing. A season where we must confront the true motives of our hearts so God can purify them. When the enemy strips us of all that glitters and shines, God gets down to the nitty-gritty of pride. He uses times of isolation to reveal our hidden intentions and the need for man's approval.

When we have nothing left but God, we discover that he is enough. When the reality of his presence becomes our top priority, our life takes a monumental turn. Here in the transparency of our need, his glory shines brightest. Our greatest honor is to bow low before our King. To recognize that every talent, anointing, favor, and creative genius is a gift from God.

Father, nothing satisfies my deepest desire like the glory of your presence. When I truly understand how valued, loved, and worthy I am to you, I stop struggling to prove it. Merely living to honor you gives my life significance and meaning. I humble myself so you can shine through.

For Your Good

Joseph's brothers lifted him out of the pit, and sold him to the Ishmaelites for twenty pieces of silver, and the merchants took Joseph far away to Egypt.

GENESIS 37:28

The Lord isn't wondering how to salvage your destiny. When the enemy throws a curveball that knocks you off your feet and into a pit, God is there to lift you out. As a matter of fact, it's usually when you get slammed and things feel hopeless that you rise stronger than ever—leaning on your beloved.

Our Father loves to take what the enemy means for our destruction and turn it around for our good. The problem is that we get so caught up in how things look that we forget how amazing God is at doing the impossible. Quite often, dank pits of despair will draw out our deepest worship and launch us into some of our greatest breakthroughs. In the darkest situations, the Savior will show up and turns things around for our good.

Father, when I find myself surrounded by darkness, I will grasp your hand and trust you with childlike abandon. This situation will not dictate how I feel. No pity-parties for me! I shake off heaviness and put on a garment of praise! You're faithful to come to my rescue. Nothing is too hard for you.

Guard Your Heart

> "No, I will mourn for him the rest of my life,
> until I join my son in the realm of the dead."
>
> GENESIS 37:35

Jacob had declared that he would spend the rest of his days in mourning for Joseph. And when the days of famine came, this stronghold of sorrow threatened to steal God's blessing for Jacob and his family. Jacob's sorrow turned into crippling fear, and his words became so powerful that they not only strangled his life but also nearly resulted in the deaths of his entire family too.

Our words are powerful. They contain the power of life and death (Proverbs 18:21). What we say gives us a glimpse into our hearts, and the meditation of our hearts will ultimately become a compass that guides our lives. When we set ourselves in agreement with the enemy and make his twisted desire a part of our everyday speech, we open the doors for even more opposition. Even in our darkest hours, we must guard our hearts and mouths.

Father, align my heart and words with the power of your truth. Regardless of how I feel when life seems to be falling apart, give me the grace to keep on believing. Holy Spirit, hold me so I won't sink into despair. Help me to guard my mouth as I stand before you in silent trust.

Discouragement

Yahweh's presence was with Joseph and he became successful
while living in the house of his Egyptian master.

GENESIS 39:2

When everything falls apart and dreams unravel, our Father steps
in and shows us a higher way. A way that maneuvers us through
the paths of pain and ultimately leads us to our greatest victories.
Success, when orchestrated by the Lord, becomes our testimony of
grace, helping others to embrace breakthroughs of their own.

The Lord is magnificent at taking what seem to be downfalls and
catastrophes and turning them into something beautiful. New
life, uncharted joy, and deep-seated faith will rise from the ashes
of defeat when we're determined to stay wrapped in his arms. In
times of confusion, discouragement, and pain, when nothing makes
sense, the Father invites us to hide in the shelter of his love. From
this place of grace, blessings flow.

*Father, don't let me get stuck in a mindset of hopelessness or
discouragement. Don't allow me to wallow in the murky waters
of defeat. Even when it seems that everything is falling apart, you
have a plan. I simply need to stop trying to figure things out and
trust you with unlimited faith.*

September

Favor Will Find You

When his master realized that Yahweh's presence was
with Joseph and caused everything he did to prosper,
Joseph found favor with Potiphar.

GENESIS 39:3–4

No matter where you are, the type of people who surround you,
and how unlikely it may seem, the favor of God knows how to find
you. You don't need to fight for acknowledgment or strive to get
the attention of those seated in places of authority; you simply need
to tune into Yahweh.

When radical faith meets absolute surrender to God, he sets you
in seats of favor. Wisdom comes. Creative ideas are unleashed.
Your gifts and anointings draw attention because the reality of
your heavenly Father saturates them. God's presence and favor will
do more for you than your skill, intelligence, and cleverness alone
could achieve. One day, things feel fruitless, and the next, the Lord
highlights you with favor. Don't despair! Just hand over every desire
and watch what God will do when you trust him.

*Father, finish the work you've started in me. Set me in seats of
favor as you see fit. I trust you with the gifts you've given to me to
share. You know how to open doors that I am not able to open. No
matter what happens, may I always live honorably before you. You
have my surrender.*

The Power You Carry

From the moment Potiphar appointed Joseph over his household,
Yahweh blessed the Egyptian's affairs for Joseph's sake.
The blessing of Yahweh was upon everything Potiphar owned.

GENESIS 39:5

Your lifestyle of wholehearted devotion attracts the blessing of
God. And when you're saturated with blessing, it splashes on those
who come near you. When you walk into a room, the substance of
his glory floods the atmosphere. Others may not understand the
significance of what you carry, but they will sense it.

The glory of God in your life is available to others. It's meant to be
happily contagious! His Spirit inside of you and all that it contains
is real. Tangible. Alive. And it is yours to share. Declare his desire
over every life so all may know. Release joy, healing, and peace
into every soul. Bless the ones Jesus gave his life for. Believe in the
power of what you carry!

*Father, when people cross my path, I want them to do a double
take. Not because of how I look or what I say but because of the
tangible glory of your Spirit inside of me. Let favor, blessing, and
life radiate from my being. May everyone I come into contact with
be blessed by what I carry.*

Through You

Potiphar placed all that he owned under Joseph's oversight. And with Joseph in charge, Potiphar had nothing to worry about.

GENESIS 39:6

Be a good steward of what you're entrusted with and the people God brings you. The world has enough harsh examples of religion. They need an encounter with a heart truly on fire with God's love. You may not agree with those you serve or work for, but how will they ever experience the love of God unless it comes from you?

When you work or spend time serving those who don't know the Lord, consider it an honor. God has chosen you to be a vessel of his grace. He has entrusted you with the souls of those he loves. Every person has value in God's eyes, so treat them with respect and show them what he's like. Work for them, as unto the Lord, and they will notice. Your values, displayed by the way you work, live, and love, will cause them to trust you and want to know you more. The more they know you, the more they will see God's glory shining through.

Father, I want to be an example of your inexhaustible grace. Give me compassion to embrace those who have yet to discover the joys of life with you. Teach me to love well and to serve people with integrity. Surround me with favor and blessing so I can share it with others.

Maintain Integrity

It wasn't long before his master's wife noticed Joseph.
She demanded: "Come make love to me."
"Never!" Joseph replied.

GENESIS 39:7–8

Self-control is a true sign of integrity. This, coupled with
commitment to the Lord, will keep you in times of temptation.
When your heart is set on the Lord and your desire is toward him,
he will strengthen you in times of weakness. In every temptation, he
will provide a way out.

Joseph may have lost his coat, but he maintained his excellent
character. He respected his master and understood the place of
honor that had been bestowed upon him. Like Joseph, when you
run to the Lord for help and remain loyal when temptation rages,
you catch his attention. You invite his grace. Nothing you do goes
unnoticed by the Lord. Sin gets easier to overcome when you desire
to live with integrity and honor.

*Father, you have paid the ultimate price to make me holy and
righteous. Now I want to shine with your character at all times.
Give me wisdom and resolve to conduct myself with integrity and
humility. Examine me. I pray you will find a heart filled with sincere
devotion, integrity, and commitment.*

Holy Vessels

"Why would I want to do such an immoral thing
and sin against God?"

GENESIS 39:9

The future ruler, Joseph, did well. He ran from temptation. Sometimes running is a mark of cowardice, and other times it is the mark of courage. Joseph would rather run in embarrassment than linger, falling into the trap of sexual promiscuity. He was a man of honor and integrity.

The Bible does not tell us to *reason* with sexual immorality; it tells us to *run*! We are vessels of the Holy Spirit. We're surrounded by angels. We are God's beloved, the ones he never takes his eyes off. If we understood how honored we are to know and be known by him, we wouldn't want to do anything to injure our relationship. Sinning against our bodies by willingly submitting them to sexual impurity darkens our awareness of him and opens the door to shame and tormenting thoughts from the enemy.

Father, I want to live my life as a vessel of honor. To be aware of you at all times. To remember who I am so I'll be strong enough to flee in times of temptation. And if I'm ever overwhelmed by the lure of sin, may I run into your arms of mercy to receive forgiveness. May I forever remain close to you.

Relentless

Yet day after day, she was determined to seduce him.
But Joseph continually refused her advances
and would not even go near her.

GENESIS 39:10

When God lifts us up, the enemy scrambles to knock us back down. The adversary knows that the only temptations worth plaguing us with are ones that entice us. Whether he's seducing us into sin, baiting our anger, or stirring our fear, he fights to grab our attention with things that matter to us. It's vital to stay close to the Lord and to pay attention to the areas of our souls that react to the enemy's devices.

Invite God into the dry, stained, and neglected caverns of our souls, and he will clean them up. He wants access to the ugliest, messiest areas. Nothing is off-limits. He hasn't missed those embarrassing thoughts, inconsistent beliefs, or dark temptations we've tried to ignore. The Lord will answer our honest and humble cries for help. The enemy may be determined to take us out, but God's faithful assistance will meet our relentless pursuit of holiness.

Father, I want to live with a pure and untainted heart. To testify that, by your grace, I am made whole. It isn't a sacrifice to turn away from temptation; it's a choice that becomes easier and easier every time I make it. My obedience flows from a heart of love.

You Will Rise

Joseph's master took him and threw him into prison,
the place where the king's prisoners are confined,
and he was left there.

GENESIS 39:20

Low points like this are difficult to go through. Betrayal, rejection,
and false accusations sting. When people sin against us, it can send
us into the most difficult seasons of suffering. Undeserved and
without reason, we're thrown into a prison of heartache. But God's
deliverance will come.

When you find yourself imprisoned in a season of pain, turn it into
a chamber of God's love. Turn your heart to the King, who holds
the key to every locked door. He knows how to heal every trauma
so that the memory holds no sorrow. Jesus suffered the darkness of
separation from God so you don't have to. He longs to reveal the
deepest love and joyous victory you've ever known. He will use
this catastrophe to launch you into your most glorious triumph. His
strength will become yours. Mercy will heal your wounded soul.
You will rise again!

*Father, pour your love like healing oil upon my heart. Let this prison
of pain become a chamber of blissful encounter. I forgive those
who have hurt me. Give me the grace to release the anger and
sorrow fully. Saturate the deepest places of my soul. Reveal your
glory in this situation.*

Testimonies of Kindness

Yahweh was with Joseph and demonstrated to him his faithful love
by giving him great favor in the sight of the warden.

GENESIS 39:21

Let's be honest—trusting God isn't always easy. Especially when life
feels like it has slammed a fist in your face. When the fog of chaos
and opposition blurs our vision, all we can do is sit at the Lord's feet
and wait. Though we want to fight our way to peace, it never works.
The flip-flops of life will never make sense, but in the center of our
chaos, God reveals his faithful love.

In the middle of difficulty, when we can barely speak, love softly
reaches from our hearts, and God rises in response. With mercy,
he turns the darkest surroundings into brilliant displays of glory. In
awestruck wonder, we watch our Father do what only he can do.
When we cannot see the way, he is working behind the scenes to
turn things around for our good. And suddenly, even in our prison,
our souls begin to sing.

*Father, I'm so grateful that your presence is always available. You
already have the answer to my situation. When I cannot seem to
find the light, your glory and grace come flooding in. You will turn
even the most unlikely situations into testimonies of kindness.*

Mysteries in the Night

Joseph said to them, "God can interpret your dreams!
Please, tell them to me."

GENESIS 40:8

God wants to unveil his mysteries. They are hidden for us to find.
To learn. To enjoy. To discover more about his love, will, and ways.
Though dreams are often wrapped in obscurity, it is our joy and
privilege to dig into their meaning with his help.

It seems our Father loves to draw us into searching mode. He
downloads dreams that spark our longing for the wisdom and
discernment that only he can give. His understanding is perfect and
cannot be learned—his Spirit must impart it. The hidden meanings
woven into our dreams leave us in awe as he reveals them one by
one. Clear interpretation comes only as the Lord reveals his secrets
to those who lean in to hear. How wonderful that he shares his
wisdom with us in such a playful and unique way.

*Father, speak to me in my dreams. Infuse my mind with holy
revelation. Draw me close to you as I sleep and unite my heart to
yours. Reveal your will and bless me with wisdom to walk in your
ways. Uncover the treasures you've hidden for me to find. I long to
hear your voice, day and night.*

Do Not Relent

"When things start to go well for you,
remember me, and please be kind and mention me
to Pharaoh so that he might release me from here."

Genesis 40:14

It hurts when it seems God has forgotten his promises to us. When year after year we declare his truth, but circumstances still haven't lined up. It's then that we must extricate ourselves from fear and embrace grace. To trust that God is working on our behalf. To partner with the character growth that is surely happening. To remember that love—God's love—is always faithful even when we're tempted to doubt it.

Joseph became a slave when he was seventeen years old, and soon afterward, Potiphar cast him into prison. It wasn't until he was thirty that Pharaoh released him from prison. Joseph was human, and waiting thirteen years probably made him weary, just as it does to us. But he continued to be a man of honor. Like him, we must hold tight to his promises. To make them a part of us and wrap them in our hearts, waiting with expectancy no matter how long it takes.

Father, no matter how long it takes for me to see your promises come to pass, I will not relent. I don't know the intricacies of what you're doing behind the scenes, but I know you will make a way. In the waiting, I know you are faithful. You will fulfill your promises to me.

Refined by Grace

"I have done nothing here to deserve being thrown
into this dungeon."

GENESIS 40:15

God will use every unwelcome situation to refine our characters
if we let him. When we're tempted to complain, lash out, react in
anger, or retaliate, we can choose to sit in the discomfort, tune into
God, and find the grace we need.

Like Joseph, there are times when we've done everything right yet
still suffer mistreatment. But it's here that he learned to rule over
his fleshly nature so God could release him to rule over others.
The same is true for us—the call to greatness always leads through
unpleasant paths where we face our weaknesses, insecurities,
and true motivations. Every situation is an opportunity to grow in
God's likeness. God will use trials to refine us until we release the
fragrance of a surrendered heart everywhere we go.

*Father, though I don't always understand the things that happen,
my heart is set upon you. When my mind overwhelms my heart
and fights for the right to complain, I will bow before your throne
of grace and yield my thoughts to you. Refine me by your grace.
Take me from glory to glory.*

Not Forgotten

The chief steward completely forgot about Joseph
and never remembered him.

GENESIS 40:23

Disappointed. Frustrated. Confused. Stuck. These are just some of
the things we feel when men let us down. Heaviness tries to weigh
on us and convince us that since we don't see deliverance coming
the way we expected, it must not be coming at all. If people don't
keep their word, maybe God won't either.

It's time to stop believing those lies! Man will fail us, but God
remains eternally faithful. The early dreams of Joseph revealed that
the Lord would exalt him. He had no clue he would be imprisoned
first. In order to become the leader that God destined him to be,
he needed refinement, his character matured. How differently God
fulfills his word to us! We believe that our dreams and callings will
be fulfilled a certain way, not realizing that God will thoroughly deal
with us before he brings our destinies to pass.

*Father, I will not despair! You have not forgotten the dreams you've
placed in my heart. You will breathe life into every desire that has
come from you. You have a purpose for my life, and even though
the process of fulfillment looks different than I imagined, I know
you will come with joyous breakthrough!*

Pray for Our Leaders

After two full years,
Pharaoh dreamed that he was standing by the Nile.

GENESIS 41:1

The One whose wisdom stretched out the expanse of sky and told the oceans where to stop hasn't been struck ignorant. He isn't wringing his hands, wondering how to get the attention of rulers and leaders, regardless of their relationship with him.

Yahweh is the Ruler of his people, the God-King over the entire earth. No city or nation is too far removed from his ability to save, heal, and intervene. But he does ask us to partner with him. To cover our leaders and countries in prayer. To bless, regardless of our differences and opinions. To uphold. To speak light into the darkness. To agree with the truth of his Word. When we, as a body, spend more time praying, blessing, and partnering with heaven for breakthrough in the hearts of leaders instead of complaining, then we will see change.

Father, though the darkness of the world gets darker still, I believe you will come in power and set things in order. You will pour out glory, and in your mercy, you will convict the shrewd. Forgive me for spending more time complaining than I do praying. Overtake our leaders with the wisdom of heaven. Enlighten their hearts to see truth.

With Him

> "I cannot do it alone," Joseph replied,
> "but God will help me."
>
> GENESIS 41:16

Whether it's interpreting dreams, praying for the sick, or living day-to-day, we all need God's help. This simple revelation abounds with truth. And if we're honest, we'll admit that we get in the flow of habits without giving him much thought. God has blessed us with talents and anointings, and at times, we step right into those gifts without acknowledging him. Still he blesses our effort. But how much more powerful and life-infused will our efforts be if we take a moment to recognize him first?

Joseph knew where his strength came from. With a simple statement of truth, he invited God's assistance. It only takes a moment to engage our spirits with his. To tune into the One who will give us grace to do things with ease, wisdom, peace, and power. To value his help in everything we do. To start our days and every task with our hearts tuned into him.

Father, I invite you to do life with me. I want to get into the habit of thinking about you all day long. I don't want to do anything without the awareness of your presence. Teach me to tune into you during mundane tasks and the most demanding situations. May all I do flow in unison with you.

Live with Dignity

Joseph continued, "Let Pharaoh select a very wise
and discerning man and set him over the land of Egypt."

GENESIS 41:33

Listen to the humility that has finally settled upon Joseph. From an eager young man who zealously shared his dreams of grandeur to a man entirely dependent upon God. Prison became his school, imparting patience and meekness. Instead of using this opportunity to beg for release from jail, he approaches the mighty Pharaoh with dignity and respect. He seeks God for wisdom and chooses to be a blessing to Pharaoh.

God wants to tenderize our hearts. In our difficult trials, we can either let ourselves grow cold and resentful or bow low and discover depth of spirit. God will not reject our humble and contrite hearts. Every choice to go low and lift others high and each time we trust God to be our Redeemer, we are stepping closer to our own victory.

Father, help me to be sensitive to your Spirit when opportunities come my way. Help me not to be so focused on myself that I miss the chance to be a blessing to someone else. I want to be wholly submitted to you without getting sidetracked by what I think I deserve. You know what I need. You are refining my character so that I can be trusted with your glory.

Give Him the Glory

Pharaoh turned to Joseph and said,
"Since God has divinely revealed this to you,
there is no one as wise and full of insight as you."

GENESIS 41:39

God makes us look good! And it's important to remember this when promotion and recognition come. All that we are, every bit of creativity and wisdom, comes from the Lord. When we understand who we are because of his mercy, favor, and anointing, it is easier to remain humble. It becomes our joy to sincerely give him the glory.

Sometimes we wonder why promotion is withheld. We know the call that burns in our hearts, yet doors of opportunity won't open. It's in the waiting that the Lord refines us. It's in the purifying of motives that we gain his perspective. And when we are dependent on God more than our gifts, callings, or the favor of man, God will set us before kings and bless us with favor.

Father, teach me who I am in you. When recognition comes, I want to remain humble, giving you all of the glory. May others see the wisdom and favor on my life and know they are your gifts. May all that I do and say point to the splendor of your Spirit within.

Suddenly

"I hereby place you in charge of all my affairs,
and all my people will obey your commands.
Only I, the king, will be greater than you!"

GENESIS 41:40

Life can change in a day! Joseph had been betrayed by his brothers, was forced into slavery, and was imprisoned due to false accusation. Circumstances certainly didn't look hopeful. Sure, he had favor in prison, but that's not exactly the place one expects dreams to come true. And those dreams he thought God gave him must have felt like a cruel joke. Life was going from bad to worse until God stepped in, and suddenly, everything shifted.

Take time to process this story, and remember that the same God who miraculously came through for Joseph will come through for you. It may have been years since you zealously believed your dreams would come to pass. Everything in your life may contradict what was in your heart. But God is still in the miracle business! Allow him to work in your heart. Continue pressing into his presence and grow in character and faith. Trust his perfect timing.

Father, I won't try to understand what I can only grasp by faith. I release my ideas of when things should happen and trust your wisdom. Nothing can stop your will from coming to pass when I live in agreement with it. I'm shaking off disappointment and choosing you, over all else.

Believe Again

He removed his signet ring, placed it on Joseph's finger,
and had him clothed with fine linen robes!
He adorned him with a golden collar around his neck.

GENESIS 41:42

In place of poverty, Joseph received the wealth of Pharaoh. Instead of restricting him with chains, Pharaoh adorned him with a golden collar of high esteem. The finest linens replaced prison robes. One moment society despised him, and the next he was leading them. God didn't restore Joseph; he gave him exceedingly more than he ever imagined possible.

God wants to lift your burdens and bless every area of your life. He wants you to know it's his will to be more radical in your restoration than the enemy is in your destruction. Spirit, soul, and body—no area is off-limits to God's burden-lifting power. It's time to believe again! Time to allow him to heal your identity and remind you who you are. Start by handing him the pain of unmet desire. Be brave. The courage to believe again happens when you stop agreeing with fear and embrace his love. God isn't done with you!

Father, I've identified with these chains for too long! But they are not my identity. You are! Your goodness and faithfulness are my portion. Your love is reason for believing again. You haven't forgotten me. I choose to be brave. I choose to believe again!

Time to Be Free

"God has made me forget all my troubles."

GENESIS 41:51

God doesn't want you to become acclimated to sorrow or to allow it to usurp your true calling. No matter how long you've suffered, he wants you to agree with heaven. To remember that hardships and pain are a part of life, but they are not your identity. He wants you to fold yourself into grace, but to do that, you must release unforgiveness and expect goodness to overtake you.

Moving forward takes time when you've been stuck in the muddy waters of suffering. It requires your agreement with one thing— God's love for you. Even in your weariness, he wants you to hold tight to his presence. To be willing to release the past so you can taste the joys of the future. It takes inviting him into your *now* so he can breathe upon the smoldering embers of faith. The mercy of God is the only thing that can cause you to forget your pain. But that mercy is reaching out to you today.

Father, I need your mercy to heal me of these unhealthy mindsets. I've been stuck in the past for too long. I lay this pain before you and ask you to be the Lord of it. To touch my soul-wounds and infuse them with your glory. I'm willing to let go. To let joy in again and finally be free.

Become Fruitful

"God has made me fruitful in the land of my suffering."

GENESIS 41:52

Agree with heaven, and soon things will change. You're becoming brave and risking joy instead of continually wearing those heavy cloaks of misidentification. Even if you're still standing in your land of suffering, you're growing wings of faith. Soon you'll be flying above the pain and looking at life from God's perspective.

Overcoming difficulty not only makes us strong, but it also creates compassion. When we let go of the past, we actually want to be fruitful. We want to share our breakthroughs. To pour out the wisdom we've gained. To share our joy. We finally understand that there are no limits to what God can do through a man or woman who has yielded his or her life entirely to him. The weight of trials is nothing compared to the weight of glory that rests on us when we embrace healing for our souls.

Father, you have done such a marvelous work in my heart. You've reached out and taken my burdens. You've shown me your faithfulness, time and time again. Now I want to share the glories of your love. I want to be fruitful by helping others embrace their freedom.

You Are a Storehouse

Because of the severity of the worldwide famine,
people from all over the world had to come
and buy grain from Joseph.

GENESIS 41:57

The wisdom, character, and compassion we gain in our trials will feed others, but we may be surprised at how far-reaching our testimony can be. Joseph once believed his family would bow to him, but he had no idea that multitudes would bow as well. The magnitude of God's plans is so magnificent that it requires the noblest and humblest of hearts to handle.

When we submit ourselves to purification in the furnace of affliction, we come out looking and smelling like God. We become trustworthy when we're saturated with his mercy and long to pour it out. When we have the Lord's heart, we become storehouses of plenty for those in famine. Though we may be locked up and sealed in the king's prison for a short time, we will soon be released. Trusted to give bread to the hungry nations of the earth.

Father, I want to be a vessel of honor. To partner with you in the wonders of heaven on earth. To do more than I have ever dreamed possible. Create a clean heart in me. Let my testimony lead others to you and become a storehouse of substance for others to feast upon.

Triggers and Healing

One day, Joseph's ten brothers came
and bowed down before him
with their faces on the ground. ...
But he pretended he didn't know them
and spoke to them harshly.

GENESIS 42:6–7

Sometimes unresolved pain hides until it's triggered. This seems to be what caused Joseph to initially react the way he did. It isn't that he didn't have the right to be angry or lash out, but God always has a higher way. It would take Joseph some time to accept this higher way. While he imprisoned his brothers, God worked on his heart.

Hardness, pain, anger, and unforgiveness often aren't revealed until they're triggered. Though it stings to come face-to-face with old wounds, it is also a blessing. It allows us to see areas that still need healing. Let's pause and pay attention to our reactions. If we don't run from the pain and instead turn to God, he will do a deeper work.

Father, shine your spotlight into the deepest wells of my soul. Help me to pay attention to the places that need the cleansing fire of your love. I want every area of my life to radiate with truth and wholeness. Heal the wounds in my soul and strengthen me by your grace.

Misunderstood

> "We're blood brothers, sons of one father."
> Joseph interrupted, "No!
> You are spies who have come here to find our weakness!"
>
> GENESIS 42:11–12

Sometimes God allows uncomfortable situations to confront us. False accusations or distorted judgments that we know aren't true seem to come out of nowhere. But God in his wisdom and mercy wants us to see our reactions.

Joseph spoke and acted in such a way that would reveal what was hiding in the hearts of his brothers. Pressure always pushes our reactions to the surface and exposes what is in our hearts. God wants us to become like Jesus—constant and unwavering under the strain of misunderstanding. He wants us to stand on a strong foundation of peace when lies swirl about. It all boils down to the heart—who are we really living to impress? When we recognize these peace-stealers, we can choose not to engage with them. Instead, we can step into the safety of God's presence where truth, wisdom, and inexplicable peace abound.

Father, I want to trust you with my reputation. Teach me how to keep my peace when I'm misunderstood. You will redeem my reputation just as you did for Joseph. Help me live in humility and not take offense so I can offer the world a true view of Christianity.

Free at Last

> "Look what's happened to us!
> We're being punished for what we did to Joseph long ago."
>
> GENESIS 42:21

The weight of sin is a burden none of us were meant to carry. That's why Jesus took it to the cross for us. He wants us to be free. To not only receive forgiveness but also to heal from the trauma of what could potentially frame our lives with sorrow and heaviness.

God always exposes sin. How else can we repent unless we first feel the fire of conviction? And this conviction is a gift given by the mercy of a loving Father. Two decades didn't remove the stain of Joseph's brothers' guilty consciences. Time will not heal the self-inflicted wounds of shame. Only Jesus can heal a torment this deep. So when we're faced with a sin we've not yet relinquished to the Lord or received forgiveness for, we mustn't ignore it or sweep it under the rug. Repentance sets us free.

Father, cleanse me with the fire of your love so that nothing hinders our communion. Examine my heart and reveal anything that would distance me from you. I won't resist your conviction. Thank you for your tender mercy. Your kindness leads me to repentance and sets me free.

The Gift of Compassion

Deeply affected by what he heard, Joseph began to weep.

GENESIS 42:24

When people are vulnerable and allow us to hear the secrets of their hearts, it affects us. It's difficult to witness another's pain or the sorrow of a soul bowed low and not be moved by it. As humans, we sometimes become stoic and indifferent to the cries of another because we're afraid to feel too much. Scared to be drawn into overwhelming compassion because it's uncomfortable.

But God never runs from our pain. He faithfully sits with us and wraps us in arms of tender affection. His love heals. And this is how we are to live. To recognize the healing power of his love that yearns for release through us. To sit in the discomfort of another's pain with nothing more to offer than a heart filled with God's tenderness. May we grow in his grace and learn to love like he does.

Father, I know your compassion is a gift, but sometimes it feels overwhelming. Bless me with the courage to embrace the discomfort of walking with others in their time of need. Give me your heart of love that heals others and keeps my heart pliable in your hands.

Mercy Triumphs

Joseph then gave orders to have their bags filled with grain,
to hide each man's money back inside his sack,
and to give them provisions for their journey home.

GENESIS 42:25

Joseph's love for his brothers, despite what they had done to him,
paid their debt. Though they deserved no grain or money, mercy
prevailed. What a beautiful demonstration of God's mercy and love
for us.

Mercy consistently triumphs over judgment. Love is always the
answer. Wisdom carefully guides us in ways that cause us to reflect
God's nature but also keep us safe. Forgiveness toward those who
have afflicted us is hard on our fleshly nature. It allows us to dig
deep and draw from the wells of God's love within. And when we
behave like our heavenly Father, the enemy cannot taint our souls
with the poison of offense. God sees everyone through the eyes of
love and grace, and he calls us higher to gain his perspective.

*Father, may your mercy always steer me in the right direction, your
truth guide me, and your love eternally surround me. I want to
follow your example and grow to emulate you more. Keep me free
from offense so I won't sin against you. May mercy always guide
my heart.*

God Is for You

Their father Jacob said to his sons, "First, Joseph is gone,
and now, Simeon! And now, you want to take Benjamin from me!
Everything is against me!"

GENESIS 42:36

What Jacob interpreted as evil was actually God working in secret
to bring about a tremendous blessing. He was stuck in the darkness
of his past and couldn't see with the eyes of faith because fear
blinded him. What he thought was his worst day was actually the
handiwork of God.

Regardless of what comes against you, God will find a way to use
it for your good. He will shake you out of your comfort zone and
make his glory known. Jacob had no clue how miraculously the
Lord was about to come through for him and his family. And though
things may look bleak and hopeless, you are going to be surprised by
God's goodness as well! His power has no limits. When it seems like
everything is against you, remember, "If God has determined to stand
with us...who then could ever stand against us?" (Romans 8:31).

*Father, even if the whole world is against me, you can turn things
around for my good. I repent for fixing my eyes on the shadows of
hopelessness. Illuminate my soul with one glimpse of your glorious
light, and I will see clearly again. You are faithful. You are for me.*

Release the Past

Jacob replied, "I can't let my son Benjamin go with you.
For his brother is dead, and...If he were to meet with disaster..."

GENESIS 42:38

Fear wants to chain us to the past and dictate the way we see our future. But God wants to overpower our former pain with his love. He wants us to recognize the way it hinders us from walking in his best so we will cry out for his healing grace.

When our eyes of faith won't focus, God wants us to quiet our souls. To be still and know that he is good, regardless of our unresolved questions. We must be honest with ourselves about where our faith is struggling. And it's easy to figure out if we listen to the words coming out of our mouths. They will prove if we're operating in doubt, fear, and unbelief. The good news is that once we face these things and are willing to release the past, the Lord in his mercy can heal even the most traumatic past.

Father, fear cannot conquer me when I remember that your love is unfailing and your goodness unmatched. You are my Shepherd, the One who fiercely protects me. You are my magnificent healer who mends my wounded heart. I turn to you with expectancy and offer you my pain.

The Greater Blessing

The famine in the land continued to grow more severe.
When all the grain they had brought from Egypt was almost gone,
their father said to them, "Go back and buy us more food."

GENESIS 43:1

Sometimes it takes a famine to awaken our desperation. It takes the discomfort of staying in our current condition to force us to do what we'd rather not do. When the thought of moving forward causes us to freeze in our tracks, God in his wisdom and tender compassion will find a way to nudge us closer to the blessing he's waiting to give us. He will smoke us out with the power of his love.

When things look bleak and you can't quite understand why things aren't turning around, seek God's wisdom. Perhaps he has something better for you that you haven't risked going after. To receive a greater blessing, you may need to first release the lesser one. Diligently seek his wisdom and peace, and they will be your compass.

Father, help me not to settle for the scraps when you have destined me to eat from the bounty. I want to courageously follow you wherever you lead. To take steps of faith without toying with fear. To experience your best so I, in turn, will be a blessing to others.

Confront Sin

Israel demanded, "Why did you make it so hard for me?"

GENESIS 43:6

One of the earmarks of maturing in the Lord is when we're honest about our reactions and take responsibility for them. Too often, we point the finger at the behavior of others, blaming them for our situations, fears, sorrow, and anger. It's easier to shift the blame on someone else than to confront our unhealthy emotions, soul wounds, or sins.

There's an awakening of truth, purity, and honesty happening within us. A gentle pulling of the Holy Spirit, leading us into revelation about ourselves. It is amazing, freeing, and often painful to unite our spirits and souls because we don't always want to admit that the two are at odds. But if we will stop blaming others for our circumstances or sinful reactions, God will help us get to the root of our problems.

Father, I'm ready to see what's really happening inside of me. To understand where I haven't fully surrendered myself to you so nothing will hinder my freedom. To stop blaming others and take responsibility for my life, attitudes, and shortcomings. Lord, I receive your correction and want to grow in your image.

October

Compassion

Judah spoke up and said to Israel, "Father, I promise to guarantee his safety with my life. You can hold me personally responsible if I don't return with him."

GENESIS 43:8

Time and experience softened Judah's heart. He understood the fear of losing the youngest son since he had lost two sons of his own. Compassion inspired him to offer his life as a guarantee that Benjamin would return with them safely.

Our greatest suffering will one day morph into deep and sincere compassion. When we understand someone's pain firsthand, we become a gift of mercy. We're moved to go the extra mile. Willing to trudge through the mud to pull out someone who is stuck. Empathy is a powerful motivator. Though it's hard to fathom when you're smack-dab in the center of your trial, God can turn every tragedy into something beautiful—not just for you but for the many you'll reach.

Father, in every trial, your presence is strengthening me. Help me to learn the lessons that will become treasures of grace for me to share. I will not ignore the cries of others who will benefit from my testimony. May my life flow with gifts of compassion, understanding, and hope. May life blossom from every tragedy I've faced with you.

Consult Him

> After considering their words, their father Israel said to them,
> "If that's the way it has to be, then do this: Load your donkeys
> with the very best gifts. ... Take some balm and some honey,
> spices and myrrh, pistachio nuts and almonds."
>
> GENESIS 43:11

Sounds like Jacob is back to resorting to works of the flesh. In his attempt to gain favor, he put together a plan rather than having faith in God. It had worked years before with Esau, perhaps it would work now.

We've probably all been there. Faced with a crisis, we rely on what worked in the past instead of turning to God. It isn't that we shouldn't glean from the wisdom of previous experience, but making significant decisions without consulting the Lord's wisdom will result in mediocre success. The truth is that when we immediately jump to do, fix, or forge ahead instead of first pausing to hear God's plan, we're acting in the flesh and not trusting God. Fear always tries to push us to act on our own. To rely on our ideas instead of the believing in for the brilliance of the Lord's.

Father, forgive me for putting pressure on myself to fix everything. With faith that pleases you, I give you full control. I release the reins of my life into your hands. I will trust. I will wait with my heart fixed on you. Let your wisdom come.

Expectancy

"May the God who is more than enough
grant you mercy and favor."

GENESIS 43:14

Not only is God more than able to take care of us, he absolutely loves to. That's the truth that will settle our souls in any circumstance if we wholeheartedly believe it. He will do the impossible when we take his promises to heart and make them our meditation.

When we agree with truth and give it more than a compulsory shrug of hope, it goes deep into the marrow of our souls. Leaning into him, fully surrendered to trusting him, causes us to sing. To rejoice in faith-filled declaration of all he will do. Soon we find it effortless to relinquish our doubts and fears because truth has filled our being. If his glory captivates our hearts every single day, a genuine expectancy of good will flood our souls. We never need to yield to fear again.

Father, you always breathe hope and joy into my soul. You push fear away by wrapping me in your love. Grace is more than enough to sustain me. Faith is rising within, reminding me that you are for me, not against me. You are powerful enough to take care of me.

Act on Faith

"As for me, if I suffer loss, then let it be so."

GENESIS 43:14

When fear has chained us within gates of complacency, it's time to do something radical. To stop cowering behind the questions and put an end to our internal debates. To face the challenges of *What if* this or that happens" and find resolve in our courageous answers.

Sometimes we just have to run as hard as we can into the unknown. To stop letting the fear of what may or may not happen hold us back. When we're frozen in place and faith feels scary, we need to find God. We need to courageously confront fear by taking a risk and moving forward. When we're not even sure if we're hearing God, let's do the opposite of what fear tells us to do. The Lord's will is revealed when we confront our questions and stop allowing them to hold us back. Faith is courageous!

Father, you know my heart's desire is to do your will. Fear of the unknown has held me back for too long. I'm going to face the what-ifs. And even if things don't turn out the way I want them to, my praise will still rise. In the fog of uncertainty, I am choosing to act on faith.

Alone

The brothers set off for Egypt.

GENESIS 43:15

Jacob's sons had left with their brother Benjamin, Simeon was being held hostage, Rachel was dead, and Joseph was gone. Jacob had nothing left. He was all alone. God was emptying him again.

In these moments when we have nothing left but God, his love shines most brilliantly. We've confronted the things that scared us. We've done all we could possibly do, and now we must wait for him to act. And in the discomfort of waiting, we mature. We learn how wild and exciting his love is. How satisfying and healing his presence is. We are welcomed into the glorious peace found in silence and rest. God wants us to find the joy of solitude. To purposefully seek out moments, days, and weeks to lock ourselves away with him. Alone with him is a great place to be.

Father, I'm so grateful for the way you zealously pursue me. For the way you set me up to discover truth. You want me to be free even more than I want to be. I'm beginning to understand how liberating it is to be yours—spirit, soul, and body. To hold nothing in higher esteem than the beauty of your presence.

The Wonders of Royalty

"Bring the men to my house and make them feel at home.
Butcher an animal and prepare a meal,
for these men are to dine with me at noon."

GENESIS 43:16

Just when we feel stuck, unsure of the future, and life seems to be handing us scraps, we're surprised by the goodness of God. To our surprise, he opens the treasures of his glory and pours out such extravagant blessings we can scarcely contain them.

God's love is immeasurable. You may not wine and dine with kings and princes, but in his kingdom, you are royalty. It's time to see setbacks, seasons of lack, and the humdrum lull of momentum as pauses before a great blessing. Too often, we cement ourselves into thinking, *This is just the way life is for me*. No! Stretch your faith! Believe for God's biggest and best surprises. Find Scriptures to encourage your heart and to declare as you agree with truth. Life can change for the better in a moment. Remember who you are. *You* are a child of the King.

Father, forgive me for partnering with discouragement. From now on, my life will be defined by what you say. I don't have to beg because you are already turning things around. I simply need to believe I am yours. I am royalty. I will focus on your love and get lost in the wonder of it all.

Expose Fear

"He's looking for an opportunity to arrest us,
turn us into his slaves, and take away our donkeys!"

Genesis 43:18

Fear always makes us jump to conclusions. To imagine the worst. It wants us to let down our guard and entertain the stress, anxiety, and worry that open the door to even worse attacks of the enemy. Fear wants to smother you. But God has a better way!

The Father wants you to see fear for what it is—an attempt to make you doubt his love. You find peace of mind by fixing your attention on his truth and love. When you lower your gaze to your situation, it stirs anxiety and causes you to falter. If you're overwhelmed, fearful, and stressed, it's not because you don't have the power to shake it off. You do! Perfect love will dispel fear. This transforming, pulsating, living substance is more than a mental grasp of spiritual truth. You must experience it. If you're overwhelmed and can't think straight, then today's devotion is for you!

Father, tear away these lies of fear that have rooted themselves in my soul. Come and flood my thoughts with your beauty and light. Illuminate my heart with truth. Forgive me for getting sucked into the swirl of worry. For forgetting that no matter what happens, I can still find the peace that passes understanding. Draw me into grace.

Gentle Reminders

"Don't be afraid. Your God, the God of your father,
must have been the one who put treasure in your bags."

GENESIS 43:23

It took one of Joseph's servants to steer the brothers' attention to the miracle-working power of God. A reminder of God's goodness and faithfulness quelled their fears. The faith and spiritual influence of his master obviously affected this servant.

It doesn't always take great wisdom or many words to turn someone's heart toward the Lord and away from fear. Sometimes the simplest response to someone's fears is the most powerful. The key is to allow the Lord to lead us in the way we speak to others. By our lifestyle of holy intimacy with God, we remain dialed into flow of his Spirit. We don't need to complicate conversations by trying to sound spiritual. We are spiritual! We are filled with hope and life that is meant to be shared. Pay attention to the people God brings across your path each day. They may need to hear the hope you carry and the truth you're meant to share.

Father, I want to represent you well and carry the beauty of your love to the world around me. Let my love be unconditional, my faith contagious, and my heart full of compassion. I want to offer the world a taste of your presence in all I do and say so they'll know how amazing you are. Lead my conversations today.

More Like Him

When Joseph came home, they presented to him the gifts
they had brought with them into the house.
They each bowed low before him with their faces to the ground.
He asked them how the family was doing.

GENESIS 43:26–27

What a drastic change this was for Joseph. The boy who blurted out
his dreams from God had become a man of maturity, wisdom, and
grace. When his brothers first came to him for help, Joseph could
have bragged about his position. He could have punished them for
what they'd done, but he remained calm and treated them well.

We often don't realize how much we've matured until we're forced
into situations that reveal our growth. Slowly, steadily, as we yield
to the work of the Holy Spirit in our lives, we're becoming more
like him. Though at times we wiggle with impatience, we resign
ourselves to the process of maturing love. And after years of setting
ourselves to seek the Lord and soak in his presence and his Word,
we begin to soar. We begin to look, sound, and behave like the
One we have set our affection on.

*Father, thank you for encouraging me. For correcting me and
allowing me to face the hard things in life so I can grow in
character. Thank you for smoothing out my rough edges so I can
shine with your glory. Each day as I walk with you, I'm becoming
more like you—my beautiful example of wisdom and grace.*

Tenderness

Joseph hastily left the room, for he was overwhelmed with feelings of love for his brother and on the verge of tears. He went into a private room and sobbed, as tears ran down his cheeks.

GENESIS 43:30

The immaturity and fears of our youth aren't meant to define us. They are meant to awaken our need for God's love and to form character. Joseph didn't let the trauma of his youth ruin the future God had planned for him. He stayed close to his heavenly Father, and instead of becoming angry and allowing his heart to harden and grow cold, it softened in God's presence.

Pain is inevitable. It's a part of life. But we must not give pain permission to dictate the way we live, speak, and behave. Only God can heal our soul wounds, but we must allow him to. We invite him into our pain, and he saturates it with healing glory. The traumas of our past become great victories when we experience his profound internal breakthrough and can then use them to help others.

Father, reveal yourself to me. Flood every memory of pain, even the ones I don't realize have formed part of my personality. Soften my heart. Make me whole. Free me so I can connect with you, myself, and others on a deeper emotional and spiritual level.

Distracted

The brothers had been seated before Joseph in their birth order...
They were all stunned when they realized the seating arrangement
and looked at each other in astonishment.

GENESIS 43:33

Perhaps if Joseph's brothers weren't so fearful, they would have
realized who Joseph was. Though it had been many years since
they saw their brother, surely he must have been somewhat
recognizable. Didn't they think it odd that he cared about their
father or knew their birth order? They were distracted and
anxious—a combination that temporarily blinds us to the provision
of God.

When fear or worry distracts us, we don't notice what's right in
front of us. We struggle to hear the quiet whispers of God's Spirit
because we're tuned into the swirls of chaos around us. That's the
enemy's plan. He wants to sidetrack us so we'll turn our attention
away from the Lord. This is why it's vital that during times of stress,
we spend extra time soaking in the Lord's presence and quieting
our souls.

*Father, forgive me for letting this mountain of stress appear more
significant than your majestic power. I still myself before you now
and ask for your grace. I will stay in your arms until my thoughts
are quiet and I can see clearly again.*

Jealousy

Eleven plates of food were taken from Joseph's table and set in front of each of them, but Benjamin's portion was five times more than any of theirs!

GENESIS 43:34

Favoritism provoked the brothers to rid themselves of Joseph. Now Joseph tested their hearts to see if favoring Benjamin would rouse their jealousy again. Would they turn on Benjamin as they had with him? Could they handle seeing one brother treated better than the others? Can we?

The only way to know what's inside of us is to bring it to the surface. When God opens doors of favor, provision, and blessing for someone else, how do we feel? Jealousy is dangerous. It throws a muddy film over our hearts, so it's important not to ignore it if we notice it stirring. Instead we bow ourselves before the Lord in humility and repentance and ask for his cleansing flow. We partner with the Lord and cheer others on just as we'd want them to do for us.

Father, forgive me for entertaining unfavorable thoughts about others. When you bless someone else, it casts a mirror in front of me so I know what's in my heart. Today, I separate myself from selfishness. Cleanse me. Help me to be genuinely excited about your faithfulness toward others.

Feast on His Love

They feasted and drank their fill.

GENESIS 43:34

God has invited everyone to dine at his table. He doesn't require us to look or act a certain way before he welcomes us in. He prepares a feast so everyone can taste and see that he is good. This banquet of his glory, love, and precious promises is ours to enjoy every day.

You can experience God's extravagant love right now. Turn your attention to him, be still, and feel his nearness. Whisper his name. See his face smiling at you. Throughout the day, drink of his presence and continually become aware of his glory. Stay in the stream of love, and you will never run dry. The world, with its counterfeits, will leave you malnourished. But when you feast upon God's love, you will have more than enough to share with others.

Father, I want to eat from your banqueting table. To feast upon your love and satisfy the true longing of my soul. Pour out the rains of your presence and saturate my soul. Let me hear your voice and feel the warmth of your embrace. I want to be so drenched with you that I drip with your glory everywhere I go.

No More Shame

"If any of your servants is found to have it, then he will die, and the rest of us will become your master's slaves!"

GENESIS 44:9

Before Joseph would tell his brothers who he was, he put them to one last test. Would they betray Benjamin and allow him to be punished for a crime he didn't commit? Or would they cry out for mercy on his behalf and demonstrate how they'd changed? If they had experienced guilt and shame over what they'd done to Joseph, their response to this test would reveal the depth of their repentance.

When guilt and shame weigh on us, our repentance can lift them. Instead of torturing ourselves with thoughts of what we did wrong, we can cry out for mercy and confess our sins. Sometimes it's easier to receive the Lord's forgiveness than it is to forgive ourselves. But Jesus bore the cross of sin and shame and suffered in our place. To hold on to guilt after we've repented is to refuse the provision of the cross.

Father, I refuse the sticky, slimy guilt of shame. I've been bought with a price, cleansed by your sacred blood. Thank you for presenting me with the choice to be free. I am not the same person I once was. Your mercy has changed me!

Every Way Imaginable

"My lord asked his servants,
'Do you have a father or another brother?'"

GENESIS 44:19

How is it that this glorious One who sits in the heavens and upon the thrones of our hearts is also our brother, Father, friend, and Counselor? He wants to bless us in every way imaginable. Where we've had poor examples of fathers, he loves us perfectly and accepts us unreservedly. When friends fail us, he never does. Not even the most experienced counselor contains the wisdom that set the planets in place. Facing each day with a faithful brother who lifts our burdens is a blessing that's difficult to describe.

The ways of God are mysterious and wonderful. They stir our souls with praise and keep us humble and grateful. Let's get to know him more! To delve into the many aspects of his love that we've yet to experience. Let's pour out our lives for this One whose love for us contains all that we need.

Father, thank you for knowing my needs and meeting them in the beauty of who you are. More than anything I ask for, I want to know you. To experience the depths of your glory that are unimaginable yet profoundly real. Lead me into encounters with every aspect of your personality.

Tender Moments

"Your servant, my father, said to us, 'You know that my wife Rachel
only gave me two sons. One is gone from me—torn by a beast!
I haven't seen him since. If you take this one also from me, and
something happens to him, you will send my gray hairs in grief
down to the grave.'"

GENESIS 44:27–29

Imagine what it was like for Joseph to hear Judah telling him this
story. It was probably chock-full of information his heart longed
to hear. Though Joseph wouldn't dare ask the brothers he hid
his identity from, the Lord knew his secret desires. He knew how
special and healing it would be to Joseph's heart to hear how loved
and missed he was.

God is so kind. So thoughtful. He not only answers spoken prayers
but also the hidden longings we don't even realize we have. This
perfect, all-knowing Father loves to swoop down and surprise us
with moments like these that remain in our hearts forever. Moments
that mend our souls wounds and remind us of his tender love.

*Father, your tender love has left me awestruck. Thank you for
reaching into my heart and giving me what I need. For surprising
me with moments that heal me in ways I didn't know how to ask
for. I feel so special to you. So known, loved, and cared for.*

Divine Exchange

"Please let me take the place of the boy,
and I will remain here as a slave to you, my lord."

GENESIS 44:33

"For the greatest love of all is a love that sacrifices all" (John 15:13). Repentance softens the heart. Mercy transforms us into a better version of ourselves. A version that resembles Jesus. Jesus revealed his great love by paying the price we were meant to pay. He took our place and gave himself as ransom so we could be free.

His act of love and unrelenting devotion has brought us into his family. It has freed us in a way nothing else ever could. This was the divine exchange of heaven. The beauty of mercy on display. Love took our sin and nailed it to the cross. Jesus became our living example of mercy and grace. He showed us how powerful compassion can be.

Father, you have greeted me with your mercy and breathed new life into my being. I'm undone by your love. Longing to draw others into the mystery of divine grace. Thank you for showing me the way. Thank you for the price you paid to free me. Thank you for your divine exchange.

Intercession

"Please let the boy go back with his brothers. How could I return to my father without the boy? I don't want to witness the woe and grief that would overtake my father."

GENESIS 44:34

You are a vessel of the Holy Spirit, filled with God-ideas and desires. If something grips your heart with passion, sympathy, and charity, it most likely echoes the desire of his. Your very being is surging with the life and heartbeat of God. You're a holy vessel, carrying his very nature. Never be afraid of what moves you. Never hold back the purity of intercession that rises from the deep wells of your spirit.

Your prayers of faith touch the heart of God. When you believe you're walking in communion with him, you intercede from a position of partnership. When you've embraced his faithfulness, you no longer beg for what you understand is his will. You simply believe and present your prayers in faith.

Father, I love doing life with you. It's the delight of my heart to pray your will over dark circumstances. To infuse faith into seemingly hopeless situations and invite you to the scene. Let me feel what moves your heart so I may pray with grace and faith.

Emotions

He began to weep so loudly that the Egyptians heard it—
even as far away as Pharaoh's house!

GENESIS 45:2

When we barricade our emotions in a protective shell and keep
them from surfacing, we deny ourselves an essential part of life.
Emotions are God's idea. They bring awareness to the dynamics of
our souls. They convey feelings and needs that connect us with the
hearts of others.

Emotions aren't shameful or wrong. Though they should not rule us,
we should not ignore them. The things that move us are important
to the Lord. We should process them with him until we find him
purifying, healing, and enjoying each one. Jesus lived emotionally
whole, and we see the depths of his emotions throughout the New
Testament. He loved fiercely, cried out from the cross when he felt
the pain of rejection, and always turned to the Father. Jesus is our
example—emotionally sound and wholly confident in the Father's love.

*Father, teach me how to embrace my emotions and to learn from
them without being ruled by them. Be the Lord of all I think and
feel. I open my heart to you. Bring wholeness into my life. Tear
down the walls that shield my emotions and flood every area of my
soul that needs healing.*

Come Close

His brothers stood there stunned, scared, and speechless.
Joseph said to his brothers, "Please, come close to me."
Inching forward, they came close to him.

GENESIS 45:3–4

How beautifully this displays the Lord's heart toward us. When we
stand in sin and shame, Jesus calls us close. When we feel we aren't
worthy, righteous, or important enough to stand in the presence
of the King, he wraps his royal robe around us and calls us family.
Nothing we have done or could ever do will separate us from
his love. Only our rejection of his mercy and love stops us from
experiencing it.

Our Father longs for you, even when you don't feel special. When
you've disappointed yourself, others, or the Lord, run to him. He's
waiting for you to draw close, regardless of how far away you feel.
His love is ever reaching to draw you in. You are family. You are his
beloved. Take a step closer to him and watch him run to meet you.

*Father, I want to see you clearly, with no shadow of sin to blur my
vision. Reveal your glory—alive and powerful within me. Burn away
the barriers I've erected that would keep you out. Fill me with your
righteousness so we may be one. I embrace your love today.*

Wholehearted Forgiveness

"Don't be grieved.
Don't blame yourselves
because you sold me here."

GENESIS 45:5

Only God can bring such profound healing to our souls that we can love our offenders. Not just love them by *faith* but honestly hold no hint of trauma, anger, or desire for revenge. This is the wonder of his glory. The power of forgiveness that Jesus has imparted to us.

There is only one prerequisite for experiencing a miraculous turnaround in how we see those who have afflicted us and caused us harm. It's a willingness to be like Jesus. Let's be honest—releasing our right to be angry or hurt is humbling. It's painful to our flesh to be transformed into his image and love as ferociously as Jesus does. But when we refuse the chains of unforgiveness, we're free to soar with him. We're able to heal the wounds of offense in others. Forgiveness is a beautiful gift.

Father, pour out your grace upon me. I want my life to be a pleasing offering—a fragrant incense rising before you. To release the beauty of forgiveness that rises from a soul set free. To be like you in every way. To welcome growth, even when it hurts, because I know you'll turn every pain into triumph.

Be Honest

"God sent me ahead of you to ensure that you would live
and have descendants. He has saved your lives through
this marvelous act of deliverance."

GENESIS 45:7

When Joseph dreamed that his family would bow before him,
he probably never imagined it would be for their benefit. With a
prideful heart, maybe he thought about how good it would feel to
finally have their acceptance and admiration. But here, as God's
purposes unfold, clarity comes. He's beginning to understand that
these abundant blessings aren't meant for him alone.

Unfortunately, this is often the case with us as well. We dream
about careers, ministry, fame, and other worldly acts with *us* on
our minds. Then God in his wisdom takes us through a long season
of purification until we finally have his heart on the matter. Once
we understand that we receive favor and anointing as a way to
bless others, the doors to our crazy big dreams start flying open.
Let's be honest about what our dreams mean to us and what our
motivations are.

*Father, my dreams are so much bigger than I am. Sometimes they
seem impossible, but maybe that's because I haven't understood
their greater purpose. If my motives haven't been pleasing to you,
show me. Purify me. Make me trustworthy. I humble myself before
you so I can flow with you in honor, humility, and total dependence.*

A Perspective Change

"It was God, not you,
who sent me here."

GENESIS 45:8

To find God's perspective, we first let go of our own. We
unreservedly release our need to control. We quiet ourselves in
his presence, and rather than talking, asking, and complaining,
we listen. If we'd stop pressing in so hard for a breakthrough and,
instead, actually believe it's coming, we'd find peace. And in that
peace, in the place where we enjoy him for who he is and not just
for what he can do, we see everything differently. Unfortunately, we
usually don't learn this lesson without suffering.

One of the things that happen when we've been broken and have
found God more profoundly than our suffering is that we begin to
see his hand in everything. (And when the enemy causes terrible
things to happen, we're immediately convinced God's good must
be on the other side.) Sometimes it takes not being able to see
straight and to be completely emptied of self to finally be able to
see through his eyes.

*Father, I want to know your heart more than I want to fight for my
own way. So I say yes to you today! Yes, to surrendering all. Yes, to
believing you can turn something terrible into something amazing.
Yes, to trusting despite what I see. Come and reveal yourself to me.
Give me your perspective.*

From Suffering to Abundance

"God has made me a father to Pharaoh,
the master of his entire household,
and the ruler over all of Egypt."

GENESIS 45:8

What does it take to become someone with immense influence and authority? Surely even the vilest, ungodliest people can step into this role. But when souls have been groomed in the presence of God through seasons of purifying and testing, they're able to serve with integrity and godly wisdom. They become a catalyst for change and aren't afraid to give God credit.

Joseph's heart was tested and proven trustworthy to handle immeasurable blessings. Like Joseph, when we feel our suffering is too much, too long, too personal, and too painful, we lean in and allow it to have its perfect work. We humble ourselves, worship (even if through tears), and yield to the Holy Spirit. Then God takes what the enemy means for harm and turns it for our good. The enemy's plan to take us out can actually set us up for God's most surprising and life-changing blessing—not just for us but for the encouragement of others.

Father, I want to be a vessel of honor. To yield myself to you over and over—as often as it takes for me to become more like you. I long to shine with your glory, but I'm beginning to understand that I must protect it with a cloak of humility. Have your way. Let the seasons of suffering make something beautiful out of me.

Freedom in Confession

"Hurry back to my father and tell him
that you have found me alive."

Genesis 45:9

There is something profoundly liberating about honesty and confession. When our hearts break open and allow truth to set us free. By admitting secret sin and asking for forgiveness. This is the opportunity Joseph was giving his brothers. By encouraging them to go to their father, Jacob, and telling him Joseph was alive, they would have to divulge a secret sin that had probably held them captive to guilt for many years.

Jesus has given us the same opportunity. He gives us the chance to experience the beauty of his cleansing blood and the power of his absolute forgiveness. All we need to do is be honest about the sins we try to ignore. We don't always need to share them with others, and if we do, it should be done with people we trust. But we can always be honest and open with the Lord.

Father, thank you for mercy. For highlighting attitudes, fears, selfishness, doubt, laziness, distractions, and even unhealthy busyness so I can lay them at your feet. When I feel the gentle nudge that things are out of balance or if I've sinned against you, myself, or others, by your grace, I will turn from sin and walk in newness of life.

The Power of Our Testimony

"Tell him, 'This is what your son Joseph says,
"God has made me ruler of all Egypt."'"

GENESIS 45:9

All that God does in us will become a testimony of encouragement for others. We're not usually thinking about the good that may come out of seasons of crisis, fear, confusion, or doubt, but what if we did? What if right in the muddied middle of our trial we use our imagination for something good? Rather than ruminating over what's afflicting us, we can dream about the many ways it will be redeemed. And one of those ways almost always comes through our opportunities to share God's faithfulness with those who need encouragement.

Your life with God—especially in times of trial and pain—becomes treasure for you to share with others. In the fires of affliction, gold has been formed in you that cannot be counterfeited. It's yours. His faithfulness to you is personal and meaningful, so share it!

Father, you've proven your love and kindness to me so many times in my life. I ask you for opportunities to pour out my truth—my treasure—into the lives of others. Help me not to miss the chances I have to share my testimony with those who come across my path.

Leaving a Legacy

"Come to me without delay. You will settle in the land of Goshen, where you will be near me—you and all your children and your grandchildren, your flocks and herds and all that you possess."

GENESIS 45:9–10

Joseph's miraculous breakthrough became a blessing passed down to his family line. What a sweet reminder for us. All that we go through, the lessons we learn, the encounters with God, the wisdom we gain, will one day become our legacy.

Let's leave behind a legacy of a passion, inspiration, and faith for generations to come by living each day in the splendor of God. Let's get to know his love and faithfulness so we can teach our children, grandchildren, and friends. When you embrace your unique personality, calling, and relationship with God, you shine with a facet of God's likeness that no one else has. Your life stands out and leaves an imprint on the hearts of those you love.

Father, I want to leave behind a legacy of endless love that reaches into hearts and memories of everyone I know. I want my life to be defined by my relationship with you. This is the legacy I will leave—a heart of fiery passion for you. Of undivided devotion regardless of temporary struggles.

Provision from Above

"For there will be five more years of famine,
but I will provide all that you need to live in Goshen.
You, your household, and all that you have will not live in poverty."

GENESIS 45:11

It's easy to get distracted by the news reports, poverty statistics, and unemployment rates, but we've been called to live from a higher reality. As children of God, we've been given the honor of living from the truth of his kingdom.

It may be a fact that you're surrounded by chaos and turmoil, but it doesn't have to be your truth. You've been given God's Word as a reminder of his will for your life. Don't let what's happening in the world determine what you'll believe. Choose to live in agreement with his Word and not with the bad news or unfavorable facts. Others may scoff at your faith, but you're called a believer, not a doubter, for a reason. Society may live by a specific set of rules and norms, but you live in the blessing of God!

Father, I say yes to your ways! Yes, to your provision. I will not be distracted by what I see and hear because I live from the reality of your heavenly kingdom. Your truth is my anchor. Your Word is my foundation and the meditation of my heart.

Family Restoration

Joseph threw his arms around Benjamin's neck, sobbing,
and Benjamin wept on Joseph's neck.

GENESIS 45:14

Restoration is a beautiful thing. A healing wonder, God's gracious gift. So many will read this verse and feel the sting of family separation. But God doesn't include these verses to burden our hearts. He blesses us to encourage us that restoration is *his* idea!

If you're feeling the heartache known by those who've experienced profound rejection or betrayal, a prodigal family member, or friends who've walked away, know that God understands your pain. But he doesn't want you to focus on the pain. He wants you to see with the eyes of faith. To pray with the understanding that his desires include healing and wholeness. With sanctified imagination, envision the day of restoration and hold it tight. Honor him by finding rest for your mind that reflects a heart of faith. To agree with him by declaring his truth and not focusing on the sorrow. Shake off the unbelief! Restoration is God's idea!

Father, I want to live with the attitude of faith that far exceeds what I see. You know my heart. You see the miracle that has to take place for things to change. But you also are filled with perfect wisdom and understand how to reach the hearts that you created. With faith, I praise you for the coming restoration!

Loved by Him

With tears streaming down his face, Joseph kissed each brother, one by one. After their tearful, emotional embrace, they took time to speak brother-to-brother.

GENESIS 45:15

God embraces the world as a whole but still takes time for each of us individually. He doesn't throw out the net of salvation and look the other way. He waits to greet us in a tearful, emotional embrace. To let us know that our lives matter to him. Each of us is important. He loves us and gave everything we need to make us family.

Ours is meant to be a relationship of interaction—personal, meaningful, and wonderfully intense. He meets with us one-on-one because he is a personal God. A personal friend. The One who dwells within us because there isn't a closer place to be. He longs to make himself known to us for no other reason than he loves us—loves *you*.

Let that sink in. Jesus loves *you*.

Father, just when it seems as though you've left and I'm feeling hopeless and alone, you remind me of your love. You rush to my side and draw me close. My heart opens to find you've never left. You're here, speaking to my heart. I matter to you. I am loved by you.

Reflect the Lord

Pharaoh said to Joseph, "Tell your brothers: 'Load your donkeys and return to Canaan. Get your father and your families and come back to me. I will give you the best of the land in Egypt, and you will enjoy the fat of the land.'"

GENESIS 45:17–18

Sometimes we forget that the way we conduct ourselves has a trickle-down effect. Our favor and reputations are meant to bless us but to also bless our families. To set them up for success. To pave the way for their dreams and callings to come to pass. To impart faith, purity, and a heart after the Lord. Our integrity will go before us publicly, but our behavior in private is also seen.

We know that only God sees the secrets of our hearts, but our families see them played out through our behavior and speech. Let's live in a way that reflects the Lord and stirs holy desire in our families. This is our blessing to give—day by day, moment by moment. And the good news is that it's never too late. As long as we're alive, we can demonstrate a heart set free. We still can model behavior that our families will remember forever.

Father, I pray that my actions, speech, and integrity will pave the way for my family. That the favor I have will become a blessing for them that opens doors for their future. Let my integrity and passion for you be contagious. And may I seek to represent you well, each day of my life.

November

Take the Risk

"Give no thought to leaving your possessions behind;
the best of all the land of Egypt will be yours."

GENESIS 45:20

When God asks us to follow him and leave everything behind,
it's much like the Scripture verse above. He already knows ahead
of time what our reservations will be, so he encourages us not to
give it another thought. There's nothing we can sacrifice that will
compare to the blessings we'll receive in exchange.

He will never push you to do something you aren't willing to do. But
if you'll let him, he'll remove every fear and show you your future
from his perspective. In tender compassion, the Lord will speak
grace and strength to every reservation. Don't be afraid of the huge
shifts in seasons—when he asks you to walk away from positions,
churches, groups, or jobs. His way is ultimately the best even if it
seems scary at first. Focus on him and take the risk. Following him is
always worth it!

*Father, I lay my fears at your feet. Whisk me away to where my
cares fade completely. Consume my every thought. I'll take the risk
and follow you wherever you lead. Fill my every step with more of
you. More of your grace, wisdom, and peace. Nothing I could ever
sacrifice compares to the joy of being with you.*

Worth the Wait

He sent his father ten donkeys
loaded with the best Egyptian goods.

GENESIS 45:23

Isn't it interesting that Joseph waited for so many years to reach out to his father? He could have told his father he was alive the minute Pharaoh promoted him. Instead, he waited for years to be reunited. This once impetuous young man had learned the importance of God's timing. Though his heart had obviously felt the weighty pain of separation, he trusted God to fulfill his promises.

Waiting on God's timing is difficult. We want to move, push, and manipulate our circumstances. We strive to make things happen because we often feel God's not moving fast enough or, perhaps, has forgotten his promise to us all together. Joseph could be trusted with the highest position in Egypt other than Pharaoh himself because he learned the value of absolute surrender to God. From the dungeons of persecution to the palaces of exaltation, he discovered that glorious breakthroughs are worth the wait. What an incredible model for us to follow.

Father, you know the desires of my heart. You understand the discomfort of waiting, and you use these times to strengthen my character and faith. I will let patience have its perfect work in me and trust your perfect timing. I will wait. I will trust. I will believe.

Grow in Peace

He sent his brothers off, admonishing them,
"Don't quarrel along the way." And they departed.

GENESIS 45:24

This is the lifestyle we've been called to. One that chooses peace above all else. One that pursues a kingdom mindset over the deafening lull of selfishness. The Lord yearns for us to mature. To step into our royal position and handle ourselves with Christlikeness. To lay aside our fleshly need to be right and have our own way.

The Lord cares about the condition of our hearts. When we notice a tendency to argue, prove ourselves right, or hold a grudge, it's time to humble ourselves in his presence. If we're honest about our short fuse or unhealthy habit of arguing and ask Jesus to get to the root of it, he will. Let's put aside finger-pointing and pay attention to what the Holy Spirit wants to teach us about our own hearts. When we choose the awareness of God's presence over our need to be right, we will grow in peace that surpasses all understanding.

Father, refine me with the flames of your sacred love. I humble myself before you and confess my tendency to argue. Forgive me for pridefulness. I want to be like you: kind, gracious, and filled with peace. I want to speak as you do. To become a true bride of Christ, shining in purity and righteousness.

Surprises

When they arrived, they ran to their father and announced,
"Joseph is still alive! Not only that, he is the ruler of all Egypt!"
The news so stunned Jacob that he nearly fainted.

GENESIS 45:26

Prayers that have long been prayed, situations that seem hopeless, the waiting that makes you wonder if he's forgotten—he sees it all, and he has the answer. In a surprising display, he will manifest his faithfulness. The Creator of all that is seen and unseen is not short on ideas for how to extend his hand of blessing. Just when you least expect it, the God of the miraculous will astonish you!

Nothing is impossible for God, and he loves to surprise you! He is the God of "suddenlies." The One who loves to breathe life into long-forsaken dreams. He has not forgotten you. In his perfect timing, he will surprise you and thrust you into the most significant breakthrough you've ever known. Never give up hope. It's not too late to step into something radical, new, and longed for. Allow your heart to dream again!

Father, even when it seems everything has fallen apart, you have a plan. My long-forgotten dreams are not forgotten by you. You will resurrect the ones you've placed in my heart. You will breathe fresh resolve and lead me by your Spirit.

Seasons of Change

Israel packed up all he had and went to Beersheba,
where he offered sacrifices to the God of his father Isaac.
God spoke to him in visions of the night.

GENESIS 46:1–2

On his way to miraculous provision and the fulfillment of God's promises, Israel pauses to honor God. He takes time to thank and worship the One who never fails. In this moment of transition, he worshiped and offered himself to God, afresh. And then, he receives a vision.

Our worship, seasoned with thankfulness and offered in total abandonment to God, will lead to fresh revelation. As we seek to honor him, especially in seasons of change, he pours out the grace we need for each new step. When doors of new opportunity open, it's important we pause and offer him our praise and acknowledge our need for his continued guidance. As we seek to keep the Lord as the center of our focus, all of the peripheral things fall into place. With eyes on him, he leads us perfectly.

Father, I bow before your marvelous splendor, knowing that without you, I am nothing. Every blessing, each surprising manifestation of your provision, humbles me and stirs me to praise. Thank you for leading me. Thank you for speaking to me during every season of change.

Adventures of Faith

"Do not be afraid to go to Egypt;
for I will make your descendants a great nation there."

GENESIS 46:3

Seasons of breakthrough are exciting, but sometimes that breakthrough is a direct result of stepping into uncharted territories. It can be nerve-racking if your focus isn't on the Lord. Fear will attempt to hold you back by reminding you of past failures or disappointments and fighting to keep you from forging ahead. But once the Lord confirms his will, don't let anything stop you!

All Jacob needed to know was that God would go with him. This is what comforts our hearts—knowing that he walks with us. We don't need all of the answers or to see the future ahead of time if we know that the King goes with us! This is our blessing—the adventures of faith that few dare to enjoy. The dawn of a new season, running with God into the unknown, means encountering dimensions of his faithfulness that you've never seen.

Father, I sense the light of a new day shining upon me. Unite my heart and mind so I can move in full cooperation with your Spirit, leaving no opportunity for the thieving hands of fear. I will stay close to you as you lead me on this adventure of faith.

Validation

They took their livestock and the possessions
they had acquired in Canaan and went to Egypt.

GENESIS 46:6

Imagine what was going through Joseph's brothers' minds as they packed up their life and moved to Egypt. They had witnessed the miracle of restoration and favor for the brother they once despised, the forgiveness they probably never imagined they'd receive, and they had bowed to him. Only God could have orchestrated something so extravagant and mind-blowing. Joseph's dreams had actually been from God!

Joseph didn't spend his life plotting revenge. Once Pharaoh exalted him, he didn't strive to prove himself to his family. He didn't brag about the favor he had. Instead, he walked before God in humility and integrity and put his family in God's hands. God was the one who validated Joseph *and* his dreams. And this is what he does for us when we live for an audience of One. Instead of striving to prove our worth, anointing, and call, we simply set our gaze on Jesus and trust him to endorse us.

Father, only you can confirm my calling. I don't need to jockey for position. I don't need to try and get anyone's attention or try to prove that my dreams are valid and God-sent. I only need to set my heart on knowing you, living for you, and obeying your voice. You will do the rest.

A Life Worth Living

Israel said to Joseph, "I am ready to die,
now that I have seen you and know that you are still alive."

GENESIS 46:30

Think of all the years Jacob spent mourning. For two decades, he gave himself over to grief, having declared from the moment he believed Joseph was dead that he would spend the rest of his life in mourning. God had spoken to Jacob before; perhaps if he had asked the Lord, God would have told Jacob the truth.

The enemy wants to trap us. To lie to us and steal our hope so we will be miserable and lose our desire to enjoy life. Many times, the afflictions seem worse than they are. We think circumstances are beyond redemption. We allow suffering to skew our way of thinking. Instead of asking the Lord for his perspective, we resign ourselves to a life of sorrow and miss discovering the surprising truth. In every moment of pain, there is always a deeper truth.

Father, I was created to hear your voice. Speak to me. Shine your light into my deepest sorrow. Reveal the truth from your point of view. I don't want to give up and waste my life. Heal my heart. Reintroduce me to faith and love so I will have a life worth living.

His Beloved

Pharaoh asked the men,
"What is your occupation?"

GENESIS 47:3

Society wants to define us by what we do. It is true that, to some degree, what we do is an extension of who we are. The jobs we have may not always show it, but instead, our actions, words, hobbies, and creative expressions do. Still, who we are is at the core of something much more significant.

When we realize our life is hidden with God in Christ, we catch a glimpse of our worth. And by accepting this love—this mysterious, spiritual, profound, and eternal love—we find ourselves. We look in the mirror and see worth and beauty. We are his beloved. And everything we do, every belief and value system, even the way we behave and the choices we make, are derived from this foundation. We are more than what we do, but let's remember that, ultimately, what we do rises from who we believe we are.

Father, I want all that I do to blossom from my identity in Christ. I want to love myself by taking care of my needs, spirit, soul, and body. I desire the grace to pursue the desires of my heart because I believe you've created me for greatness. But most of all, I want to know you because by knowing you, I will discover my true self.

Impart His Blessing

Jacob blessed Pharaoh.

GENESIS 47:10

You will reign with Christ for all eternity, but he has called you to begin that journey now. To be confident in your identity so that you can stand before the world's most famous men and women as the Lord's mouthpiece.

As royalty, it's time to think differently. To behave with dignity, grace, compassion, and wisdom. To season our words with the flavor of heaven and release his heart. To impart a blessing and represent God's kingdom to those who don't know him. The things that move society mustn't move us. It crucial we guard our hearts against offense. Regardless of the caliber of people we stand before, whether we agree with them or not, God calls us to impart his blessing. It's his blessing that softens a hardened heart.

Father, I believe that when the words I speak are in agreement with yours, it will cause shifts in the atmosphere. Help me behave wisely and to be above reproach. May I represent you well—a bride arrayed in splendor. May I stand in confidence, wholly relying on your grace.

Hold On to Faith

> "If there are any competent men among them,
> put them in charge of my own livestock."
>
> GENESIS 47:6

Not only did Pharaoh give Joseph's family provision, but he also appointed some of his brothers as his official herdsman. The blessings of God were continuously flowing because of Joseph—the man who suffered long but kept his mind fixed on God.

Too often, we focus on negativity. Those times we're slammed with one bad thing after another. Just because we go through seasons (sometimes long seasons) of difficulty doesn't mean it's our lot in life. We must be careful not to agree with opposition as if it's the way life will always be. Joseph lived for many years without any sign that his dreams would come to pass. The family who was supposed to love him had rejected him. But suffering didn't become his mindset. He held on to faith. Held tightly to the Lord, and eventually, everything changed. Now, the blessings of God were continuously flowing not only for Joseph but also for his brothers!

Father, forgive me for the times I've viewed my life from the standpoint of disappointment, pain, and disillusionment. Today, I choose the mindset of an overcomer. I set my gaze on you and choose to believe that you are turning things around for my good. Everything can change in a moment.

Wisdom

Joseph said to the people,
"Today I have acquired for Pharaoh you and all your land."

GENESIS 47:23

Joseph's wisdom resulted in one of the greatest transfers of wealth ever recorded. The years he spent listening to God's voice resulted in his total dependence upon God and absolute trust in following his instructions. Now, his finely tuned ear and willingness to act on what he believed God said became an extravagant blessing for Pharaoh. More than likely, as Pharaoh witnessed Joseph's God-given wisdom, it led him to seek God for himself.

Wisdom isn't meant for us alone. It is designed to guide our lives and be dispersed to those around us. God wants us to discern his voice. To take risks when we believe we've heard him but aren't sure, so we will grow in confidence. As we do, we increase in wisdom that will not only change our lives but also the lives of those around us.

Father, I ask for the wisdom that only time with you can bring. Give me ears to hear and a heart to understand. Strengthen me and give me the courage to follow even your faintest whispers. I bow before you today, knowing that no matter how smart or talented I am, I need you. I need your wisdom.

Represent Him Well

"You may keep the rest for planting your fields and for food
for yourselves and your families to nourish your household
and your little ones."

GENESIS 47:24

With the gift of wisdom comes compassion. It's impossible to have the mind of Christ without experiencing his heart. Wisdom sees beyond itself. It gives us eyes to view trials and predicaments with hope. We believe that God alone holds the answer, and he is willing to share it with us.

Joseph's wisdom resulted in Pharaoh's exceeding wealth, but it also provided for every person affected by the famine. He became a testimony not only of wisdom but also of God's abundant compassion. He never abused his authority and resisted the temptation to become opportunistic. Joseph was a man of integrity and honor who represented God well. May we learn these lessons of humility, integrity, confidence, and absolute dependence upon God that not only set us up to be blessed but also enable us to be a blessing to others.

Father, awaken me to the truth of who I am in you. Give me the grace to stand tall and the courage to bow low. Thank you for allowing me to know the joy, honor, responsibility, and humility of carrying your glorious Spirit within me. May I always represent you well.

Awaken Dreams

Jacob lived in Egypt for seventeen years
and lived a total of one hundred and forty-seven years.

GENESIS 47:28

The kindness of God is astounding. He not only blessed Jacob and Joseph with sweet reunion, but he also gave them seventeen years to spend together. How healing this must have been! After many years of grieving, Jacob experiences the therapeutic streams of joy.

This God of restoration has not forgotten you. Nor has he given up on the dreams you thought had died. What were they? Family restoration, freedom for a lost one, desire for ministry or career— whatever desires stirred in your heart that were placed there by God (not by the well-meaning confessions of men) are still important. If you once burned with hope and faith, absolutely convinced that a particular desire was his will, awaken that hope again! Time gives us wisdom to discern where we've missed him or heard him clearly. And if we heard him, we mustn't give up! Our latter years can be sweeter than our former.

Father, I have no idea how you'll make my dreams come to pass. Some things have long been forgotten but not by you. In this season, remind me of the desires that came from you. It's not too late for you to extravagantly change my life. I will partner with faith as you lead the way.

Eternally Faithful

"When I go to rest with my fathers, I want you to carry me
out of Egypt and bury me where they are buried."

GENESIS 47:30

At the end of his days, Jacob asked to be buried in the land of
promise, near the spot where the Messiah would one day be
crucified. Like his father Abraham, he was looking for a city whose
builder and maker was God. His heart longed to see the fulfillment
of the Holy Scriptures in regards to Christ. This man of faith looked
forward to his day of resurrection. And the day Jesus rose from the
dead, his prayer was answered as "holy ones" came out of their
graves (Matthew 27:52–53).

God knows every desire of our hearts. Every outlandish, extravagant
longing that leads to him touches him and catches his attention. When
our deepest longings point to the Lord, he does not dismiss them.
Even at the end of our days, he does not ignore sacred yearnings. We
may not understand delays to prayer, but we can rest assured that
God is eternally faithful. He will answer our purest desires.

*Father, I long for you to manifest yourself more clearly. But as I
wait, I'm pressing into your presence. Catching glimpses of your
beauty as I sit with you. Through the power of your resurrection,
I access your glory by faith, until the day I see you face-to-face
without hindrance.*

Our Strength

Israel worshiped and leaned on the top of his staff.

GENESIS 47:31

At the end of his days, Israel leaned upon God. His strength was not his own. He had learned the lesson we all must learn—that God alone is our source of strength. Through the things Israel suffered, he learned that God is greater, more powerful, and more faithful than he ever imagined. And now, he worshiped.

This story reflects so many of our lives. In the ups and downs of life, through sorrow, joy, and suffering, we are continuously learning. Constantly discovering the beauty of life with the Lord. In each season, we grow into his image. Becoming more dependent upon him until we are convinced that surrender to the Lord allows *his* strength to shine through. From our posture of humility and deeper understanding, we worship with pure hearts. Let this be our testimony—that at the end of our days, we are joyfully dependent upon the One who is our strength.

Father, your faithfulness is proven to me over and over. The longer I walk with you, the more sincere my praise. You are the reason I sing. You are the desire of my heart more than any other. I lean upon you now and forever. You are my strength.

Destiny

Jacob said to Joseph, "The God who is more than enough appeared to me at Bethel...where he blessed me! He said to me, 'I will make you fruitful and multiply your descendants until I have made you a company of nations.'"

GENESIS 48:3–4

Our destiny is bigger than ourselves. It affects our families and those who surround us. It's vital that we take our calling to heart, as we are a part of an ongoing strategy to reveal Jesus in his fullness. It's time to live, move, and have our being saturated in the reality of the Lord so it drips from us everywhere we go.

More than anything we seek to accomplish, we must find ourselves by finding Christ. Who we are and are meant to be is found as we live for him. Destiny is wrapped up *in him*. He is our inheritance. His glory is the destiny we're meant to pass along! The life we live in his presence must be imparted to our children (physical and spiritual). It's so important that we share the wisdom and revelations he's given to us. To impart a blessing that others will carry long after we're gone.

Father, I want to live a life worth replicating. To instill a longing for your presence to those who spend time with me. To be so lost in you that I find myself. Reveal yourself to me, speak to my heart, and I will release the reality of your love to others.

Yes, He Can

> "Yes, I claim Ephraim and Manasseh as mine."
>
> GENESIS 48:5

The name *Manasseh* means "God made me forget." This was Joseph's proclamation of God's goodness when he named his firstborn son. God wants us to be so overwhelmed with his goodness that we forget the pain of our past.

The healing power of God isn't just physical. It extends to every part of us—spirit, soul, and body—so we can be whole. It's God's will for us to believe for something not even the best therapist can help us achieve—to be set free from the pain of a memory. God alone can do this. He can drain previous traumas of lingering poison because he is the antidote. He is the One who still does miracles. He is the One who does the unimaginable. He is the One who sets us free!

Father, I've lived for too long with memories that cause me pain and sorrow. Today, I'm stretching my faith to believe for freedom. I invite you into these memories. Show me how you see them. Let me find your redemption and healing for each one.

Double Blessings

"Yes, I claim Ephraim and Manasseh as mine."

GENESIS 48:5

The name of Joseph's second-born, *Ephraim*, means "double fruitfulness." It was a declaration of thanksgiving and praise as Joseph conveyed the abundant faithfulness of God in his life. God not only rescued him from the dungeons of tragedy, but he also set him up to be as influential and esteemed as Pharaoh! He gave him abundance that overflowed into every area of his life and radically affected the people of his day.

This is God's way! It's time we stopped settling for sprinkles of his goodness and believed for the radical blessings. God wants to exceed our wildest dreams—not simply so that we'll be blessed but so we can also share his overflowing kindness with others. It's time for the upswing!

Father, now I understand that every extravagance is given to me to share. You want me to experience your abundance, and I want to be a good steward of your heavenly rewards. As your blessings overtake me, I will keep my heart set on you. Escort me into deeper waters of your inexplicable glory so that I may release it everywhere I go.

Hear God

"...my two oldest, Reuben and Simeon."

GENESIS 48:5

The record of Jacob's twelve sons gives us a type of self-portrait. From the sins of his first four children to the last two who were without fault, we find symbolic meaning, which points to Christ and his redeemed church. In the meaning of his sons' names, we catch a reflection of ourselves. A hint of our prophetic destiny.

For example, the name *Simeon* means "one who hears." This is the blessing that has been bestowed upon us. We are those who know the sound of our Father's voice. We're blessed to recognize the internal whispers of his love as they play a chord in our hearts. Without striving or doubting, we simply lean into his presence and commune with him in the chambers of glory. He created us for this. Designed us to hear the sweetness of his love that is deeper than external, audible words.

Father, there's so much on my mind. So many things I could pray about, but instead, I simply want to be with you. To sense your tangible presence as you manifest yourself. To honor you with an attentive heart. Speak to me. I'm listening.

Mercy's Kiss

Joseph then removed them from his father's knees and bowed low
in respect before his father with his face to the ground.

GENESIS 48:12

What a tender, moving, and powerful moment for Jacob and
Joseph! Jacob had just blessed Joseph's sons. A moment in time
they probably never thought would happen. God is kinder than we
imagine. He will do more than we hope for if we continue to set our
affection on him and keep him first.

God's kindness opens our eyes so we can see his love in a new light.
It leads us to repentance and draws us into joy. It's overwhelming,
better than wine. Relentlessly, he pursues us, knowing that we can
find in him what we desire most in this life. His love is both a tender
and powerful kindness. The way he invites us close, despite how far
we may have drifted, is mercy's kiss upon our life.

*Father, to be loved by the very One who is love is the most
extravagant of blessings. How undone I am by your kindness and
affection. Every breath I breathe reminds me of your faithfulness.
Each moment in your arms reminds me of your love.*

A Legacy of Devotion

"May the God of my fathers, Abraham and Isaac,
who lived devoted to him..."

GENESIS 48:15

During Jacob's final days, he spoke of his ancestors with well-deserved respect. The greatest honor he could give them was to convey to his son and grandsons the legacy they had left—lives served in devotion to the Lord. This was how he remembered them.

How will we be remembered? What is the testimony we will leave behind? Let's not forget that our zeal for the Lord is contagious—passed down to future generations. Let's leave an inheritance worth imitating and a legacy of righteousness, holy devotion, and radical zeal. When love for God and others is our life's quest, those we love will remember it in their hearts and minds. Our family will remember not only how much we love God but also how well it shines through our life.

Father, my heart's cry is that I will live with a sincere and evident devotion to you that others will want to follow. I want to live a life worth imitating. A life of unquenchable devotion and obedience to your every word. I want love to be the driving force behind all I do and say.

The Will of God

"Not that way," Joseph said to his father,
"Here, father, put your right hand on the firstborn's head."
But his father refused and said, "I know, my son, I know."

Genesis 48:18–19

As the Spirit of prophecy fell upon Jacob, he knew it was God's will to bless and honor Ephraim above his older brother Manasseh, as was the custom. Though Joseph stepped in and tried to correct the seeming error, Jacob remained firm. This was the will of God, and the desire of man would not sway him.

God's blessing always wins over maneuvering and posturing for favor. Though we may desire to force his hand or manipulate circumstances in our favor, the most significant promotions come from God. When God chooses to bless us, no one can stop him. Blessing is his choice. Let's learn the lesson it took Jacob a lifetime to master. It is far better to wait until the blessing of God is seen than to force something that either isn't his will or isn't in God's timing.

Father, forgive me for trying to force things to happen ahead of your schedule. You know my heart. You know the areas I must mature before promotion comes. Pour out your grace so I will learn the lessons I need to learn. With patience, I will humbly trust you.

Lessons in Reflection

"The Angel who has delivered me from all harm..."

GENESIS 48:16

Instead of moaning and complaining about his hardships and the things he had to endure, Jacob declared that the mercy of God preserved him. Amidst his wrestling and immaturity, he learned the Lord was gracious and faithful. It took many years for Jacob to understand this lesson.

As we look back over trials and suffering, it's beneficial to pause and reflect on the many ways God met us. What did we learn? How did we grow in character and maturity as a result of God's mercy? Where did we see his hand of protection? Christ, the Angel of the covenant, redeems us from all evil, but sometimes we take it for granted instead of thanking him. Let's purposefully reminisce with the Lord and call to mind the many times he's delivered us from harm and directed our lives. Let's take time to process and even journal the essential things he's taught us, so we won't forget.

Father, I don't want to waste one trial. I want to be intentional about growing in character and Christlikeness. Instead of walking away from pain, I will sit with you and process what I'm learning about your love, power, and kindness. I want to hear both your encouragement and correction.

Transformation

Jacob blessed them that day.

GENESIS 48:20

The hands of Jacob that once deceived and grasped for what wasn't his finally become hands of blessing. Out of his brokenness comes an overflow of life. The *heel-holder* becomes the *blessing-giver*. God knows what he's doing. He understands that the hardships we go through will serve to refine, strengthen, and purify us if we lean upon him.

Transformation in the way we think, our lifestyle of extravagant faith, and our levels of surrender to God take time. But as we walk with him day after day, we're growing. Sometimes he carries us over the tumultuous terrain, sometimes we stumble, but most often, we get stronger, become more nimble and more focused. And soon, we're guiding others along these unleveled paths, helping them find their way.

Father, have your way in me. Transform me into your image so I reflect your light. Strengthen and uphold me with your righteous right hand. Change the way I think. Refine every motive. Mend my brokenness with your golden glory so nothing but beauty comes pouring forth.

Listen

"Let me prophesy to you about your future destinies."

GENESIS 49:1

God wants to speak to you, and he wants to speak through you. Others may agree with the darkness and gloom of this world, but his words will bring life to your soul and strength to your heart. When your mind is consumed with thoughts of God and you turn away from the chaos, you'll notice his Spirit bubbling up from within. All you need to do is posture your heart in agreement with his and believe that he wants to speak to you.

Sometimes he will show you images—glimpses of his plan. Sometimes his voice sounds like peace: quiet, reassuring, and contradicting fundamental understanding. Often, Scripture will alight upon your heart, reminding you what he's already said. But in all these ways and more, you *do* hear him.

Father, you created me to hear your voice. I don't have to be good enough to listen to my Father. I don't have to beg. You've already paid the price for me and invited me to come close. I simply need to believe that you long to speak to the ones you love.

Declarations of Truth

"Come together and listen to me,
O sons of Jacob."

GENESIS 49:2

One of the shocking things in the Bible is that the names of Jacob's sons are inscribed on heaven's gates of pearls. As spiritual sons and daughters, the history and transformation of Jacob's sons reflect our lives. We, too, are transforming, maturing, growing in the ways of holiness.

Only God could have given Jacob such profound insight and revelation. In the natural, he couldn't have known the significance his sons (who were not all gems but rather contaminated by sin) would carry into eternity. God can transform the worst of humanity and turn them into pearls. We may not always understand the power of the prophetic declarations we speak, but he does. We may not understand how light can chase away the darkness, but it does.

Father, I'm so glad you see the end from the beginning. By your great wisdom, you not only declare the truths that contradict natural circumstances, but you also share that wisdom with me. You are God. You are the One who transforms us into vessels of righteousness.

A Warning and an Example

"Reuben, my firstborn, you are my strength and the firstfruits of my manhood. You are preeminent in pride."

GENESIS 49:3

When pride stands at the forefront of our lives, it steals our blessing and perverts our identity. It isn't wrong to know your place in God's kingdom, but with that knowledge, humility must also come. It is by grace alone we stand. This truth keeps us free from the sin of pride.

True spiritual maturity understands its worth but doesn't flaunt itself. Jesus was our example of selflessness. Our Lord, the true firstborn and honored Son. The strength of heaven revealed to us. Confident and compassionate, he lifted others up when he bowed low to carry the weight of our sin. He excels them all in honor! He is our example to follow.

Lord, you are glorious and excellent in all you do. Prince of glory, all blessing and honor are yours forever! You are the pattern I want to follow. The example of strength and humility I want to emulate. I want nothing to do with pride. I humble myself in your presence and ask you to examine my heart.

Purity

"You will no longer excel,
for you have slept with my concubine
and defiled yourself in your father's bed!"

Genesis 49:4

Joseph received Reuben's birthright because he fled from the very corruption Reuben indulged in (Genesis 39:7–12). The double portion inheritance of the firstborn, the possession, and privileges, Reuben forfeited because of immorality. Joseph didn't lie with Potiphar's wife and gained by purity what Reuben lost by defilement.

We must take the message of purity seriously. It may be easy to dismiss sexual promiscuity as an acceptable part of our ever-changing society, but holiness is still God's way. For those who sin, mercy is always available—ready to make us white as snow. But there is often a price to pay. Like Reuben, sinful acts can disqualify you from spiritual privilege and leadership.

Father, I submit every thought, each desire, and every part of myself—spirit, soul, and body. I want to be a vessel of purity. Give me the grace to stand firm in my convictions and to honor you with my lifestyle. Cleanse, restore, and forgive me for any time I've given myself over to immorality. Thank you for being the God of restoration and forgiveness.

Powerful Intercession

> "You are unstable—
> as turbulent as floodwaters."
>
> GENESIS 49:4

Reuben had lost his birthright because of sin. It seemed his fate was sealed, and the inheritance destined for his family forsaken. But four hundred years later, Moses prayed for Reuben's tribe, and restoration came. Because of Christlike intercession, his descendants finally received a *grace-blessing*. Standing in heaven right now is a pearly gate with the tribal name of Reuben.

We've seen the price of sin visited upon sons and daughters for generations. Addictions, poverty, hopelessness that run in the family. But faithful intercession can change everything! Jesus has the power to reverse every curse. He holds the key to turn away death (loss of inheritance) and cause multiplication. Regardless of what the past has held, our grace-blessing can still be released. If we've learned anything from the story of resurrection, it is that it's not over even when it's over.

Father, release your blessing. Restore the families of those whose sin has stolen their inheritance. Reverse the curse! Let mercy wash away the past and set them up to receive a glorious inheritance. Resurrect the destinies that the enemy has stolen.

December

Lay Aside Anger

"Cursed be their anger,
for it is fierce."

GENESIS 49:7

It's time to part with everything that doesn't reflect the beauty of the One who lives inside us. It's a privilege to live in the glory of freedom. It's our destiny to be known as people of joy, peace, and grace.

When we lay aside our right to be angry or hurt, we are stepping into an eternal blessing. We're experiencing the freedom we were created for by letting go of offense. Our words hold the power of life and death, so we must choose them wisely. Let's not ignore the emotion of anger rising within us but submit our feelings to the Lord, quickly. Even if we need to speak a word of rebuke or correction, he will show us how to do it in a way that doesn't belittle someone. God alone can give us peace in place of anger, but it's up to us to value it and reach for it.

Father, have mercy on me and give me grace! Help me to guard my lips so I don't hurt others with my words and sin against you. Teach me when to speak and when to stay silent. Let everything I say be seasoned with love and integrity. Instead of feeling empowered by holding on to anger, I will enjoy the power of hope and joy.

Priesthood

"Simeon and Levi, you are two of a kind
and brothers in crime."

GENESIS 49:5

Our choice to embrace change and become who God created us to be is monumental! We are able to impact generations we may never meet on this side of heaven. Leaving our sin behind, we go forward into the ways of priesthood—pouring out love to our heavenly Father and ministering his presence and blessing to others. The power of our transformed lives is often far-reaching in ways we never imagined it would be. Just look at Levi and the impact his life continues to have!

Because Levi's natural ways were transformed, he was privileged to carry God's Urim and Thummim as a priest (Deuteronomy 33:8). The Levitical priesthood became his legacy. From the story of the Levites, we learn that God can redeem and transform us even if we have lost our blessing because of past failures.

Father, I want my life to be a testimony of your merciful redemption. I long to live before you in purity and power, ministering to you in intimate worship. Change me, day by day, moment by moment, until I reflect the glory of the One within.

Let Us Roar

"Judah, you are like a young lion
who has devoured its prey."

GENESIS 49:9

Judah is a wonderful picture of the One known as the mighty Lion of Judah. This is the prophecy of Jesus, who came from Judah to devour his prey. He is not a raging lion but a resting one who has conquered every foe. He crouched and took up his cross but now lies down in perfect peace. His victory is complete.

Our Savior-King has destroyed the power of death when he was raised and seated at God's right hand. Today, like a lioness, he guards us with tender love and compassion. He has taught us to roar at injustice and exposes every lie. Let's not be passive! Let's exercise our faith and follow in his footsteps. Let's be bold and do great exploits. When fear is conquered within us, giants are defeated around us. Let a roar rise from within, and it will silence the voice of the enemy.

Father, when darkness screams and hope fades, you roar with truth. Teach me to be like you—defeating my foes from the posture of peace and confidence. Thank you for devouring the plans of the enemy and securing my victory in you, mighty Lion of Judah!

Represent the King

"The obedience of nations belongs to him."

GENESIS 49:10

Jesus. All-powerful, all-knowing, all-wise. Unshaken by the turmoil in the nations. Looking for those who will boldly live in partnership with him—unafraid to stand in their identity. To be pure. To be confident. To burn. He is with us. And everywhere we go, we represent our King.

It is time for us to join him in unrelenting faith. To pray for the nations. To cry out for mercy. To know his justice will have its way. It's vital we stand in holiness. Crucial that we become the people of faith, action, love, and compassion he's called us to be. There's a shaking in the heavens that's awakening the earth. A call to remember that our merciful King has called us to rule and reign with him. It's time to take a stand. To know what we believe so we can burn with power that sets souls ablaze. It's time to remember that the nations belong to him. Let's love them. One person at a time.

Father, I want to carry your Spirit with honor. To part with what's culturally acceptable and burn with what's eternally true. To love others fiercely and see souls set free. I want to live unafraid. Your partner. Your bride. Your set-apart one.

A Servant's Heart

"He will tether his donkey to the vine."

GENESIS 49:11

Jesus has tethered his servant nature to us, the vine. He has given us an example to follow that contradicts the ways of the world. The need to be right, feel entitled, be easily offended, and fight for our own way is contrary to an unselfish heart. The Lord came to teach us that the greatest among us came to serve. He did not seek his own way but did what he saw his Father do.

To emulate the Lord, we, too, must tether ourselves to him and his giving nature. We aren't afraid to serve, but we also find balance by following the leading of the Holy Spirit. We are compelled to love not out of obligation but as an extension of his Spirit inside. Today, let's pay attention to the needs of others and demonstrate the nature of God.

Father, if there are any selfish, lazy tendencies in me, reveal them. I want to shine your brilliant compassion and servant's heart into the lives of those you bring before me. You are my example. May I take what you've given me and release it freely as your Spirit leads.

Tap into Glory

"...and his purebred colt to the choicest branch."

GENESIS 49:11

We are the choice branches Jesus has chosen to share his glory with. It is through our servant nature that we tap into the glory of our Savior. His righteousness and purity have paved a golden pathway into his presence. He is the way, the truth, and light guiding our lives.

Humility and servanthood demonstrate our ability to handle the riches of his kingdom. We can be trusted to carry his anointing when our aim is to make him famous and not ourselves. We are the seekers of his heart. Servants dedicated to the message of the cross. Willing to believe for the outrageous miracles by bowing low and giving ourselves to this one holy pursuit—that he will be magnified on the earth.

Father, may the confession of my mouth, the humble posture of my heart, and the actions I take point to you. Thank you for sharing your glory with me. For inviting me to partner with you in both servanthood and the manifestation of your power. Release yourself through me.

The Anointing

"He will wash his garments in wine."

GENESIS 49:11

The garments (gifts) of the Lord have been washed in wine (soaked in the anointing of the Holy Spirit). It is this anointing that has made you a fruitful vine. The sweet fragrance of his life is meant to be shared through you.

The Lord's robe of righteousness wraps around you. The crown of divine royalty sits upon your head, and the anointing of his Spirit dwells within you. Jesus had made you worthy. Standing beside you is your greatest cheerleader. The One who celebrates you and reminds you who he's called you to be. He equips you with all you need to walk in victory and to release it to the world around you. His anointing will do through you what you cannot do alone, but it's up to you to step out of your comfort zone and do what he's asking you to do—moment by moment, situation by situation. You are anointed!

Father, sometimes I get stuck in my head. Trying to reason away the things I think you want me to do because they seem so much bigger than myself. The truth is they are bigger! But they all point to you. So meet with me as I step out. Flow through me as I give the world a taste of your love.

Gloriously Redeemed

"He will wash...his robe in the blood of grapes."

GENESIS 49:11

The righteousness purchased through the precious blood of Jesus robes you. No longer does the cloak of heaviness weigh you down and confuse your identity. Clothed in splendor, you look a lot like your Father. Everywhere you go, you carry within you the absolute holiness, purity, and power of heaven itself.

For all eternity, you are clothed in radiant splendor—wrapped in the finest linens of extravagant love. Look in the mirror and see what Jesus sees—you—beautiful, powerful, confident, and compassionate. You will never be the same now that you have awakened to the truth of who you are. Stop looking around you for someone to confirm your worth. Jesus already has.

Father, thank you for reminding me that I am a vessel of honor. Shame, guilt, and lies of unworthiness are not going to hold me back. I am a child of God! I have been gloriously redeemed by the price of sacred blood. I am yours, and you love me exactly the way I am.

His Gaze

"His eyes are more exhilarating than wine."

GENESIS 49:12

Come face-to-face; look into his eyes. The Lord's sight is set on you. Do you see your face reflected in the brightness of his gaze? His intentions are fixed on you. You are the object of his affection. You have captivated him.

The intoxicating sweetness of his love is better than wine. It is more alluring and fulfilling than the pleasures of this life. With relentless zeal, he's pursuing you. So drink deeply. Satisfy every longing by drinking in the splendor that flows from his heart. Feast on his Word. Taste the glory of his truth. Once you experience this love, nothing else could ever fulfill you. Nothing else is as exhilarating. His truth gladdens the heart. He is the new wine that flows within.

Father, your eyes are upon me—empowering me and not condemning. I have found my worth in the passion of your gaze. Because of your suffering love that brought me near, I stand before you now—finding confidence in the price you've paid. Your love pierces my heart and sets it ablaze with unquenchable zeal to know you more. My eyes are locked on yours. I cannot look away.

Found in Him

> "...and his teeth whiter than milk."
>
> GENESIS 49:12

The Lord's white teeth speak of the vigor and healthy power of his person. He is rich in love! Abundant in power! He has drunk deeply and without measure of the Holy Spirit, eating honey and milk from the heart of God. He is steeped in wonder. Offering you his cup of revelation.

The Lord wants you to sink your teeth into the truth of who you are in him. You are not insignificant and powerless. It doesn't matter what the world says about you or how it has smothered you in its lies. Shake off everything that contradicts the reality of what he has said. All that he's done, everything the Lord says about himself, is now a part of who you are. His strength is yours. His wisdom is readily available. His anointing, peace, creativity, favor, and everything else you need are gifts found in him.

Father, that's it! I'm done agreeing with doubt, fear, guilt, or lies of insignificance. You have carved my worth into your hands for all to see. I am beautiful. Worthy. Strong. Desired. All that I am or ever hope to be is determined by the person and victory of Jesus!

Beyond Borders

> "Zebulun will settle along the seashore
> and become a safe harbor for ships,
> and his borders will extend to Sidon."

GENESIS 49:13

The Lord calls you to extend the testimony of Jesus far behind the borders of culture and religious belief. The anointing and glory you carry speak volumes when you present it in love. Truth spoken in love, seasoned with wisdom, and empowered by the Holy Spirit demolishes walls of separation.

Sometimes we complicate things. It's not our job to convince people of the truth; it's simply our job to introduce them to the love of God so his love can woo their hearts. It is the anointing that sets people free, and very often, our daily acts of friendship, kindness, and love release that anointing. Yes, love speaks truth, which is sometimes hard for people to hear, but if the Holy Spirit leads us, he'll weave his truth in with tender care.

Father, help me not to miss the divine appointments—those invitations to pour your love into someone else. Forgive me for not paying attention. I don't have to worry about touching the multitudes—I just need to notice the one in front of me.

The Honor of Prayer

"Issachar is a strong donkey
lying down between its saddlebags."

Genesis 49:14

A horse loves speed, but a donkey is made for carrying burdens. A horse needs blinders, or distractions will easily spook it. A donkey is focused and sure-footed—attention fixed on the trail ahead, enduring hard conditions with little rest. This sounds like an intercessor!

The men of Issachar are noted in Scripture as those "who understood the times and knew what Israel should do" (1 Chronicles 12:32 NIV). Those who pray God's heart are unshaken by shifting conditions. They're convinced God's Word is true. They stand in faith with nothing but a firm belief directing their focus. Issachar was the smallest, least mentioned tribe in the Bible. Intercessors may feel insignificant, but they are the powerhouses. They are the ones who hold the promises of God with conviction and focused intent. They are the ones who believe God is worth believing.

Father, there is nothing as amazing as knowing your heart. You are the reason I stand in faith when the odds seem to be against me. Your Word is the foundation I stand upon. Your love is the conviction that sets my soul ablaze.

His Resting Place

"When he sees that his resting place is good..."

GENESIS 49:15

The rest of God is available in every season. Whether you're experiencing a stretch of busyness, a time of sorrow, or a period of joy, the peace and rest of God are always available because they are found *in him*. You don't have to be in a season of stillness to take time to bask in his love.

When unpleasant circumstances pile up on you, slamming you with one thing after another, finding time to be quiet in the arms of God is vital. Pay attention to your body and your emotions. If you notice that you're physically tired, easily triggered (quick to anger, etc.), or feel overwhelmed, it's time to love yourself. It's time to rest. Start by physically resting (let the chores go undone for a day) and then intentionally soaking in the presence of God. *His resting place is good.*

Father, there's nothing like resting in the stillness of your love. Each moment I'm in your arms, rivers of peace cascade over my soul. Each movement of your heart silences the noise in my head. I'm so grateful for this love.

His Portion

"His portion is so pleasant..."

GENESIS 49:15

All that Jesus is—every victory and every provision—is ours. Paid for by his precious blood. Even during trials, his presence is our place of refuge. Right now, as we stand on earth, facing whatever joys or sorrows, the Bible says we are also seated in heavenly places (Ephesians 2:6).

Heavenly life is the portion he shares with us. It's the peace that blossoms from our history with God. It taps into grace. Builds pleasant walls of faith that may shake but will never crumble. This is our portion—Jesus. He is the undeniable reality that comforts us even when life has dealt a weighty blow. Everything we need to walk in victory is already ours. So let's align our thinking with his promise of grace. This is our portion and our inheritance.

Father, I invite you into my daily, my mundane, and my outrageous. Be Lord of it all. May peace be my portion, wisdom be my guide, and favor pepper the atmosphere around me. In every season, be my friend, Savior, and hero. The One who never leaves and who has become my portion.

True Potential

"Dan will provide justice for his people
as one of the tribes of Israel."

GENESIS 49:16

Though Dan was called to provide justice for God's people, pride hindered him and his tribe from reaching their full potential. This tribe, which was strong (with men like Samson), did win a victory for Israel (Judges 18). However, it made Dan independent and proud. This fall became a stumbling block for the nation.

Each of us has the potential to bless or hinder God's people. Our lives of holy devotion and absolute trust in God set us in position to be blessings. But pride and self-sufficiency will leak from us like poison. We must never buy into the lie that our decisions affect only us. This is far from the truth. Let's embrace the promises of God over our lives, walking out their fulfillment, and leaving imprints of his glory for all to see.

Father, you are my joy and example of true love. Let my life be an offering of total and complete devotion as I seek to release your glory on the earth. I don't want to reach my full potential; I want to surpass it by the greatness of your Spirit inside me! May every word and deed be rooted in your holiness so it will draw others to you.

Confident in Him

"I wait in hope for your salvation, O Yahweh!"

GENESIS 49:18

Jacob prophetically understood that where Dan would fail to judge rightly, Jesus would succeed. The righteous judge of all the earth would provide justice for his people. The promised One would victoriously lead us to salvation.

Our hope for deliverance and justice must rest in him, not the frail efforts of man. In their most valiant attempts, they still fall short. Only Yahweh walks in complete victory. He will do what no one else dares to believe is possible. Without him, everything seems an insurmountable obstacle, but with him comes unrelenting power! Like Jacob, let's declare our expectancy! Let's turn our hope into confidence—not just for what he will *do* but also for who he *is*.

Father, breathe upon the embers of my faith. Ignite my heart afresh so I will stand confident and whole. I don't need to scream at the enemy and beat the air to see your salvation in the circumstances of my life. You are my deliverer! You restore the ways of justice!

Overcomer

> "Gad will be raided by raiders,
> but he will raid at their heels
> and overcome them at last."
>
> GENESIS 49:19

Gad symbolizes the victorious, resilient life of an overcomer. And it would become the sixth stone on the breastplate—a diamond! Throughout the Scriptures, hidden like sacred jewels for us to find, are whispers of God's encouragement. Let this truth breathe hope and faith into you again.

You are his jewel. His beautiful resilient one whose arms are still lifted in surrender. Whose heart is still bowed in love. Though the fires of affliction burned furiously against you, the Lord surrounded you. He was with you in the fire and, in the end, caused it to serve you. To purify you. You did not give up. Even when you were weak with grief and questions bombarded your mind, the flickering ember of faith still burned. You have found your strength in him. You are an overcomer!

Father, thank you for your mercy. For never abandoning me. For the way you hold me and whisper words that inflame my faith. You have filled the vacancy in my heart with your tangible presence. You gave me strength when I had none left.

The Oil of His Presence

"Asher's food will be rich,
and he will provide delicacies fit for a king."

Genesis 49:20

Moses said of the tribe of Asher in Deuteronomy 33:24–25 that their feet would be "bathed in oil." Oil soaked feet speak of walking in the anointing and richness of the Holy Spirit. This is the lifestyle God invites you to enjoy.

As you step into the presence of your Father today, the fragrant oil of divine love bathe each step. You are his. He is yours. He offers to anoint you with the oil of gladness in place of sorrow. To pour the warmth of his healing love over every wound. To bind your longing heart to his with the golden glory that streamed from a bloody cross. His presence is saturating you. Today. Dripping from you, everywhere you go.

Father, smother every part of me—spirit, soul, and body—with the anointing and blessing of your Spirit. Awaken my senses to the nearness of your holy presence. Desire to know you more than anyone else ever has is swelling within me. May I drink eternally of the reality of your love.

Skip over Mountains

"Naphtali is a doe set free."

GENESIS 49:21

Christ is not only the victorious lion but also the resurrected doe skipping over the mountaintops in joyous freedom. He is the resurrected doe beckoning you to dance with him into victory. Awakening you with radiant hues of morning glory!

Redeeming love will set you free. Strengthen you so you can skip over the mountains of difficulty, laughing with Jesus. His victory is your gift. His joy is meant to be shared. He is reaching for you with nail-scarred hands that purchased your freedom. You are destined to reign with him as you take your place beside him as his chosen bride. Stay close to the Lord, and soon, with the agility of a gazelle, you will frolic with him in situations that once caused you to cower and hide.

Father, I want to dance with you on top of mountains whose peaks no longer scare me. You are the resurrected doe whom I willingly follow. I say, yes! Yes, to experiencing the thrill of victory. Yes, to your strength and joy within me! Yes, to your gift of freedom!

Beautiful You

> "...who bestows beauty on his offspring."
>
> GENESIS 49:21

The same beauty surging from Jesus lives inside of you. It wraps around you like a diamond-flecked cloud. In him, you live, move, and discover how fearfully and wonderfully made you are. Created in his image, he has made you beautiful.

Do you see him smiling through your eyes when you look at your reflection? Take a look! It's time for you to see what the Father sees when he looks at you. The love of an earthly parent cannot compare to what he holds in his heart for you. He's already given all he had to prove your worth. Like a caterpillar, you are being transformed. Emerging from your season of hiding because you have ravished his heart.

Father, all I can do is stand in awe at who I've become. You have set me free in every way. I'm lighter. Happier. Clothed in your radiance. Confident in the beauty you have bestowed upon me. Thank you for your grace. Thank you for who I am because of you.

Fruit for Sharing

"Joseph is a fruitful vine,
a fruitful vine growing by a spring."

GENESIS 49:22

Like Joseph, you are a fruitful vine. An unending source of living water surges within you. The wine of the Holy Spirit is invigorating you and making you come alive. You are not just a garden of fragrant beauty; you have become a nourishing and bountiful vineyard.

In the secret garden of his presence, you're empowered to fulfill your destiny. You have cast aside your garments of heaviness and run with joy and humble confidence as you feed others. Within you are the fruits of spiritual maturity. Clusters of sweet fruit now adorn your life. Because they have blossomed from your history with the Lord and are treasured by you, they will not be stolen. Share the fruit of your life with others.

Father, your presence within me is a fruitful vineyard of extravagant, unending provision. You are joy, hope, healing, and saving love. Thank you for pursuing me and never giving up. For lifting my head to drink of your goodness and satisfying the longings of my soul. Now, I will release your hope to those in need.

Unstoppable

"...whose branches run over a wall."

GENESIS 49:22

As branches abiding in the vine, you are unstoppable! As resilient and nimble as Jesus is. The walls the enemy erects are getting easier and easier to scale. When you remain close to the Lord, drinking each day from the wellsprings of his love, you're growing stronger. Finding the courage to face the lies that fight to hold you back. Truth is setting you free.

The longer you walk with the Lord, the more you look and sound like him. You bear his likeness and the fruit of his life is in you. Feast on the truth of his Word and it will be your continual joy. Vitality, strength, and bravery are launching you out of the pit that once hemmed you in. Now you do more than wish for the blessings of God; you run toward them with faith that no one can deny.

Father, steep me in the oceans of your eternal love. Cause me to be so confident in who you are in me that I am unstoppable. Unable to be restricted by the fear that once blocked my vision. In your presence, I see clearly. By your grace, I am empowered to leap over these walls.

Our Vindicator

> "Persecutors fiercely attacked him;
> they pursued him with their bow and arrows."
>
> GENESIS 49:23

Arrows are often used metaphorically for slander and false accusation. Joseph was a victim of both. But the slander and abuse of others couldn't keep him from his destiny, and if you set your intentions on pleasing God, it won't stop you either!

Let's be honest: it hurts when we're falsely accused and mistreated. At times, it may even seem that the lies hurled against us are hindering God's will. But when we set our hearts on God and live with the conviction that he is our righteous vindicator, he steps in. He knows how to set us on paths of grace that lead us where he wants us to be. We can rest in the revelation that he is our faithful defender.

Father, step in and set things right. Unfurl paths that have been twisted by the words of malice. Cover my reputation with your merciful truth. I choose to trust you despite this swirling opposition. I release the right to stay mad or be consumed by indignation and unforgiveness. Have your way. I will keep my heart set on you.

He Is Strong

"The power of the Mighty One of Jacob strengthened him."

GENESIS 49:24

In every dark corner, Jesus is cheering you on. Reminding you who you are. Encouraging you to gather your courage and stand back up. Partner with this truth, and it will empower your faith—he is by your side. He is enough.

Allow this message to permeate your thoughts—the might of his Spirit, which has no rival, fills you. The same power that raised Christ from the dead is surging through every fiber of your being, right now! Hand him your weakness and watch it transform into something extraordinary. Jesus will strengthen you and give you wisdom. He will lead you down paths you didn't know existed. He will be your joy when sorrow has stripped you bare. So arise and shine! Your Light has come.

Father, breathe upon the smoldering remnants of my hope. Set me ablaze with holy fire that burns away every lingering doubt. I can do all things that you have called me to do because you are with me and never leave. You are igniting my faith afresh! You are the strength of my soul.

The One We Worship

"...by the name of the loving Shepherd,
the Rock of Israel."

GENESIS 49:24

The King of glory, the Shepherd, and keeper of our hearts is also the Rock upon which our entire existence rests. All that we are or ever hope to be is wrapped up in the beauty and grace of our Lord and Savior, Jesus. This beautiful One who deserves all honor, glory, and praise draws us close. The One whose breath creates life sees fit to call us beloved, friend, partner, and child.

How magnificent! How utterly unimaginable are his love and mercy! There is no other name in all existence that deserves every ounce of our tear-drenched devotion. He alone is God. The unchanging One who saves, delivers, and does miracles every day. This is who we worship!

Father, your glory leaves me undone. Everything about you is lovely. I'm struck with wonder at the beauty of your holiness and the splendor of your majesty. Moved by the way you welcome me into your presence. With hands lifted high and heart bowed in loving surrender, I honor you. I'm so grateful to be yours.

More than Able

"He will bless you with the blessings of heaven,
blessings of the deep that lie beneath."

GENESIS 49:25

God is not short on ways to take care of you. Where man fails, he comes through. The same God who placed a coin in the mouth of a fish (Matthew 17:27) knows how to provide for you. He will move the hearts he created just to get his blessings to you.

The blessings of heaven are his promise to you. Regardless of your previous experiences—no matter how much or little you've received—there is always more. Always enough bread at the Father's table. Copious joy to replace mourning. Healing for every physical and emotional pain.

Be careful not to limit God based on your understanding. He is God, after all! He is more than able to do the unimaginable if you will set yourself in agreement with him.

Father, forgive me for any way that I've held back your blessings due to unbelief. I lay my doubt at your feet and ask you to free me from fear. I'm choosing to believe, and I will not relent. I will meditate on your Word until it becomes the truth my heart agrees with and the confession my mouth declares. You are more than able!

Carrying His Name

"Benjamin is a ferocious wolf.
In the morning, he devours his prey;
in the evening, he divides the spoil."

GENESIS 49:27

Benjamin, the favored son of Jacob, whose name means "son of my right hand," is a picture of the last day church. We are those called to live with purpose and identity. Seated at the right hand of God, ruling with the power he's entrusted to us.

When Sarah gave birth to Benjamin, she wanted his name to portray her sorrow, but Jacob favored him and wouldn't allow it. Instead, he blessed his son with a name that carried prophetic destiny. In like manner, our fate has not been sealed by the sorrow we've caused but by the purpose and meaning Jesus has given to our lives. He has brought us close, as sons and daughters, to the place of strength and authority. We are his favored ones.

Father, thank you for giving me a purpose and an untamable hope for the future. For blessing me with the pleasure of living in you and with you. For the joy of holding your hand as I walk by your side. These are the inexplicable mysteries I'm privileged to enjoy. This is the honor of carrying your name.

Speak Life

These were prophetic words their father spoke to them
when he blessed them.

GENESIS 49:28

Your words matter, so speak life. Declare the blessings of God over your loved ones. Be mindful of the frame you're placing around children of God because they will live to fill it. Do all you can to help them see themselves through the eyes of his truth and love. Love that creates boldness and envelops them with confidence so they can fearlessly stand in their identity.

There is something precious, powerful, and fearful about the blessings and curses of our lips. Our words release power. They attract whichever kingdom they agree with. They can build up and tear down. Use them wisely. Dare to speak extravagant words, dripping with generosity and outrageous faith. Let them hear words of love, encouragement, and hope. Speak the words of life that align with the value Jesus has placed upon them.

Father, thank you for awakening me to the power of my words. Teach me to only speak things that edify and encourage. Show me others as you see them. When people spend time with me, let them walk away feeling valued and cared for. May my words echo your heart for everyone I meet.

Seasoned with Grace

But Joseph dried his tears and said,
"Don't be afraid. How could I ever take the place of God?"

GENESIS 50:19

Joseph remained honorable even in his grief. He comforted his brothers who, after the death of their father, feared Joseph would now give them the punishment they deserved. Instead, he behaved with righteous compassion and acknowledged his submission to God.

Humility will always be our safety net. Even when we're confronting sin, lies, or mistreatment, we are still required to carry ourselves as children of God. To see people through the eyes of our heavenly Father. To stand up for righteousness but to remember that truth, spoken in love, contains power. Condemnation does not reflect the character of Christ. Even when Peter betrayed Jesus, the Lord never condemned or guilt-tripped him. Rather, Jesus offered him three redeeming chances to profess his devotion. Let's choose our words carefully and not allow our right to lash out darken our path.

Father, teach me to speak words of truth with compassion, wisdom, and love-infused boldness. May everything I say reflect your heart and not my own need for revenge. Help me to carry myself with dignity and grace as I aim to submit every emotion to you.

The Grace to Forgive

With more kind, reassuring words,
Joseph comforted his brothers.

GENESIS 50:21

Only God can equip us to comfort the very people who were once
our enemies. To love and forgive in a way the world finds almost
impossible. To care for those who sought to slice our reputations
with razor blades of accusation. To see them through the eyes of
the One who longs to win their hearts.

Mercy can do that. His forgiveness is contagious. God not only
heals our trauma, but he also causes us to feel the pulse of his
compassion. All he asks is our willingness to release the pain and
anger. He will do the rest. The ability to love our enemies is a gift
unwrapped by faith. And if we will consent, Jesus will soften our
hearts in a way that makes no sense to our natural understanding.
Yes, God can do that!

*Father, I've decided to hold nothing back from you. No aspect of
my life is off-limits. I want you to be the Lord of every thought and
secret musing. Give me the grace to forgive. To see those who have
hurt me through the lens of your unbiased mercy.*

A Life Framed by God

Joseph declared to his brothers, "I will die one day,
but God will certainly come to you and fulfill his promises."

GENESIS 50:24

Throughout his life, Joseph was known as a man of integrity, honor, humility, and graciousness. An incredible testimony, which framed his reputation. A history that pointed to the goodness and faithfulness of God.

Regardless of how many years have passed, God allows us to walk in newness of life. Each new year becomes an opportunity to start again. To attune our hearts to his and become the person he has created us to be. Let's release the past, cast off unbelief, and find the courage to love without condition. Let's laugh, shed more tears of worship than sorrow, and notice the blessing of each mundane or busy moment. Jesus is with us every single day. And these are days worth living.

Father, my greatest desire is to be found in you. Wrapped so completely by your glory that I'm unrecognizable. In you, I come alive and understand my identity. Without reservation, I am yours. May my lovesick heart and unrelenting devotion to you define my life. May my love for others reflect your heart.

About the Authors

Dr. **Brian Simmons** is known as a passionate lover of God and the lead translator of the Passion Translation, a new heart-level Bible translation that conveys God's passion for people and his world by translating the original, life-changing message of God's Word for modern readers. Brian and his wife, Candice, travel full time as speakers and Bible teachers.

*G*retchen Rodriguez has co-authored three books with Brian Simmons: *Prayers on Fire*, *The Divine Romance*, and *Ever Present Love*. Her heart burns with one main message: intimacy with Jesus and discovering the reality of his presence. She and her husband invested nine years as missionaries in Puerto Rico, along with their three daughters, and now make Redding, California, their home. For more about Gretchen, see her website: gretchenrodriguez.com.